"Kris Vallotton builds a solid case for why women should be allowed to excel and lead. He courageously addresses the challenging Scriptures, the ones that have kept women from taking their place in shaping the course of history in church life. This profound work is a must-read for men and women alike; it has the potential to instill courage in the hearts of men to see women around them empowered more fully, as well as give women permission to dream again."

Bill Johnson, senior leader, Bethel Church, Redding, California;
author, *When Heaven Invades Earth* and *Hosting the Presence*

"Kris does an exceptional job at unraveling societal and cultural dogma in relation to a woman's place and position in God's Kingdom. In truth and conviction, he presents God's rightful place for women as co-heirs of the same promises that men have in Christ. *Fashioned to Reign* empowers women to walk in their God-given identity and men to understand women's God-given destiny. This book is a must-read for everyone!"

Dr. Ché Ahn, senior pastor, HRock Church, Pasadena, California;
president, Harvest International Ministry;
international chancellor, Wagner Leadership Institute

"Even though there is ample evidence in the Scriptures that women share an important part in the unfolding of God's eternal purpose, the marginalization of women still holds sway in the minds and practices of many who profess Christ. Let us remember that the image of God is far from complete unless it is understood as 'male and female He created them.' This compelling work reveals the way God has raised up women to be powerful and mighty and to move the hearts of the masses; it will elevate your awareness, challenge some presuppositions and invite you to grow in the grace and true, experiential knowledge of the Lord Jesus and His Church."

Dr. Mark J. Chironna, Church On The Living Edge,
Mark Chironna Ministries, Orlando

"*Fashioned to Reign* is off the charts and worthy to be read and studied by all. My favorite part is Kris Vallotton's narration of Adam. Wow, what insight! Once you start it, you won't be able to put the book down."

Patricia King, founder, XP Ministries

"I love the heart behind this book. Finally, a biblical perspective on female leadership that encourages women to remain themselves and still take their God-given places of leadership. Imagine leading—like a woman—in church! This extraordinary book gives women freedom and biblical confidence to co-labor with men and with God."

Stacey Campbell, author, *Ecstatic Prophecy* and *Praying the Bible*;
co-founding pastor, New Life Church, Kelowna, British Columbia;
founder, Canadian Prophetic Council

"This must-read gives answers to solve the biggest crime in women's lives, and that is identity theft. This book will empower you to regain your identity that Satan stole and find your place in God to live the life He created you to live. 'As [Jesus] is, so are we in this world' (1 John 4:17 NKJV)."

Cynthia Brazelton, pastor, Victory Christian Ministries International

"This is an evolving and desperately needed conversation in a rapidly changing Church, where the religious mind-set is being challenged and roles redefined within the context of godly leadership. It serves as a prophetic declaration on the role of women as agents of change globally."

Dr. Ayoade Olatunbosun-Alakija,
international development expert, health and gender specialist

Testimonies from Some Who Have Been Impacted by Kris Vallotton's Teaching on Women

Fairly early in the year, when I was a first-year student from England at Bethel's School of Supernatural Ministry, Kris was doing a Q&A with our class. One girl stood up on the other side of the room and asked, in response to 1 Corinthians 14:34, if it was okay for women to speak up in church. Kris responded by taking five minutes to briefly talk through his biblical understanding of the strength and calling of women. Then he talked for the rest of the class about his biblical understanding of the strength and calling of women.

In all honesty I cannot remember the details of what he said that day because everything in me was leaping for joy. I knew through and through that what he was saying was right and that, without knowing it, this was the freedom and release I had been waiting for.

The ministry that followed was one of the most memorable moments of the entire year for me. After Kris finished, one of the other pastors asked those of us women affected to stand. He then asked the male students to gather around us, to hold our hands and to apologize for where men had held us back in the past. Then they prayed for us, released us, blessed us and prophesied over us. The testimony I fed back to my church and friends in England led men in my congregation to apologize to the women, to pray for them, and to bless and release them.

This teaching has had a ripple effect—ripples of freedom. I will never be the same.

Jessica Wilde

My interaction with women has been hindered because my view of them has been very shallow. I have not valued having influence with them because I did not see them as influencers or difference-makers. I have honored the women I worked for because the Bible says to do this, but in my heart I never truly respected their strengths or wanted to submit to them.

Then I listened to Kris's podcast on women. Shortly afterward I came to work as a personal trainer at a small gym where the demographic is about ninety percent women. Women in a fitness environment typically view men as prideful and arrogant, and men are not always welcome there. But since starting to work there, I have been viewing women with a renewed mind and have created many fruitful relationships. In fact, my classes have grown two to three times in attendance because the women tell their friends about me. They have also complimented me to the gym owner, a former corporate wellness director in charge of seven hundred people.

The owner told me recently that I have given her new hope for her business that she would never have imagined possible. Praise the Lord!

Tony Rhine

Between Kris's message on women and his Facebook updates and excerpts, I am reminded constantly why I should step out in faith and walk in my calling. Kris and many like him are taking risks and spending their lives on making a way for women—too many for me not to walk down the path chosen for me by God and made possible by the help of His chosen people.

With thoughts lingering in my mind about feeling condemned by loved ones, I am still more excited than ever about my calling and am willing to pay my portion of the price. There is too much to be done on this earth and too many people to be loved on for me to say no to my calling because of someone else's unbelief.

I am forever grateful for Jesus calling me, and for those like Kris who are paying the price so that I can be embraced by the church and freely tell the nations about the love of Jesus. I am ridiculously excited for the holy chaos this new book will create. I will be one of the first to buy it. I am equally excited to be part of the calling, sharing the Gospel in the streets and in the pulpit. Imagine all the women who will read this book and become all that God has created them to be!

Sarah Walsh

I was stepping out of a violent marriage, one I had been for in twenty years while seeking help from thirteen counselors. Four different pastors had given me various renditions of why I was to blame, why I was not doing my wifely duty and why I needed to stay married. The classics were "It's not our job to deal with abuse, so you're on your own" and "Angry is not okay."

I knew what I was hearing was wrong. I knew that the Scriptures were being quoted out of context. But I lacked clear understanding until I heard Kris's teachings. From the very first teaching I heard via podcast, I started weeping and did not stop. I had not realized how hurt I had been by the male-dominant structure of the churches I had grown up in until I heard the life-breathing message Kris taught. I was delivered instantly!

4

What has happened in my life in the past two years—in part as a result of being set free from the oppression we women have faced in the church—is nothing short of miraculous. Today I am confident in who I am in God the Father, and in His love, strength, gifting and position of greatness in the Kingdom.

Kathryn Blair

This teaching is the first I heard that completely blew the doors open on what I had always wanted to hope was true but had been raised to believe was not. I was to accept my own inferiority. The implications: a lifetime of imposed conformity; a lineage of tyranny and abuse; ministries of childcare and singing in the choir—the only options for godly service and the underlying reasons many of our mothers searched outside the walls of the church for validation, enduring scorn by both men and women of the church and being dubbed "Jezebel."

This understanding has been the reality that played over and over in my head for these forty years of my life and in the lives of the women in my family before me—until now. What began for me as a teaching of validation has become a complete life transformation as the Spirit of God has stepped in, torn the veil hiding my worth and calling even from myself, and whispered the possibility of emancipation for women throughout the world.

To actually lift my head and not be ashamed of something I never asked to be; to know that I am the last generation of women in my lineage to be scarred by not correctly discerning the Father's heart; to watch a brother take the stage to defend those who have been despised for centuries . . . There are simply no words for this! This truth has forever changed our course.

Nancy Ross

My life has been changed radically by Kris's teaching on women. I feel as if an invisible structure has been broken over my life. My attitude toward myself has been transformed.

When I listened to Kris's podcast, I could see for the first time the high esteem in which Jesus held me as a woman, and I felt healed in an area I did not even know I needed healing in. I had harbored no doubt that God loved me, but now I know in a new way that He loves me as the woman He created me to be.

I am grateful to God for all He has revealed to me through this teaching.

Stephanie Tompson

Navigating this world as a powerful woman and desiring with all my heart to be godly has proved one of my life's greatest challenges. I have lived both ends of the spectrum. After starting as a career woman who fought through the corporate ranks in the retail world, and running my own business while raising two girls, I then became the flip side of the coin: a docile doormat, erasing all hobbies, business pursuits, relationships, even personality traits in a valiant attempt to conform to the prevailing model of what a "good Christian woman" should look like.

Then I heard Kris stand up and make a case for the strong woman. I was afraid he stood for the very thing I wanted no part of. But as I listened, truth from the Bible began to rise up. I realized God loved me as He had made me—a powerful woman. I did not need to kill off anything else in me, or in anyone else either.

There is something uniquely beautiful and just about men standing up for women. Our partnership is neither a rough-and-tumble football game nor a chatty quilting bee. It is a dance in which together we create a world that looks like the full spectrum of the nature of God in all its brilliant diversity.

Carol Goble

I grew up in church and have served in leadership roles as a staff member and elder. I always realized God opened these doors for me and that my gifts edified the Body of Christ; but I wrestled in my heart. Although the staff embraced my serving in these roles, there were Scriptures, people and situations that made me wonder if I was stepping outside of God's design for me as a woman by accepting positions that were considered equal with or over men.

Kris's teaching on women set me free. With each Scripture he explained and with each revelation he shared, I was released from questions and doubts that have plagued me much of my life. By the end of his podcast, I was weeping, overwhelmed by the heart of my Daddy. My spirit always knew He was good, but I needed another lens through which to view His Word, the Scriptures.

I will be forever grateful to Kris for giving me that lens. God has empowered me to embrace my gifts and use them without hesitation to destroy the works of the devil.

Angie Byrne

FASHIONED TO REIGN

Other Books and Messages by Kris Vallotton

BOOKS

Fashioned to Reign

Heavy Rain

Moral Revolution

Outrageous Courage

Poverty, Riches and Wealth

School of the Prophets

Spirit Wars

The Supernatural Power of Forgiveness

Destined to Win

Developing a Supernatural Lifestyle

The Supernatural Ways of Royalty

Basic Training for the Supernatural Ways of Royalty

Basic Training for the Prophetic Ministry

MESSAGES

Casting Vision, Catching Hearts

Developing a Legacy

Is Your House Haunted?

Fighting for Your Place in History

For the Love of God

From Paupers to Princes

Fear Is Not Your Friend

From the Pool to the River

Mercy Triumphs over Judgment

Leadership for an Epoch Season 1, 2 & 3

The Tipping Point

Living from Eternity

These and many other titles are available at
www.krisvallotton.com

FASHIONED

to

Reign

Empowering Women
to Fulfill Their Divine Destiny

KRIS VALLOTTON

Chosen

a division of Baker Publishing Group
Minneapolis, Minnesota

© 2013 by Kris Vallotton

Published by Chosen Books
11400 Hampshire Avenue South
Bloomington, Minnesota 55438
www.chosenbooks.com

Chosen Books is a division of
Baker Publishing Group, Grand Rapids, Michigan

Paperback edition published 2014
ISBN 978-0-8007-9619-8

Printed in the United States of America

The Library of Congress has cataloged the hardcover edition as follows:
Vallotton, Kris.
    Fashioned to reign : empowering women to fulfill their divine destiny / Kris Vallotton.
        p. cm.
    Includes bibliographical references and index.
    Summary: "Bethel pastor and bestselling author Kris Vallotton delivers a powerful, liberating teaching for women, revealing the special role and vital purpose God has for them"—Provided by publisher.
    ISBN 978-0-8007-9560-3 (cloth : alk. paper)— ISBN 978-0-8007-9577-1 (international trade paper : alk. paper)
    1. Women in Christianity—Biography. 2. Women—Religious aspects—Christianity.
I. Title.
BR1713.V35 2013
248.8'43—dc23   2013017675

Unless otherwise indicated, Scripture quotations are from the New American Standard Bible®, copyright © 1960, 1962, 1963, 1968, 1971, 1972, 1973, 1975, 1977, 1995 by The Lockman Foundation. Used by permission.

Scripture quotations identified CJB are from the Complete Jewish Bible, copyright © 1998 by David H. Stern. Published by Jewish New Testament Publications, Inc. www.messianicjewish.net/jntp. Distributed by Messianic Jewish Resources. www.messianicjewish.net. All rights reserved. Used by permission.

Scripture quotations identified ESV are from The Holy Bible, English Standard Version® (ESV®), copyright © 2001 by Crossway, a publishing ministry of Good News Publishers. Used by permission. All rights reserved. ESV Text Edition: 2007

Scripture quotations identified GOD'S WORD are from GOD'S WORD®. © 1995 God's Word to the Nations. Used by permission of Baker Publishing Group.

Scripture quotations identified THE MESSAGE are from The Message by Eugene H. Peterson, copyright © 1993, 1994, 1995, 2000, 2001, 2002. Used by permission of NavPress Publishing Group. All rights reserved.

Scripture quotations identified NIV are from the Holy Bible, New International Version®. NIV®. Copyright © 1973, 1978, 1984, 2011 by Biblica, Inc.™ Used by permission of Zondervan. All rights reserved worldwide. www.zondervan.com

Scripture quotations identified NIV1984 taken from the Holy Bible, New International Version®. NIV®. Copyright © 1973, 1978, 1984 by Biblica, Inc.™ Used by permission of Zondervan. All rights reserved worldwide. www.zondervan.com

Scripture quotations identified NKJV are from the New King James Version. Copyright © 1982 by Thomas Nelson, Inc. Used by permission. All rights reserved.

Scripture quotations identified KJV are from the King James Version of the Bible.

18 19 20 21 22 23 24   10 9 8 7 6 5

Dedication

*I dedicate this book to all the women in my life whom I have
had the privilege of loving and who have loved me.*

To my mother: Thank you for enduring the hard times and always loving me in
the midst of them.

To my wife, Kathy: You are the most amazing woman I have ever known in my
life. I thank God for the gift of grace you are to me.

To my daughter Jamie: I love your passion, your sense of justice and your love for
adventure. You are a beautiful woman and an amazing leader.

To my daughter Shannon: Your life inspires me, and your love for the unlovely
and the broken is a beacon of light in a dark and troubled world. You are a lovely,
grace-filled woman.

To my daughter-in-law, Lauren: I will be ever indebted to you for all that you have
done for my son and grandchildren. You are a woman full of strength and dignity
who carries herself nobly.

To Mesha, my oldest granddaughter: You are a one-of-a-kind woman whose passion
and sense of justice will establish you as a profound, beautiful and powerful leader.

To my granddaughter Rilie: Your servant's heart and steadfast spirit are the hall-
marks of your beautiful nature. I love your affectionate character. You bring joy
to my heart.

To my granddaughter Ella: The strength of your character, your passion for life
and your fearless nature are God's gift to the world through you. You are simply
amazing! May you never change.

*To all the women in the world to whom I have had the privilege of being a spiritual
father:* May God free you and empower you to transform the world!

Contents

Foreword by Jack Hayford   15

Acknowledgments   17

Introduction   19

1. The Saddest Story Ever Told   23

2. Hold On, Adam—Help Is on the Way   39

   Mother Teresa: The Courageous Power of Compassion   51

3. Who Was That Masked Serpent?   55

   Joan of Arc: The Prophetic Warrior   69

4. I Believe Every Word of the Bible   73

   Harriet Tubman: Leader of the Underground Railroad   97

5. Jesus: Founder of the First Women's Liberation Movement   101

   Rosa Parks: Founder of the Civil Rights Movement   130

6. The Misunderstood Apostles   133

   Joyce Meyer: A Matriarchal Legacy   162

Contents

7. Excavating Restrictive Foundations   165

   Aimee Semple McPherson: Founder of the Foursquare Movement   186

8. Women, Take Your Places   189

   Sarah Edwards: The Mother of a Legacy   206

9. Empowering Strong Women   209

   Epilogue: Powerful Women   237
   Notes   243
   Scripture Index   249

Foreword

I urge Church leaders to read, weigh and embrace the spirit, truth and heartbeat of Kris Vallotton's book *Fashioned to Reign*. Its biblical approach rightly addresses unright arguments of strained interpretations that have too long succeeded in resisting the simplicity and wholeness that God's Word presents.

Fashioned to Reign not only speaks clearly to long ensconced issues and arguments against a woman's place in Church leadership; it proposes that a tasteful, righteous and sensitive invitation be extended to the believing woman who evidences the gifts, calling, character and conduct answering to biblical standards. He adds a worthy note urging women be *more* than merely allowed to lead in the Church. He urges that she be welcomed as a lady-leader who may "elegantly, gracefully, intuitively and compassionately" lead with the dignity and purity of a truly God-honoring femininity and thus "join in leading the great task of nurturing an ailing planet back to health." Such balance and beauty makes sense and offers wisdom. I say, "Amen!"

Pastor Jack W. Hayford, chancellor, The King's University, Dallas/Los Angeles

Acknowledgments

Beth Chiles: Thank you for helping me complete this project. Your extensive research, insight and writing have helped make this book a reality.

Beni and Bill Johnson: I want to thank you for teaching me how to love and empower my wife and raise my children. The two of you have molded the way I view life, family and especially women, and I am eternally indebted and grateful to both of you.

Danny Silk: Thank you so much for encouraging me to take a stand against the oppression of women. You inspired me to write this book.

Rich and Danielle Schmidt: Thank you so much for your inspiring article on empowering women. It was informative and encouraging.

Introduction

I wrote this book because I wanted to incite a revolution that empowers the women I love so dearly. I have an amazing wife, two daughters, a daughter-in-law and three granddaughters (not to mention thousands of other spiritual daughters) who wake up every day to a world of discrimination simply because of their sex. The most troubling aspect of this oppression is that the Church of Jesus Christ is often found leading it! Somehow, many believers have developed a theology that proactively uses the Bible to disqualify women from the most formidable leadership roles, especially in the Church. I am appalled by the number of Christian leaders who are convinced that women are not as qualified, not as called and/or not as gifted to lead as men are.

I want to prove to you throughout the pages of this book that this disempowering thesis is not only illogical; it is also completely unscriptural. Let me give you just a little foretaste of some of the truths that will unfold in the following chapters. Were you aware that men commit more than 80 percent of all of the crimes in the world? In America alone, 92 percent of prisoners are men, while women commit only four-hundredths of a percent (.04) of all violent crimes.[1] Men are also responsible for starting most of the wars, committing the worst atrocities ever chronicled and inciting nearly ever genocide in the history of the planet. It was Hitler who slaughtered the Jews, men who massacred the

Native Americans and men who enslaved the African-American. Men account for most of the rapes, serial killings, thefts and even white-collar crimes. And it was men who put Jesus on the cross. Not a single female was involved in the crucifixion. As a matter of fact, Pilate's wife tried to talk her husband out of crucifying Jesus.

Now, do not get me wrong. I am not saying that women are innocent of sin or are somehow inherently righteous. I am simply pointing out the fact that if the devil's plan is to steal, kill and destroy, then men are at least five times more likely to help him fulfill his devious mission.

Furthermore, while ten apostles huddled up in a house trying to save themselves, it was three women (and John) who stayed at the cross to comfort Christ in the dark night of His soul. Although Jesus had been telling His disciples for months that He would be crucified and would rise on the third day, it was only the two women who visited the tomb to check out the story. When the women found the tomb empty and encountered excited angels, they ran back to the village to tell the hiding world changers that the stone was rolled away and Jesus was gone. Yet only Peter and John even bothered to see if there was any truth to their story, while the rest of the apostles refused to believe. It was Mary Magdalene who first encountered the risen Christ, and she was the only person who touched Jesus before His ascension. It was Christ who instructed *her* to go tell His disciples that He had risen.

Long before that, under the Genesis curse that placed husbands above wives, Old Testament women were empowered as prophetesses, judges, queens and leaders. The book of Proverbs even depicts wisdom as "female."

Yet in spite of all of this, in the name of the Bible many Christians have disempowered women and relegated them to the backseat of the bus in society and in the Church. When Jesus died on the cross, He became sin for us and destroyed the curse propagated against us—including the curse that caused men to rule women. But for some reason, two thousand years later much of the Church still has only applied His blood to one sex and has relegated women to the ball and chain of

Eve's deception. In the last hundred years, many countries of the world have begun to champion women, giving them places of leadership in politics, business, education and in every realm of society, while most of the Body of Christ will not even allow women to be elders in the Church. What we have failed to realize is that Jesus founded the first Women's Liberation Movement.

After years of research, I am convinced that there are four basic reasons why men and women are not empowered equally in society. First of all, the devil hates women even more than he hates men. Remember, the curse God pronounced over the *serpent* was that women would be hostile or angry at the devil. Therefore, demonic warfare is more often focused against women. Second, most men are insecure, and reducing women helps them feel more powerful. Third, many Christians have misunderstood the Bible with reference to women, and they do not want to violate their understanding of the Scriptures to empower women or be empowered as women. And fourth, as a people group women tend to be less competitive than men. They are not typically fighters; they are prone to be more humble and gentle, and they lean toward understanding men instead of resisting them. Maybe this is because women gave birth to everyone on the planet. Men mistakenly interpret these attributes as weaknesses and believe that women are not as qualified to lead, which results in women being promoted less frequently than men and in men purposely oppressing women.

We need matriarchs to step up into their rightful place alongside our patriarchs in every realm of society, including the Church. It is only then that we can see the *full* manifestation of the glory of God cover the earth as the waters cover the sea! Encouraging women to live powerfully is the mandate and mission of this manuscript.

In the midst of reading these pages, you may so strongly disagree with my reasoning at times that you will want to throw this book in the garbage. I challenge you to read the entire book before you form your final opinion about my perspectives. The chapters build on one another, and they fit together like pieces of a puzzle. Toward the end of the book, a clear picture will emerge that clarifies my point of view, which I believe will deepen your understanding of God's most beautiful creation, women. May God Himself meet you in these pages and give you a deeper revelation of His invisible attributes, His eternal power and His divine nature as you ponder the profound purpose of women.

1

The Saddest Story Ever Told

Not too long ago, I was reading the creation story as God recounted it to Moses in the book of Genesis. Suddenly, I began to envision Adam narrating the story, as if I had unearthed some lost journal hidden deep in an Iraqi cave that once lay in the midst of the beautiful Garden of Eden. I imagined myself sitting in a dimly lit cavern, poring over a tattered scroll thousands of years old. I envisioned the scroll reading like an ancient documentary, told in first person by Adam himself. I listened as Adam recounted his walk with God in the Garden, his exhilaration at waking to see woman for the first time and his agony at being expelled from the Garden. I became so captivated by the vision that I could actually feel Adam's loneliness as he longed for a companion. I was mesmerized by my thoughts as God searched for a solution among the living creatures, and tears rolled down my face as I pictured Adam waking up to the woman of his dreams.

This experience gave me a new perspective on mankind's journey and helped me understand what it might have been like at the dawning of creation. Let me make it clear, however, that this Genesis story I am about to tell is simply the way I *imagined* Adam recounting it. I am *not* claiming that the Holy Spirit in any way inspired this narrative. Let the journey begin . . .

Creation through Adam's Eyes

The other day I was walking through the Garden with God and feeling kind of sad. He was teaching me some new words, but I felt preoccupied and disconnected. He gently put His large hand on my shoulder and looked deep into my soul. His intensity made me uncomfortable. It seemed as though an eternity passed as we stared at each other in silence. Tears formed in His eyes, and He said, "Adam . . . Adam, you're lonely, aren't you?"

"God," I responded, "I'm not lonely when You're with me. I just have no other friends like You. You complete me. I feel whole and happy when I'm around You. But when You're not with me in the Garden, I'm bored and disinterested in the others. I need someone I can relate to in the same way I relate to You. I long for a companion, a soul mate, someone I can share life with. I want to be with someone who needs my protection, who longs for my affection and who can help me understand how to deal with my vulnerabilities the way You do when You're with me."

"Adam, you're right—it isn't good for you to be lonely. I have someone in mind designed especially for you."

We walked into a beautiful meadow full of flowers. The Tree of Life stood in the middle of the meadow. God picked me up and sat me on one of its large branches. I watched in complete and utter amazement as He reached down into the meadow, scooped up soil from the ground and formed creatures from the dirt. He carefully molded each one with His hands and then breathed on it. When He did that, the creatures would suddenly come to life—flying things, crawling things . . . some small and others massive. God's creativity was infinite!

At first I thought these creatures were just random manifestations of God's creativity. But as I watched more carefully, I realized that every creature unveiled some secret mystery of His divine nature. He received so much joy from fashioning each beast and bird that He chuckled out loud as they ran off or flew away. When God had finished creating all of the animals, He looked over at me and said, "Adam, now name all of the creatures I just created."

Three winters passed as God looked on patiently while I named the living creatures. They migrated by species to the place where the four rivers met in the land of Havilah in the Garden of Eden. I sat on a big boulder at the mouth of the river, with water gushing out beneath me, and God sat by my side. All the animals were rather docile as they drank from the river. Distinct pictures began to emerge in my mind as I observed each creature that came forward to drink. All of a sudden, a name for it would settle in my heart. Because of the look He had on His face, somehow I think the Lord was taking part in all of this. He laughed when I yelled out each name, as He had taught me to do.

For instance, the other day I was watching this passive animal, so meek and shy, drink from the river. Suddenly, this picture surfaced in my mind of the animal aggressively sneaking through the brush, running like the wind and roaring loudly. I pointed to the creature and shouted, *"Lion . . . your name shall be called Lion!"*

The large, docile beast looked up at me as if to say, "What did you just do to me?" Immediately, it let out a loud roar that echoed through the Garden, and it ran fiercely into the brush. I got scared and covered my ears. God chuckled and said, "You're helping Me." I did not understand what He meant, but it sure was fun. I felt as though I were co-creating with God. He formed the animals and gave them life, and I called them by names that determined their nature.

When I finally finished naming the living creatures, God looked over at me and said, "Adam, what do you think?"

"I like them all, God, but I don't think a pet will fulfill my need for companionship. I want someone. . . someone who isn't just with me, but is part of the very essence of who I am."

"Adam, it's important for you to remember what you learned about the animals. Although they're amazing, they'll never meet your need for companionship," God responded.

We walked through the meadow for a while in complete silence. (God is always quiet when He is "imagining.") Some time passed, and suddenly He got this curious look on His face. "Adam," He said with a chuckle, "you're going to really love this."

By now God was beaming all over. (I had a feeling that whatever He was about to do had actually been in His heart for a long time.)

"What . . . what do you have in mind?" I pressed.

"It's a surprise, son . . . but you're going to be so happy!" God teased. "Lie down right here in the tall flowers, and I'll show you."

The last thing I remember was asking God a bunch of questions, and then *bam*, I was out cold. I must have been asleep all night, because I woke at sunrise. I sat up in the tall grass and tried to understand what had happened to me. I felt strange . . . different . . . changed. It is hard to explain what was going on in my heart. My left side was kind of tingling. I reached my hand over to feel it and discovered a long scar that was completely healed. I looked down in the grass where I had lain and saw a small puddle of blood and water. I sat there for a long time trying to get a grasp on my condition. Something essential and significant was missing from my being. I sensed that aggression had dramatically increased in me, and I was less intuitive. I was mystified, and my feelings perplexed me.

In the midst of my bewilderment, I heard a noise in the trees nearby. I knew it was God because the ground always shook when He walked. I stood up to greet Him, and then I saw the most beautiful creature I had ever seen in my life holding His hand. She started giggling innocently as they drew near. I ran to meet them, completely losing control. I was so excited, I could not contain myself. I began jumping around and yelling, "*She is bone of my bone and flesh of my flesh! She is bone of my bone and flesh of my flesh! She is booone of myyyy booone and flesh of myyyy fleshhhh!*" God was laughing so hard as He watched me jump and shout, "*She shall be called Woman because she was taken out of Man!*"

I started touching Woman's skin. It was so soft! Her long hair glistened in the sunlight. She sort of clung to God while I stared at her, waves of passion flowing through my soul in a way I had never felt before. I began yelling again, *"A man will leave his mother and father and cleave to his wife . . . and the two shall become one flesh!"*

I grabbed Woman by the hand and gently pulled on her arm. She looked up to God as if asking if it was all right to go with me. God let go of her other hand and motioned for her to follow me. (He obviously had not had time to teach her to talk yet.)

"Adam, you watch over Woman and be gentle with her," God instructed.

"I will!" I answered excitedly. We were both laughing as we ran through the meadow all the way down to the river. Many different animals were drinking along the bank. I was eager to show her everything God had made. She kept pointing at the wildlife and smiling. Sometimes she would say, "Wow, wow!"

I would say a creature's name out loud as she pointed to it. She would try to repeat the name after me, and we were having so much fun! Suddenly, a lion emerged from the trees with a loud *roar*. Woman became so excited that she began running toward the lion. I could hear her breathing hard as I pursued her.

"I think the lion is showing off for you!" I shouted as I chased her. I finally caught up to Woman in the meadow, put my arms around her and held her near me. She seemed to like that. She laid her head on my shoulder as I stroked her long, beautiful hair. "The lion always acts tough," I said, hoping she would understand, "but I think the lion likes you. Everything God created tells us something about Him."

I do not think she understood much of what I was saying to her in those first several days, but it was fun to tell her things anyway. I was eager to show her the part of the Garden I was cultivating. I took her by the hand and led her downriver to an orchard God had planted. I had been working there, and I picked some fruit from a tree, took a bite of it myself and then handed it to her.

"Taste it—you'll like it," I said as I nudged her hand to her mouth. She reluctantly took a small bite. Suddenly her eyes lit up. She looked over at me, smiled and ate the rest of the fruit. It was funny watching her experience eating for the first time. Juice ran down her face as she devoured the fruit. After that, Woman loved eating any kind of fruit.

I looked up and saw God watching us in the distance. Obviously, He was happy. I waved at Him and mouthed, "Thank You!"

He smiled and mouthed back, "I love you!"

"God is awesome," I mused out loud.

Many seasons have come and gone since the day that I first met Woman. At first, God often joined us in the cool of the day and walked with us through the Garden. It did not take long to teach Woman how to talk. She is really smart and learns certain things much faster than I do.

One day God approached us in a serious mood. He took us both by the hand and walked with us to the middle of the Garden. I knew then that we were going to have "the talk." God took us over to the two trees in the midst of the Garden and began His firm exhortation. (He had already talked to me about these two trees a long time ago.)

"This is My favorite tree," God said, showing us the fruit. "It's the Tree of Life. You may eat from it whenever you like." Then His voice became stern as He turned to the second tree. He said, "This is the Tree of the Knowledge of Good and Evil. *Do not ever* eat from it because it will kill you in one day."

I did not say anything to God, but the fruit from the Tree of Life did not look very inviting. It was kind of a thorny fruit. The other tree had beautiful fruit on it that made you want to taste it. Woman and I glanced at each other, and I could tell she was thinking the same thing. It was a little hard for me to see God being so intense, but Woman seemed to process God's urging differently. I was not sure why at the time, but later I realized that she was much more intuitive, which often caused her to understand God from another perspective.

The season was beginning to change, and it was getting cold at night. We stayed closer to the cave that God had made for us to stay in when it was chilly. Woman liked to decorate the cave walls by etching pictures of the animals, or of me, on them. She is really good at etching and often spent several days at a time working on the walls. After some time, she had the idea of using her pictures to tell stories about the things we were experiencing so we would not forget them. Woman is so creative and intuitive. Whenever God was with us, she seemed to know what He was thinking before He talked. After God would leave, she and I would have long conversations about the things that she would *feel* when He was near.

One time I got alone with God in the Garden and told Him what Woman was feeling. He nodded in agreement and smiled at me, as if to say, "Adam, you just don't get it, do you?" The truth is, I do not understand how she knows things about God (and about me) that He has not told her. But I seem to remember having similar experiences before the Woman was taken out of me. I will have to learn to trust her ability to understand things intuitively that I cannot seem to recognize logically.

One day while I was down by the river planting corn, Woman was walking by herself through the meadow and looking for colored stones to use for her etchings. A beautiful creature met her in the midst of the meadow and engaged her in conversation. I had caught glimpses of him hiding amongst the trees of the forest long before God had made the animals and let me name them. This creature was much taller than I was and had long blond hair. His eyes were deep blue and his body was shaped much like mine, except his skin glistened like the sun. He had two awesome wings on his back, but I never saw him fly. Later, Woman told me that the beautiful creature's wings had been broken in a great fall. She told me that he blamed God for this. Maybe that is why the beautiful creature never came around when God was hanging out with us.

One time I was down by the river getting some water when I suddenly came upon this beautiful creature. I must have startled him, because he immediately disappeared. I could sense that he did not like me. A few minutes later, I felt the ground trembling beneath my feet and knew God was near. The animals often heard Him coming before I did, and the Garden would become charged with excitement. The birds especially liked to put on a show for God, flying around and around Him, while the animals all rushed to be near Him. God enjoys all His creatures. He often laughed as we watched them play together.

I decided that I would bring up the beautiful creature that day. "God," I said rather sheepishly, "there's a creature I didn't name who keeps watching me from the trees in the distance. Today I saw him down by the river, and I must have surprised him because he took off running. I can tell that for some reason he doesn't like me." I looked up into God's eyes and added, "I'm sorry, but I don't trust him!" (I was a little uneasy telling God this; I am never allowed to talk negatively about any of the creatures He has made because He says they are all very good and display different aspects of His nature.)

God stared back at me in silence. His face grew somber, and His eyes were full of disappointment. He frowned and said, "It's the serpent."

God did not have to say anything else; somehow I understood that the serpent was an ancient rival from a past age. God shook His head as if to say, "Trust your instincts." Then the silence was broken as Woman came running through the meadow and jumped into God's arms. She was kissing Him on both cheeks, and He was teasing her. I always loved it when God played with us. He is so funny, and we were having so much fun that day that I forgot to tell God about seeing Woman talking to the serpent.

Over the next year, I saw the beautiful serpent interacting with Woman several times in the meadow. I expressed my concerns indirectly to her because she seemed to like him, and I did not want to hurt her feelings. Woman is sensitive. I also did not tell her about my conversation with God concerning the serpent. Looking back now, I wish I would have.

None of the animals can talk, so it was easy to see why Woman liked the serpent. Woman enjoys talking much more than I do, and the serpent's beauty was spectacular. When I went off to work in the Garden, she would often walk through the orchard and pick fruit. The serpent met her there more and more frequently. I do not know if I was jealous of the serpent or if I just did not like him, but I knew that God did not trust him either. Woman is much more intuitive than I am, so I thought she would know if the serpent was bad. But Woman kept telling me about all the things she was learning from the serpent. It confused me. The serpent seemed so intelligent, and he was much more beautiful than any of the other living creatures. Woman appeared mesmerized by his splendor and wisdom. He must have known that I did not like him, though, because he disappeared any time he saw me coming.

On the saddest day there ever was, Woman and I were standing in the middle of the Garden between the two trees God had planted. Woman picked some fruit from the forbidden Tree of the Knowledge of Good and Evil.

"We're not supposed to mess around with the fruit from that tree!" I said. "Woman, you know what God told us about that tree!"

"Adam," Woman responded in a sweet voice, "the beautiful creature said that the fruit from this tree tastes great and will make us smart, like God. He asked me why God would plant a tree in the Garden if He didn't want us to eat its fruit, and he said God is trying to keep us from being as smart as He is."

Before I could say anything else, Woman took a bite from the fruit. Instantly her eyes lit up, and she shouted, *"Wow! This fruit is amazing!"* She began to speak about things that I have never heard God talk to us about. "Adam, you *have* to try this fruit! It tastes so good, and it's opening up my mind to comprehend things in a new way. Whoa! Adam, come on, honey, take a bite! Oh my goodness, come on, just one bite—if you don't like it, you can spit it out!"

Woman looked so happy that I decided to try the fruit myself. She fed me a piece, and as soon as I took a bite, my eyes were also opened. *"Wow!"* I shouted. I felt amazing and took another bite. *"Something's awakened in me,"* I said with a loud voice.

As the day wore on and the sun began to set in the distance, our consciences slowly awakened. We somehow realized that we were naked, and we felt embarrassed. I grasped Woman by the arm and pulled her into the trees. We both wept because we felt so guilty. We quickly gathered some leaves and tried our best to weave them together to cover my penis and her vagina. I knew something had gone terribly wrong because the Garden grew silent . . . even the birds stopped singing.

Moments later, I felt the ground beginning to vibrate beneath us, and I knew God was near. Woman and I rushed into the forest to hide ourselves because we felt ashamed and did not want to face Him. He stood in the meadow, weeping and waiting. My heart broke as I peered through the bushes and saw the look on His face.

"*Adam . . . Adammm!*" God shouted in a somber voice. "*Adammm, where are you?*"

The entire earth shook, and the animals fled as God yelled my name. "*Adam, son, did you eat of the tree from which I told you not to eat? Adam and Woman, come out here and speak to Me right now!*"

I had never heard God talk to us in that tone of voice before. Trembling from head to toe, I made my way out of the brush. Woman followed, weeping uncontrollably as we emerged together from the trees. I will never forget the look on God's face as we approached Him.

"Adam," God said with a deep sigh, "what have you done?"

I was so scared that I could hardly form the words. "The Woman . . . You gave me the Woman . . . and the Woman *You* gave me talked me into tasting the fruit," I said, staring at the ground.

"Adam, look Me in the eyes!" God said. "You haven't just disobeyed Me—you have obeyed your wife *instead* of Me!"

He turned to Woman next. "Woman, what have you done?" He asked in an angry voice.

Weeping hard, Woman faltered, "I don't know! I . . . I listened to the serpent, and he lied to me! It's not my fault, God! It's not my problem!"

"Adam, Woman, I gave you both leadership over the world, and you chose to change masters and obey the serpent. I told you both not to eat from the Tree of the Knowledge of Good and Evil, but the serpent told you to eat its fruit and you chose to obey him instead of Me."

I caught a glimpse of the serpent hiding in a grove of trees; he was watching us from a distance with a sinister look on his face. He mocked us (especially Woman), snickering with a creepy laugh as God reprimanded us. Suddenly God looked up at the serpent and commanded him to come. The serpent trembled as he obeyed. He could not look God in the eye.

God's voice thundered through the Garden as He shouted at the serpent, "*You are cursed—cursed beyond all cattle and wild animals— cursed to crawl on your belly and eat dirt all of your life!*"

God continued, "I declare that from this day forth, the Woman will be at war with you. All of her children will hate you for the rest of your days. They will stomp on your head so hard that they will bruise their heel!"

Woman and I watched in shock as the beautiful serpent was transmortified before our eyes. He groaned in agony as his skin was suddenly covered in scales. His arms and legs withered up and he crashed to the ground with a loud thud, his head hitting the dirt first. His wings and hair disintegrated like dust. He slithered off into the weeds that were now rapidly overtaking the Garden.

God turned to Woman, who was trembling uncontrollably, and whispered, "I'll multiply your pain in childbirth; you'll give birth to your babies in pain. You'll want to please your husband, but he'll lord it over you."

My heart broke as I listened to God's curse over Woman. Next, God turned and looked me in the eyes. Tears were streaming down His face, which was ridden with betrayal.

"Adam," God said, His voice quivering with emotion, "because you listened to your wife instead of to Me and ate from the tree I forbade, the very ground is cursed because of you. Getting food from the ground will be as painful for you as having babies is for your wife. You'll work in pain all of your life. The ground will sprout thorns and weeds. You'll get your food the hard way, planting and tilling and harvesting, sweating in the fields from dawn to dusk, until you return to that ground yourself, dead and buried. You started out as dirt, and you'll end up dirt."

When God had finished cursing us, He said sternly, "Wait here!" Woman and I watched as He disappeared deep into the forest. A short time later, we heard a terrible sound off in the distance. God emerged from the wilderness at sunset with two animal skins that He had fashioned into clothing for us.

"Put these on," God said sadly. "They will cover your naked bodies so that you won't live in shame."

The skins fit perfectly, but I was struck by the grief I could feel emanating from God's being. I knew then that one of His precious creatures had died to provide these skins. Then God sent us into the cave while He stood in the meadow, near the Tree of Life. Woman and I both fell asleep, but early the next morning we woke to voices talking in the meadow. The ground was trembling more violently than I had ever experienced before. Woman and I rushed to the mouth of the cave to see what was going on. We saw the Godhead talking together. Two huge, heavenly creatures flew in a circle above them. Woman got scared and ran deep into the cave, as if she somehow sensed the outcome of their discussion. I stood there trembling in awe as the Godhead conversed. I could hear them somberly talking about the ramifications of Woman and me eating from the Tree of Life now that we had eaten from the other forbidden tree. They discussed the possibility of creation living in this broken condition for eternity. I heard something about a Lamb that was killed long before the world was created, but I did not understand why or what it all meant.

When the conversation was over, God commanded the heavenly beings to land on the earth and guard the Tree of Life. The beings pulled out flaming swords from their sides and patrolled the Garden in every direction. They were terrifying to watch. The rest of the Godhead disappeared, and God began walking toward the cave. My heart was beating out of my chest as He drew near.

He called in a stern voice, "Adam, Woman, come out here now!"

Trembling, we both emerged. We were terrified! I remembered God's words to me many seasons ago: "In the day that you eat from the Tree of the Knowledge of Good and Evil, you will die."

God looked at us with tears in His eyes and said, "Get out of the Garden right now! Go!"

Woman hurried to gather her stones that she used to etch the cave walls, but God stopped her. "Woman, leave your things and do what I told you! Don't you understand Me? Run! You've given the authority I gave you to rule the earth to the serpent. Now you must stay away from the Tree of Life, lest the world live in this condition forever."

We fled the Garden, and suddenly I felt so dead inside. *How can we live without a relationship with God?* I wondered. I could tell that

Woman was struggling, too. We had been put in charge of the earth, and now we had lost our authority. Surely the ugly serpent, cursed by God, would not rule the world now . . . or would he? Grief and confusion plagued my soul.

The relationship between me and Woman also changed. I began to rule over her, so we were no longer coequals; now she was subject to my will. Woman did not like having me tell her what to do, but I secretly enjoyed it. Woman excelled at leading in the Garden, which is why I listened to her so often. The serpent must have realized how much I respected Woman's leadership ability. I am certain he knew that if he could get control of Woman, I would follow her lead. I should have realized that she also had vulnerabilities, especially when she told me to disobey God.

Another season passed, and then one afternoon while we were taking a walk through a field full of weeds, I recalled how I had helped God create the animals by naming each one of them. Woman had not yet had any children, so I decided to change her name to something that would empower her to bear children. I turned to her and said, "Your name shall be called Eve, the mother of the living!"

Woman smiled and seemed to like her new name. A few days later we had sex together, as God had instructed us many seasons before, yet this time Eve got pregnant. We were both so excited! Because it had taken us so long to have children, Eve said that God had helped her get pregnant. It was good to feel that God was still involved in our lives even though we had chosen not to obey Him.

Many days passed, and finally it came time for Eve to give birth to Cain, our firstborn. She crouched down early in the morning on a bed of hay I had made for her. Struggling to give birth, she screamed in intense pain and labored deep into the night as I stood by helplessly. Listening to her wailing and watching the agony on her face, I prayed for the first time that God would not let Eve die. I felt powerless listening to her beg for mercy as the child slowly emerged from her womb.

Cain was born late into the night. Eve, soaked in sweat, passed out from exhaustion as I cared for our firstborn son. I wrapped him tightly in a fur that I made for him during the winter, then I held him close and rocked him in my arms. I grieved for Eve and at the same time rejoiced for Cain. A short time later, Eve got pregnant again and gave birth to Abel. We loved them both so much. I think having our own children helped us understand God's intense love for us for the first time.

God started coming around more often after the boys were born. Abel enjoyed God's company and loved to bring Him great gifts from the flock of animals that he raised himself. Cain took after me; he liked to cultivate the ground and grow fruit trees. Cain never showed much interest in spiritual things and was always jealous of the way Abel got along with God. When Cain saw Abel giving God gifts, he would grab something out of his orchard and give it to God, too. Most of the time, it would be an unripe or rotten piece of fruit. He showed little respect for God; consequently, God favored Abel over Cain.

Eve and I worried about Cain because he often was depressed. God had told him one day that if he would stop being selfish and start serving others, he would feel much better about himself. But Cain never seemed to listen to anyone, including God. Cain lived with a lot of anger toward Abel, even though Abel treated Cain well. One day Abel went to Cain's field to try to show some interest in his brother's work, as his mother and I had advised him to do. We were all trying to find ways to dispel the jealousy that enraged Cain, yet the nicer Abel was to his brother, the angrier Cain became.

One morning, Cain rose up and killed our beloved Abel. God broke the news to us after He had confronted Cain. Eve and I grieve for Abel to this day! We miss him so much. We often walk together among his animals and remember how much joy he received from raising them. He loved to show them off to God.

Many seasons have come and gone since the first day that God brought Woman to me in the Garden. Eve and I experienced so much pleasure there, but we have experienced so much pain since the sad day we chose to change masters. We dream often of God finding a way to restore our beloved children back to the Garden. We talked to God about it a short time ago.

God promised us, "I will send another Adam. He will defeat the serpent and put all our enemies under our feet. In that day, the second Adam will break the curse over all of creation so that men and women can again walk hand in hand with Me in the Garden. Dominion will return to them, and creation will rejoice at their crowning. Until then, all creation groans under slavery to corruption, waiting eagerly for the revealing of the glorious children of God to emerge. When that day dawns, the morning star will rise in their hearts, and shouts of joy will return to the earth."

As God spoke to us, I thought back to the day when I first met Woman and joy rushed over my soul. Tears filled my eyes as I wondered to myself if things would ever be the same again. Eve must have sensed what I was feeling. She took me by the hand and tried her best to comfort me. To this day, I thank God for Eve as I cultivate the ground by the sweat of my brow and look for the dawning of that new day and the restoration of all things.

2

Hold On, Adam—Help Is on the Way

or thousands of years, forces that are out to destroy the dignity, glory and self-respect of the human race have been at work in our world. The brunt force of this battle predominantly has been executed against women. It is a battle that puts the sexes at war with each other as each sex creates standards from its own strengths that demean the other. The majority of the contention has involved men requiring women to measure up to masculine standards, while ignoring the superior strengths of feminine virtues (which we will investigate in-depth in the following chapters).

Before we narrow our focus to the plight of women, though, let's use our Google map controls, so to speak, and pan out to a more global perspective. Let's talk about one of the most destructive weapons of warfare ever unleashed on this planet—Darwinism. At the turn of the century, Darwinism began to seep into every crack of society. But before you throw this book in the trash, thinking I have some kind of antiscience agenda disguised as a book on empowering women, I want you to know that nothing could be further from the truth! I actually love science and have great respect for most scientists, so let me explain my perspective. Darwin did not just advocate evolution; he was the father of *inner-species* evolution. Whatever your take is on evolution, there is a *huge* difference between a species evolving to adapt to changing climates, cultures and so forth and an amoeba evolving into all of the species on the planet.

It is important to understand that Darwin's scientific theories have led us into cultural mind-sets that have been extremely destructive to the dignity of both women and men. Darwinism basically said that all life, including human life, evolved from the same source over billions of years through the process of natural selection. This argument created two important core transitions in our thinking. First, instead of women and men being created in the image of God, as people once commonly believed, Darwinism taught us that our ancestors were not divine. Instead, they were apelike and had ultimately evolved from an amoeba. This transformed the way society valued human life because it reduced humans down to the level of smart apes.

Second, Darwin's theory of evolution taught us that we came about through a series of genetic mutations that transpired over billions of years. This meant there was no divine design or purpose for which we came about and no Creator who loved us enough to die for us. We are just the human race . . . all alone on this God-forsaken rock we call Earth, floating through the cosmos on a purposeless journey to nowhere.

Darwin's theory taught us that we are born to die with no eternity before us and no heaven after us. John Lennon captured Darwin's mind-set in the beautiful hit song "Imagine." John sang us into a new way of thinking when he told us to imagine that there is no heaven above us and no hell below, and that people are just living for today.

Although Darwin's theory of evolution has been around since the mid-1800s, it really gained a foothold in modern thinking during the sexual revolution. The sexual revolution created the perfect environment in which Darwinism could thrive because people were violating their own moral values and were looking for a way to avoid answering to God for the guilt they were experiencing. Charles Darwin gave the world the excuse it needed to live like hell and not have to answer to heaven.

The Bible teaches us a polar-opposite perspective on the origin of life, giving believers a radically different perspective on creation. Let's look at a portion of the creation story and see if we can dislodge Darwin's myth, which has devalued and disgraced humanity for decades.

> In the beginning God created the heavens and the earth. . . . God created the great sea monsters and every living creature that moves, with which the waters swarmed *after their kind*, and every winged bird *after its kind*; and God saw that it was good. God blessed them, saying, "Be fruitful and multiply, and fill the waters in the seas, and let birds multiply on the earth." There was evening and there was morning, a fifth day.
>
> Then God said, "Let the earth bring forth living creatures *after their kind*: cattle and creeping things and beasts of the earth *after their kind*"; and it was so. God made the *beasts* of the earth *after their kind*, and the cattle *after their kind*, and everything that creeps on the ground *after its kind*; and God saw that it was good.
>
> Then God said, "*Let Us make man in Our image, according to Our likeness*; and let them rule over the fish of the sea and over the birds of the sky and over the cattle and over all the earth, and over every creeping thing that creeps on the earth." God created *man in His own image, in the image of God He created him*; male and female He created them. God blessed them; and God said to them, "Be fruitful and multiply, and fill the earth, and subdue it; and rule over the fish of the sea and over the birds of the sky and over every living thing that moves on the earth."
>
> Genesis 1:1, 21–28, emphasis added

Did you notice a common phrase in the verses above? You guessed it—the catchphrase is *after their kind*. Remember, Darwin's theory of evolution stated that *all* life evolved from the *same kind*. As God progressed through creation, check out the contextual momentum leading up to the creation of mankind. He created:

- Great sea monsters—*after their kind*
- Winged birds—*after their kind*
- Living creatures—*after their kind*

41

- Cattle—*after their kind*
- Creeping things—*after their kind*
- Beasts of the earth—*after their kind*
- Man—*in our image and likeness* (after their kind)

Did you get the progression? God is saying that He made everything *after its kind*, including humans. When He said, "*Let Us make man in Our image, according to Our likeness*," He was saying that we were created *after the God kind*! We are not intelligent apes, mutated amoebas or cosmic accidents; we are the offspring of God, with the divine purpose of reigning over the earth and the heavenly destiny of living with God throughout eternity. The great apostle Paul put it this way:

> You have received a spirit of adoption as sons by which we cry out, "Abba! Father!" The Spirit Himself testifies with our spirit that we are children of God, and if children, heirs also, heirs of God and fellow heirs with Christ.
>
> Romans 8:15–17

The Bible clearly states that we were created to be godlike. God *is our kind*, and although we are not God, He is our Daddy. That is why the Bible says, "Be imitators of God, as beloved children" (Ephesians 5:1). When we are acting like God, we are being ourselves! The ramifications of having God as our Daddy (rather than some ape dragging his knuckles in the African jungle somewhere) is life changing. I hope you can see that what you believe about your origin makes a difference in the way you value yourself and humanity in general.

Female Adam and Woman

Now let's get back to the Genesis story. We just read in the first chapter of Genesis that God created Adam both male and female, and then He immediately commanded them, "Be fruitful and multiply" (verse 28). Next, let's look at the creation story as it is recounted in Genesis chapter 2.

Then the LORD God formed man of dust from the ground, and breathed into his nostrils the breath of life; and man became a living being. The LORD God planted a garden toward the east, in Eden; and there He placed the man whom He had formed.

Genesis 2:7–8

I am sure you noticed that God *formed* Adam from dirt and then breathed life into him. The next thing we read is that Adam is alone and God begins to look for a suitable helper:

Then the LORD God said, "It is not good for the man to be alone; I will make him a helper suitable for him." Out of the ground the LORD God formed every beast of the field and every bird of the sky, and brought them to the man to see what he would call them; and whatever the man called a living creature, that was its name. The man gave names to all the cattle, and to the birds of the sky, and to every beast of the field, but for Adam there was not found a helper suitable for him.

Genesis 2:18–20

Do you see any problems here? "Well, chapter 1 is an overview of creation," you reason, "and chapter 2 gives us specific details about the way God created mankind and the animals, right?" That is very possible and has to be at least partially true, but it still leaves us with a strange situation. Let me explain. The Hebrew word for man is *Adam*, therefore the names *Adam* and *man* are interchangeable throughout the entire Old Testament. When God created Adam (man) in Genesis 1, He created them both male and female. The first instruction God gave them in that first chapter was to be fruitful and multiply. So the first challenge we have is this: When God said in Genesis 2 that it was not good for man (Adam) to be alone, did He mean that Adam was by himself? If Adam was alone in the sense that there were no other humans on the planet, then Adam could not procreate or reproduce, as God had instructed in Genesis 1. That sounds fine, right? Yes, *except* for the ramifications of defining Adam as being alone in this way, which leaves God looking for a "suitable helper" for Adam among the animals!

This scenario creates an awkward picture that is not only perverted, but is also unbiblical. Remember what we learned above—God caused everything to reproduce *after their kind*. "Adams" would not have been reproducing *after their kind* if they somehow could have procreated with the animals. (I understand that this is gross, but stay with me because I have a point to all of this.) I know what I am about to suggest here sounds crazy, but is it possible that Adam (man) was originally created without separate sexes? Is it possible that man was originally created as an inter-sexed being, male and female? In other words, when God told Adam, both male and female, "to be fruitful and multiply" in Genesis 1, was He speaking to "Adams" who were intersexed and who individually had both male and female organs, and who therefore could procreate together?

I know what you are thinking: *Kris, you've really lost your marbles now!* Maybe I have, but let's look more closely at the creation of woman:

> So the LORD God caused a deep sleep to fall upon the man, and he slept; then He took one of his ribs and closed up the flesh at that place. The LORD God fashioned into a woman the rib, which He had taken from the man, and brought her to the man. The man said,
>
> > "This is now bone of my bones,
> > And flesh of my flesh;
> > She shall be called Woman,
> > Because *she was taken out of Man*."
>
> Genesis 2:21–23, emphasis added

Did you notice where God got the woman? He took the woman "*out of Man*." When Adam was put to sleep, the Creator literally took the *she* out of the *he*. That means that the woman must have been *in* the man, or God could not have taken her *out* of him.

In case it is not yet clear to you, what I am proposing is that the female Adam spoken of in Genesis chapter 1 ("male and female He created them") is *not* the woman who was taken out of the man in Genesis chapter 2. I am suggesting that "Adam" (both male and female) was "alone" in the sense that "Adam" (both male and female) was designed for intimacy with God. When God was present in the Garden, He completed "Adam" and fulfilled that longing for wholeness inside. Yet when God was not walking with "Adam" in the cool of the Garden, "Adam" was alone (but not by himself/herself). Man was created in the image of God, therefore man was designed for intimacy . . . not just for mating for reproduction.

We Were Made Godlike

One of the Hebrew names for God is *El Shaddai*, which literally translated means "the multibreasted one." God is describing Himself as a nurturer, the breasted one, which is primarily a female characteristic. The primary male personality trait is to provide and protect. When God put Adam to sleep, He "separated" the image of Himself into two distinct persons, man and woman. He not only took the "female" out of the man; he also took the "woman" out of him. Men and women are more than just physically different; all the strengths of womanhood were removed from the man.

God literally took Adam and broke him in half. The Bible says that God made a "helper suitable" for Adam (Genesis 2:18). The Hebrew word *suitable* means "corresponding to or opposite of." Adam would no longer be alone because he would now need his woman the way he needed God. Women would complete men in the same way that Christ completes us when He is joined to His Church. The apostle Paul put it this way:

> For this reason a man shall leave his father and mother and shall be joined to his wife, and the two shall become one flesh. This mystery is great; but I am speaking with reference to Christ and the church.
>
> Ephesians 5:31–32

Marriage makes man whole, complete and intact as the strengths of womanhood are once again joined to the strengths of manhood. This concept is further clarified by the Hebrew word *ezer*, which is translated "helper." *Ezer* is used nineteen times in the Old Testament, twice to describe a wife and seventeen times to describe God Himself. Here are two examples: "Our help [*ezer*] is in the name of the LORD, who made heaven and earth" (Psalm 124:8), and "How blessed is he whose help [*ezer*] is the God of Jacob, whose hope is in the LORD his God" (Psalm 146:5).

This is a real blow to those who want to use the word *helper* to reduce women to a subservient role. But it also helps us understand the place that God originally intended for a wife to have in her husband's life and the way she would relate to him.

I should make it clear that I am not saying a man's wife should be a god to him. I am simply trying to point out that as men are incomplete without God because they were designed to be completed by Him, so also men and women are incomplete without each other. It is common for people to tell a guy that he needs to get in touch with his feminine side. I would like to suggest that when the woman was taken out of the man, the feminine characteristics were removed from his *side*. The only way for a man to get in touch with his feminine side is to marry. Marriage merges the two so that they reemerge as one again. This holy union gives a husband access to his wife's strengths and vice versa. (I do not mean that a single person cannot live in wholeness, of course. I will return to that thought a few pages ahead.)

Here is another interesting side note that emphasizes the biblical point that the two sexes are actually one. Did you ever notice that God never counts women in a crowd? For example, the Bible recounts in the gospels that Jesus fed four thousand or five thousand *men*. Although the writers sometimes acknowledged that women were in attendance, the women were never counted (see Matthew 14:21; Mark 6:44; Luke 9:14). Why? It very well could be that God is reemphasizing His point that the two sexes are one by refusing to count them twice.

Or Maybe . . .

Let's investigate the other more commonly held possibility that Genesis 1 is the overview of creation and Genesis 2 is the detailed version of the same story. This, of course, would mean that Adam was all by himself, with no other humans on the planet. In this scenario, God could have been looking for a suitable helper among the animals so that Adam would understand—after naming all the living creatures and still being unfulfilled—that pets could never meet his longing for wholeness. But whether you believe Adam was intersexed (male and female) and was lonely for intimacy with God, or whether you believe Adam was the only human being in the Garden and no animal could fulfill his need for companionship, the truth remains that God somehow took the woman out of the man. Adam now had someone he could relate to in the same way as he connected to God.

A great example of this relational connection is found in the way that the Bible describes Adam impregnating Eve with Cain and later Abel. Genesis 4:1 says, "Now the man had relations [*yada*] with his wife Eve, and she conceived and gave birth to Cain, and she said, 'I have gotten a manchild with the help of the LORD.'" The word *relations*, which some Bible versions translate as *knew*, is the Hebrew word *yada*. It means "to be aware, to experience, to know very well, to understand, to learn and to regard." The Hebrew word for intercourse is *zera*, which means "to sow seed" or "to have sex" (see Leviticus 18:20, 23; Numbers 5:13, 20).

The interesting thing is that God often uses the word *yada* to describe how He relates to His people. For example, David writes, "Search me, O God, and know [*yada*] my heart; try me and know [*yada*] my anxious thoughts" (Psalm 139:23).

In other words, the Bible assumes that you know Adam had intercourse [*zera*] with Eve in order to get her pregnant. But what God does not take for granted is that you understand that Adam and Eve had *yada* with one another. Cain and Abel were not simply the result of a sexual union between two people; they were the offspring of a deep personal relationship. Adam had this kind of relationship with God before he ever had it with Eve. God took the woman out of the man so that they could experience *yada* with each other the way Adam did with God.

Formed and Fashioned

The Bible says that Adam and the animals were both *formed* from dirt (which explains why our DNA is so closely linked). The Hebrew word *formed* is *yatsar*. But God *fashioned* (the Hebrew word *banah*) the woman out of more sophisticated material. She is a second-generation creation. (Of course, women have been into "fashion" ever since!)

After forming Adam, God breathed into his nostrils—unlike with any of the other creatures He made—and man became a living soul (see 1 Corinthians 15:45). It is intriguing that the likeness of God and the breath of the Almighty is what separates humankind from every other living creature God made. But it is what happened when Adam met Woman for the first time that most intrigues me. Let's look at the passage again:

> The LORD God *fashioned* into a woman the rib which He had taken from the man, and brought her to the man. The man said,
>
>> "This is now bone of my bones,
>> And flesh of my flesh;
>> She shall be called Woman,
>> Because she was taken out of Man."
>
> For this reason a man shall leave his father and his mother, and be joined to his wife; and they shall become one flesh.
>
> Genesis 2:22–24, emphasis added

When Adam saw Woman, he began to prophesy to her, much as he did when God brought the animals to him to name. I believe that Adam was not just calling the creatures Spot, Fee-Fee and Trigger; he was prophesying their very creature distinctions into being (see Genesis 2:19–20). Remember, God spoke most of creation into being, but He seemed to be silent when He began working with His hands. Was it God's silence that became an invitation to Adam to co-create with God, or was it just the nature of God in Adam that caused him to help mold Woman's distinctions through prophetic declarations? I am not certain what inspired Adam, but his words to Woman became a powerful declaration that launched women into their destiny. "She shall be called Woman, because she was taken out of man," Adam declared (verse 23). In other words, "She is much more than a man; she is a womb man."

Just as God created man to cultivate, Adam's prophetic decree helped fashion woman into an incubator. This became part of the circle of life. Man cultivates the ground and brings Woman food from the garden. She incubates the gift and makes it a meal. He cultivates his trade and builds her a house. She incubates the atmosphere and makes it a home. He cultivates his love for her and gives her sperm. She incubates his intimacy and gives him a baby.

I write the above paragraph about men cultivating and women incubating metaphorically, of course. It is not meant to determine the roles of men and women. I am not saying that men cannot cook or women cannot be carpenters or gardeners. I am simply trying to put into words the different way in which men and women process life.

Beware, men, what you are cultivating in your woman. Remember that she is incubating what you have been cultivating in her. Be sensitive to what is gestating in the "womb" of your wife, or you could become the victim of your own poisonous garden.

Adam continued his prophecy, "A man shall leave his father and mother, and be joined to his wife" (verse 24). It is important to remember that Adam and Eve had no mother or father except God. Adam is therefore prophesying into the nature of the masculine and feminine roles. He is not saying, "When two people get married, the husband should leave his parents' house and move in with his in-laws." No way! Adam is prophesying gender distinctions into the relational foundation of humanity. He is saying that women will be adored and pursued, while men will be pursuers and protectors. The man leaves the protection of his father and mother and creates a safe place for his wife.

Singleness

At this point you may be asking, *What about the ramifications of singleness?* The apostle Paul addressed this issue when he wrote his first letter to the Corinthians. He told them that he felt it was better for people to remain single for ministry if they could (probably because of the intense persecution of his day), but he went on to say that "each one has his own *gift* from God" (1 Corinthians 7:7 NKJV). The Greek word *charisma*, translated "gift" in this passage, means "a supernatural endowment from God." The same Greek word is used in 1 Corinthians 12 to describe spiritual gifts such as healing and miracles.

In other words, we were not designed to be alone, but God can and often does give people the supernatural gift of singleness so that they can live in wholeness without marrying. Of course, all of us need the gift of singleness for a short season in our lives, at the very least. God has a way of supernaturally grafting us into wholeness through His ever-present Spirit who lives in us.

Please do not mistake my motive for writing this chapter by feeling as though you are only half a person if you are single now or choose to remain single. I am simply pointing out that it takes both women and men to accurately represent the Godhead, as we were both created in the image of God. God is not human, but neither is God a male. It takes both feminine and masculine characteristics to represent God to the world.

In the next chapter, we will discover why the serpent hates people so much—especially women—and how he managed to weasel his way into the life of the first family. You might be surprised by the intense prejudice the devil has toward women!

Mother Teresa

The Courageous Power of Compassion

One of the most awe-inspiring and well-known women in modern history is Mother Teresa. She spent her life feeding and caring for the poor, while simultaneously building a charitable organization called Missionaries of Charity. Her ministry, which began with just 13 people, has grown to more than 600 missions in 123 countries.[1]

Mother Teresa is also one of the few women in history to receive the Nobel Peace prize, not to mention numerous other humanitarian awards. But how did this radical woman, who gave herself for the poorest of the poor, build such an astonishing ministry? Why was this powerful woman able to be "in the ministry" and run a massive organization with hardly any male opposition?

One of the reasons Mother Teresa was able to accomplish so much was her unwavering conviction that God had called her to care for the poor and destitute. She was a woman possessed by her mission. She wrote, "My mission is to care for the hungry, the naked, the homeless, the crippled, the blind, the lepers, all those people who feel unwanted, unloved, uncared for throughout society, people that have become a burden to society and are shunned by everyone."[2]

This nun refused to quit. With the tenacity of a pit bull, she simply would not take no for an answer. Mother Teresa intimidated government officials, church authorities and even military leaders with her intense persistence. Though she was barely five feet tall, she was a giant in the Spirit. In 1985, with the TV cameras rolling, she insisted that a government leader from Ethiopia give her organization two abandoned buildings to use as orphanages. The leader clearly did not want to concede, but when the smoke cleared and the crowds dispersed, the 75-year-old nun stared down the Ethiopian official on his own turf.[3] (Frankly, I do not blame the guy for conceding. I would have given her the buildings, too!)

Mother Teresa gained so much worldwide influence that in 1982, at the ripe old age of 72, the woman negotiated a ceasefire between the Israelis and the Palestinians so she could rescue 37 orphans trapped in the war zone. With the battle raging around her, bystanders watched in amazement as she bravely approached the battlements. Finally, the gunfire ceased as the nun and her team navigated the battlefield and carried the children to safety.[4]

Most male leaders probably did not resist Mother Teresa's leadership because she was doing a work that, for the most part, men did not want to do. Caring for the poor in India was a function most men thought was better performed by a woman who was a nun, anyway. Many of the people she cared for were dying of gross diseases like leprosy, where people's flesh literally rots off. These patients had no money to pay for medical care and no family to assist them; they were the scourge of society. Yet without fanfare, Mother Teresa quietly went about her business of rescuing the downtrodden such as these for decades.

Although most leaders appreciated Mother Teresa's compassion, she was often criticized and condemned for her views against abortion and divorce. She refused to let the opinions of others derail her ministry. She insisted that her workers ignore her critics and not defend her values. Some people also questioned the long-term effects of her work with the poor. Her critics only served to forge her determination. They would often ask why she did not teach the poor to fish, instead of giving them fish to eat. She would respond, "My people can't even stand up, they're sick, crippled, and demented. When I have given them fish to eat and they can stand, I'll turn them over to you, and you can give them the rod to catch the fish."[5]

In the early years of her ministry, Mother Teresa faced many financial hardships. Even though she had received permission from her leaders to start her organization, they refused to fund her ministry, leaving her begging for food and supplies. Many times, she was tempted to abandon the difficult ministry of serving the poor and return to her life as a teacher, but instead she strengthened herself in the Lord and pressed on toward her mission. Her persistence finally paid off, and volunteers began to join forces with her. As her momentum grew, financial support began to pour in from governments as well as churches.

There were no borders between religious and nonreligious praises for Mother Teresa's work, and to this day she remains one of the most admired public figures of all time. As a woman, her heart of compassion, nurturing spirit and humility were strengths that she brought to her ministry. But equally important, Mother Teresa had a natural gift of administration and organization that dramatically multiplied the impact of her ministry. Her legacy is carried on through the lives of thousands of people working in orphanages, hospitals and charity centers worldwide. To this day, the ministry she left behind continues to care for refugees, the blind, the disabled, the aged, the addicted, the poor and the homeless. The organization she founded, Missionaries of Charity, also cares for the victims of natural disasters throughout the world.

The revelations that emerged after Mother Teresa's death about her struggles with depression and doubt threw some people for a loop, but these struggles actually showed more strength of character in Mother Teresa than the world even recognized when she was alive. In spite of her personal challenges, Mother Teresa marched through life determined to change history. She was unwavering in her call. She refused to see womanhood as a disadvantage. In fact, it is possible that her role as a nun benefited her call to the poor and actually helped increase her favor with global leaders.

Yet the sad truth remains that although Mother Teresa was the founder and leader of one of the greatest charity organizations in the world, she would not have been allowed to be an elder in most churches! It simply does not make sense that a godly and powerful woman like Mother Teresa can lead a ministry, but cannot be a leader in the Church of Jesus Christ. Let's give the Mother Teresas of the future an opportunity to be as powerful in the Church as they are on the mission field.

3

Who Was That Masked Serpent?

*I*n the height of his arrogance, Satan reached for the pinnacle of God's divine order and grasped for the very nature of God's majesty. Delusional with pride and overcome by ego, he said to himself, "I will ascend to heaven; I will raise my throne above the stars of God, and I will sit on the mount of assembly" (Isaiah 14:13). But in the next scene of God's motion picture, we hear God say, "You will be thrust down to Sheol, to the recesses of the pit" (verse 15).

The devil was forced out of God's beautiful heaven onto a cold, dark rock floating through space that (maybe) billions of years later would be known as planet earth. Sheol would be just the beginning of Satan's eternal sentence before he finally would be thrown into the lake of fire located in the midst of hell itself. Sheol is not hell; it actually means "the place of the living dead."

The book of Genesis gives us a little insight into our planet's horrible original state. It says, "The earth was formless and void, and darkness was over the surface of the deep" (Genesis 1:2). Let's see if we can picture the condition of this planet at the beginning of the serpent's imprisonment. The Hebrew word translated "formless" is the word *tohu*, which means "confusion," "desolate" and "chaos." The Hebrew word translated "void" is *bohu*, which means "emptiness" and "without purpose." And finally, the word translated "darkness" is the Hebrew word *choshek*, which carries the concept of being pitch-black or "glowing with darkness."

I picture this freezing cold planet with no orbit, direction or destination, with strong cosmic winds whistling through the surface of its deep pits and crevices. Like a wandering star aimlessly floating through a black hole in space, its darkness was so vexing, so black and so deep that its essence seeped into the serpent's very soul, creating disorienting hopelessness and unimaginable despair.

A thousand millenniums pass, and suddenly the serpent heard these words echoing out of the cosmic darkness, traveling at the speed of thought: "Let there be light." Without a moment's hesitation, light began to emanate from an indistinguishable source (the sun was not created yet). Simultaneously, the Spirit of God, brooding over the planet, created favorable conditions, life-giving ecosystems and shifting atmospheres. A few moments passed while God separated the light from the darkness and called the light "day." The serpent realized that the Creator had just invented time—the finite suddenly exists within infinite.

More days passed as light and life began teeming from every imaginable molecule, glimmering forth at the velocity of God's imagination. Birds flew through the midheaven, singing out their sounds of approval as they soared above the surface of the deep, while waters retreated to fill oceans and seas, leaving land exposed. Then vegetation, trees, grass, beautiful flowers and plants of all kinds began sprouting spontaneously from the ground, while rivers and springs started flowing all over the earth. Spectacular waterfalls initiated their descent, winding their way through the majestic mountains, pooling in the valleys below.

The sun was created, and the planet began its yearlong journey around the cosmic star. Earth proceeded to rotate on its axis, which separated the night from the day. God filled the heavens with stars that glistened at night, and He strategically placed the moon in its orbit to radiate at night as the sun set slowly in the west.

Then God filled the oceans, rivers and seas with living creatures: fish, whales, seals, porpoises and all kinds of great sea monsters. After that, God focused on the land and began creating beasts: bears, deer, elephants, monkeys, gorillas, cattle and every kind of animal that roamed the surface of the earth.

Finally, God planted a stunning garden called Eden with His own hands in the midst of four rivers. The Garden of Eden centered around two trees: the Tree of Life and the Tree of the Knowledge of Good and Evil.

By now, Satan must have been mesmerized by the immense beauty of God's tremendous creation. I wonder if he thought, *Maybe God has relented and is turning this prison into a magnificent paradise for me . . .*

I can picture the serpent hiding in the foliage as he watched the God he once had served create life all around him. For the first time in eons of ages, a small flicker of hope seeped through the demented mind of the devil. But then suddenly, a chilling sensation shimmered up his spine as he heard the majestic Creator enunciate these powerful words: "Let Us make man in Our image, according to Our likeness; and let them rule . . ." (Genesis 1:26). God made it very clear (mentioning it seven times in one paragraph of His Word) that He made every living creature, every animal and every bird *"after their kind,"* but that now He was producing a creature "after the God kind."

Satan wanted to be like God. He wanted to sit in the high places like God. He wanted to rule like God. God thrust him down to a dark and chaotic planet to serve out his death sentence. Then, in the midst of the devil's misery, God remodeled the planet and placed godlike creatures there who could reproduce other godlike creatures, after their kind. The devil could only look on in terror as God unveiled His divine creation and unearthed His ancient strategy for them to rule over everything that creeps on the earth. The war of the worlds was about to commence, but the victory had been predetermined before the foundation of the world.

Do you want to know why the devil hates you? Because you were born in the image and likeness of God, whom Lucifer was determined to imitate. We received through creation what the devil was striving for through self-promotion, jealousy and arrogance.

Cohabiting the Earth

Have you ever wondered why God put us on the same planet as the devil, when there are billions of other planets He could have placed us on? Why do we cohabit on this planet? Our coexistence on this earth has a couple of dimensions. First of all, we are here to do damage to the devil by worshiping God while the devil watches. Most theologians believe that Lucifer was the third archangel and was responsible for leading worship around the throne of God. When referring to a being that most theologians believe is Lucifer, the prophet Isaiah mentions "your pomp and the music of your harps" (Isaiah 14:11). But the most intriguing passages concerning Lucifer were written by the prophet Ezekiel. (You will notice that Lucifer is called the king of Tyre in the following passage, but he could not literally have been an earthly king because Ezekiel said that he was in the Garden of Eden.)

> Again the word of the LORD came to me saying, "Son of man, take up a lamentation over the king of Tyre and say to him, 'Thus says the Lord GOD,
>
> > "You had the seal of perfection,
> > Full of wisdom and perfect in beauty.
> > You were in Eden, the garden of God;
> > Every precious stone was your covering:
> > The ruby, the topaz and the diamond;
> > the beryl, the onyx and the jasper;
> > the lapis lazuli, the turquoise and the emerald;
> > And the gold, the workmanship of your *settings and sockets*,
> > Was in you.
> > On the day that you were created
> > They were prepared.
> > You were the anointed cherub who covers,
> > And I placed you there.
> > You were on the holy mountain of God;
> > You walked in the midst of the stones of fire.
> > You were blameless in your ways

From the day you were created
Until unrighteousness was found in you.
By the abundance of your trade
You were internally filled with violence,
And you sinned;
Therefore I have cast you as profane
From the mountain of God.
And I have destroyed you, O *covering cherub*,
From the midst of the stones of fire.
Your heart was lifted up because of your *beauty*;
You corrupted your *wisdom by reason of your splendor.*
I cast you to the ground;
I put you before kings,
That they may see you.
By the multitude of your iniquities,
In the unrighteousness of your trade
You profaned your sanctuaries.
Therefore I have brought fire from the midst of you;
It has consumed you,
And I have turned you to ashes on the earth
In the eyes of all who see you.
All who know you among the peoples
Are appalled at you;
You have become terrified
And you will cease to be forever."

Ezekiel 28:11–19, emphasis added

A few interesting things stand out to me in this passage. The first one is that Lucifer seems to have been in the garden of God called Eden in a much different condition than the way he appears at the Genesis Garden of Eden. I would like to propose that the Garden of Eden in Genesis was a replica of the garden in heaven. It could very well have been a kind of "on earth as it is in heaven" concept.

The next thing that stands out in Ezekiel's discourse is that it is very possible that God had fashioned musical instruments into the body of Lucifer, the covering cherub. Ezekiel said Lucifer had "settings and sockets" within him (verse 13). The Hebrew word for "settings" is *toph*, which can mean "tambourine" or "timbrel," and the Hebrew word for "sockets" is *naqab*, which can mean "bored holes such as in a flute."[1] He goes on to say, "In the unrighteousness of your trade you profaned your sanctuaries" (verse 18). Many take this to mean that when Lucifer led worship in the sanctuary of heaven, his beauty and splendor undermined his call to worship. In other words, his pride and arrogance caused him to draw attention to himself instead of directing worship toward God.

One other profound truth really captured my attention as I was preparing to write this chapter. God said that Lucifer was extraordinarily beautiful and full of splendor. A few different Hebrew words are used for "beauty" or "beautiful" in the Bible, yet all but three times, those Hebrew words are used to describe people and are always in reference to women. Much like Lucifer, the covering cherub, women are described as beautiful 26 times in the Old Testament alone, while men are only described as handsome three times (handsome has the same Hebrew root word as beautiful).

What is my point? Before Lucifer was reduced to an ugly, grotesque snake eating the dust of the earth, he was God's most beautiful creation in heaven. Not only are women created in the image and likeness of God; they were also fashioned to be God's most stunning creation. I would like to suggest that the once-beautiful cherub, Lucifer, who corrupted his trade and was cast out of heaven for being arrogant about his beauty and splendor, became extraordinarily ugly and now seethes with jealousy toward the King's gorgeous daughters. It is just another reason why this fallen angel hates women more than he hates men.

Back to the Garden

Now that we have some insight into the fall of Lucifer and his inherent hatred toward humankind, let's journey back into the Garden and pick up where we left off in the Genesis story. It appears that between the time Eve was fashioned and the time Cain and Abel came along, the serpent began to weasel his way into the life of the first family. Remember that he was speaking to the woman as a beautiful, majestic-looking serpent, not a slimy snake slithering on his belly. He stood upright and could speak their language, which was probably refreshing for Eve considering that God apparently only came into the Garden in the cool of the day. This situation left Eve alone with Adam and a bunch of animals most of the time. Let's face it—most guys are not famous for their great communication skills, which probably made talking to a brilliant serpent pretty intriguing for Eve. According to the following passage, evidently Adam viewed the serpent as some sort of talking animal since Genesis names him among the beasts of the field. Look at the dialogue that ultimately brought on the downfall of mankind:

> Now the serpent was more crafty than any beast of the field which the Lord God had made. And he said to the woman, "Indeed, has God said, 'You shall not eat from any tree of the garden'?" The woman said to the serpent, "From the fruit of the trees of the garden we may eat; but from the fruit of the tree which is in the middle of the garden, God has said, 'You shall not eat from it or touch it, or you will die.'" The serpent said to the woman, "You surely will not die! For God knows that in the day you eat from it your eyes will be opened, and you will be like God, knowing good and evil." When the woman saw that the tree was good for food, and that it was a delight to the eyes, and that the tree was desirable to make one wise, she took from its fruit and ate; and she gave also to her husband with her, and he ate. Then the eyes of both of them were opened, and they knew that they were naked; and they sewed fig leaves together and made themselves loin coverings.
>
> Genesis 3:1–7

Several things come to light as we study this passage. First of all, it is important to note here that man and woman were already co-reigning in the Garden. The serpent knew that Eve was no slave. This is evidenced by the fact that the devil spoke to her instead of to Adam, and the reality is that without hesitation, Adam trusted his wife's insight over

God's command. We can therefore conclude that Eve was a powerful and influential person, not a subservient maid living mainly to keep the cave clean.

The next thing we see in this Scripture is that the serpent was tempting them to perform so they could be like God. He told Eve that on the day they ate the fruit (performed), their eyes would be opened and they would be like God. The truth is, Adam and Eve were *already* like God because they were created in His image and likeness. The serpent was trying to get them to perform for what they already had! The moment they ate the fruit, religion came into the world. People were suddenly subject to the curse, which caused them to perform for identity instead of operating out of their identity. This has led to all sorts of perversions—people working for love instead of from love, for instance, and men and women measuring their relationship with God by their disciplines instead of by their passion.

The most important truth we learn from this passage is that Adam and Eve did not stroll through the Garden one day and decide to try some fruit from the forbidden tree. No! Contrary to popular opinion, Adam and Eve did not simply disobey God—they obeyed the serpent. God had said, "Don't eat from the tree." The devil came along and said, "Eat from the tree and be wise, like God." When Adam and Eve ate the fruit, they changed masters. Because they were given authority over everything on the planet, the entire earth came under the control of the serpent when they yielded to him, and he became the master of mankind.

The last thing I want to point out from these verses is that when Adam and Eve ate the fruit from the forbidden tree, they felt guilty about being naked even though they were alone in the Garden. The simple truth is that religion has more rules than God has. When we leave an intimate relationship with Jesus, we begin the downward spiral into escalating rules that lead to increased guilt. Most of us respond to this condemnation by working harder to feel better about ourselves. This becomes a cruel hamster wheel and an evil ecosystem that can only be broken through the power of the cross.

The Not-So-Cool Day

When God showed up in the Garden in the cool of that particular day, instead of rushing to meet Him as they usually did, Adam and Eve hid from Him. God began calling out to His beloved son and daughter, "Where are you?" (You know you are lost when God cannot find you!) Adam stepped out from behind some shrubs and yelled back, "I heard the sound of You in the garden, and I was afraid because I was naked; so I hid myself" (Genesis 3:10).

God responded, "Who told you that you were naked? Have you eaten from the tree of which I commanded you not to eat?" (verse 11).

Then the age-old game of passing off the responsibility for sin onto somebody else began. Adam responded sheepishly, "The woman whom You gave to be with me, she gave me from the tree, and I ate" (verse 12). Adam's implication was, "How can this be my fault? It was Your idea to give me this woman! I mean, how can You blame me for this problem? I wasn't even awake when You decided to take the woman out of me."

"Then the LORD God said to the woman, 'What is this you have done?'" (verse 13). God's implication to Eve was, "I put you in Adam's life to stand beside him and help give him perspective. Instead of offering your wisdom, you helped inspire him to disobey Me!"

Instead of repenting, Eve perpetuated the blame game and said, "The serpent deceived me, and I ate" (verse 13).

I often wonder if God would have responded differently if Adam and Eve had taken responsibility for their own disobedience and sin instead of passing it off on somebody else. I guess we will never know the answer to that question.

The Curse against the Serpent

God did not bother to ask the serpent what *he* was thinking. God knew that Satan is the father of lies and that no truth resides in him, so God began by cursing the serpent:

Because you have done this,
Cursed are you more than all cattle,
And more than every beast of the field;
On your belly you will go,
And dust you will eat
All the days of your life;
And I will put enmity
Between you and the woman,
And between your seed and her seed;
He shall bruise you on the head,
And you shall bruise him on the heel.

Genesis 3:14–15

The serpent is suddenly transformed from a magnificent and beautiful creature that wooed Woman through his deceptive nature into an ugly, snakelike creature slithering in the dirt. And let's not miss one of the most powerful revelations of the Genesis story—the curse spoken over the serpent was that there would be *enmity*, which means "hostility," between the serpent and women. I never realized until recently that part of the serpent's curse was that women would be hostile toward him. This curse was never meant to be against women, but against the devil!

In other words, God told the serpent, "Women will be your enemy; they will hate you and be hostile toward you from this day forward. Furthermore, the hostility women have toward you will be reproduced in everyone they give birth to, until a woman ultimately births the Savior of the world, who will stomp on your head so hard that it will bruise His heel."

This is obviously a prophetic declaration about the crucifixion and resurrection of Christ. Jesus was "bruised" on the cross, but He "crushed the head" of the serpent when He defeated sin, death, hell and the grave. I think it is important to point out here that although the devil hates mankind, the spear point of spiritual warfare is womanhood! It is women who emulate the beauty of God more than men and thus remind Lucifer of his former glory. It is also women who carry a deep-seated hostility toward and hatred of the serpent.

It is no wonder that ever since the Garden of Eden, the devil has worked so hard to oppress women. He knows that if women are empowered, there will be a new depth of compassion, love, understanding, caring and peace on this planet, and also a deeper hatred for everything the serpent gives birth to. Many generations later, King David expressed it like this:

> The LORD gives the command;
> The women who proclaim the good tidings are a great host:
> "Kings of armies flee, they flee,
> And she who remains at home will divide the spoil!"
> When you lie down among the sheepfolds,
> You are like the wings of a dove covered with silver,
> And its pinions with glistening gold.
> When the Almighty scattered the kings there,
> It was snowing in Zalmon.
>
> Psalm 68:11–14

Although this psalm most likely had some practical application in King David's day, the apostle Paul quotes verse 18 in his epistle to the Ephesians and relates it to Christ's ascension into heaven. Let's examine it together:

Therefore it says,

> "When He ascended on high,
> He led captive a host of captives,
> And He gave gifts to men."

(Now this expression, "He ascended," what does it mean except that He also had descended into the lower parts of the earth? He who descended is Himself also He who ascended far above all the heavens, so that He might fill all things.)

> Ephesians 4:8–10

In other words, if Paul viewed this psalm as having both natural and spiritual applications, then it is well within the realm of the rules of interpretation to view these kings, who are fleeing before a host of women, both as natural kings of the earth who lived during the days of David and as demonic authorities that war against us in heavenly places (see Ephesians 6:12). The English word for "host" is the Hebrew word *tsaba*, which means "an army of warriors." David goes on to say that it was "snowing in Zalmon" when the Almighty scattered the kings there. The name *Zalmon* comes from the Hebrew word meaning peace.

Knowing all that, this psalm can give a beautiful picture of what happens in the demonic realm when women share the Gospel (glad tidings). They become like a mighty army (host) who are commissioned by God to drive out spiritual forces of wickedness (kings), which are ruling in the places of authority (mountains). Snow is often synonymous with purity (see Psalm 51:7; Isaiah 1:18), and it begins to snow on the mountain of peace during these women's exploits. In other words, God is driving these demonic princes off of the mountains of influence through a purity movement led by women.

The Curse against Women

God went on to pronounce a curse against women when He said, "I will greatly multiply your pain in childbirth, in pain you will bring forth children; yet your desire will be for your husband, and he will rule over you" (Genesis 3:16). Some people point out that the Bible does not use the word *curse* when God speaks to Adam and Eve, but those who insist that mankind was not cursed after the Fall bewilder me. The ramifications and manifestations of God's proclamations were definitely negative, and the pretext had already been established that God was cursing them.

One of the curses over women was increased pain during childbirth, but the verse that had the greatest negative impact on womanhood was God's proclamation that their husbands would rule over them. The Hebrew word for "rule" is *mashal*, which means "to have dominion." It is important for us to realize that before the curse, husbands and wives were commissioned to co-reign together (see Genesis 1:27–28). It was only after the curse that husbands were given dominion over their wives. But the apostle Paul said, "Christ redeemed us from the curse of the Law, having become a curse for us—for it is written, 'Cursed is everyone who hangs on a tree'" (Galatians 3:13). When Jesus died on the cross, He broke the curse off mankind. Paul also said, "For the law of the Spirit of life in Christ Jesus has set you free from the law of sin and of death" (Romans 8:2).

In light of these things, my question is, "What makes us think that men were set free from the curse of the Law at the cross, but that women should still be under the curse that allows husbands to dominate them in the name of God?" In fact, Christian women who have been redeemed and transformed by their Savior ought to be among the most powerful people on the planet. Instead, many believers insist that while a woman in the world can be the president of a company or the queen of a nation, a woman cannot even be an elder in the Church of Jesus Christ. Do you perceive any incongruity in our thinking here? (We will talk more about this later on.)

The Curse against Men

The final curse that day in the Garden was spoken over Adam. God said,

> Because you have listened to the voice of your wife, and have eaten from the tree about which I commanded you saying, "You shall not eat from it";
>
> > Cursed is the ground because of you;
> > In toil you will eat of it
> > All the days of your life.
> > Both thorns and thistles it shall grow for you;
> > And you will eat the plants of the field;
> > By the sweat of your face
> > You will eat bread,
> > Till you return to the ground,

Because from it you were taken;
For you are dust,
And to dust you shall return.

Genesis 3:17–19

Adam was not cursed because he listened to his wife, but because he valued her opinion more than God's command. The ramifications of any curse are that you can do the right thing, but the wrong thing still happens. In this case, Adam was told that he would work hard in the Garden, but in spite of his efforts, the land would yield *thorns* and thistles. In other words, instead of creation cooperating with men, it would resist them.

When Jesus died on the cross, the soldiers placed a crown of *thorns* on His head. Why *thorns*? God wanted to make it clear that the curse over mankind in the Garden of Eden was broken by Christ in the Garden of Gethsemane. No longer would our efforts be doomed from the start; no longer would we work hard, yet not reap the benefits of our labor. From the time of our redemption on, it would be true that "whatever a man sows, this he will also reap" (Galatians 6:7; see also 2 Corinthians 9:6).

It is time for women and men to receive the full benefit of the redemptive act of our Savior's death on Calvary's cross. After all, Jesus died to provide us with abundant life and everlasting joy. It is high time that both women and men are empowered to reach their full potential in Christ.

Joan of Arc

The Prophetic Warrior

oan of Arc is one of the most amazing and unique women in all of history because she was a warrior with a divine call. For thousands of years, society's stereotypes decreed that a woman could not be a soldier. Joan shattered that myth and proved that women could not only serve in the military, but could lead armies to victory. Her tenacity and boldness, combined with her fierce conviction that God had called her, opened the door to favor and gave her such influence with leaders that it literally changed the course of a nation.

Joan of Arc was born in France in 1412, right in the midst of the Hundred Years' War with England. The war dragged on for decades as the English army marched across the land, crushing the French resistance. The French had not won a single victory in generations, which humiliated the entire nation. With morale at an all-time low and France on the verge of a complete collapse, times were desperate. Suddenly, out of nowhere, a sixteen-year-old girl appeared on the scene. Joan was impetuous and brash. She had no problem speaking her mind. She announced to the commanding officer that she not only wanted to join the army, but that she was called to lead his troops!

What on earth would possess a young girl to leave the comforts of home and risk her life to fight a war? At the age of twelve, Joan had heard an audible voice tell her she was to "help drive the English out of France." After that, nothing could stand in her way. Her radical God encounters gave Joan an intense passion to rid France of English control and see Charles VII crowned king of France.

Joan's task was not as easy as she had hoped, however. Even though she pleaded with the commander, he was unmoved by her request and promptly sent her home. Undeterred by his resistance, she returned again the following year. This time she came armed with a vision from the Lord, and she predicted a military victory in a key city. When her prophecy miraculously came true, the commander allowed her a private conference with Charles VII, the future king of France.[2]

History does not record exactly what happened at Joan's meeting with Charles VII that day. But we can only imagine how tough it must have been for a fiery, passionate sixteen-year-old *woman* to try to convince the noble court that the "voice of God was instructing her to take charge of her country's army and lead them to victory."[3] Yet France had grown so desperate that they were willing to consider nearly any plan. With the favor of God on her, she convinced Charles that she was a trustworthy and loyal subject. He immediately granted her permission to join the army.

With absolutely no military experience and armed only with the knowledge that God had commissioned her to win the war, Joan of Arc rallied the French troops, imparting fresh passion to them.[4] She gave the lethargic, halfhearted army a vision for freedom and independence from England. She resolutely began marching across France, leading the troops in capturing several English fortresses. As her list of successes grew, the French army slowly embraced her leadership. Her fearlessness and determination inspired the warriors to greatness. But most importantly, Joan gave them a leader they could follow. It did not seem to matter to them that she was a woman!

As inspiring as Joan of Arc was on the battlefield, she did not always endear herself to other leaders. Her overzealousness frequently landed her in trouble. At times the leaders would exclude her from war council, which infuriated Joan. At other times, if she disagreed with certain decisions, she would go ahead and do her own thing. On one of these occasions, the leaders secretly met without Joan and decided not to attack a fortress until reinforcements had arrived. When she discovered their plan, she insisted on attacking the fortress immediately. During the battle she was shot in the neck with an arrow, but she refused to retreat and continued to lead the attack. Consequently, the French captured the fortress, and of course, Joan was considered a heroine.[5]

Joan of Arc's divine leadership ability resulted in Charles VII being crowned king and France regaining control of their country. After a century of war, the English finally proposed a truce. The truce was short-lived, however, and soon Joan was defending France against another English attack. This time, Joan was captured in battle. She proved a fearless prisoner. She attempted several escapes, including a leap from her prison cell from a seventy-foot tower.[6] The girl was crazy!

Once they had her, the English government wanted a reason to kill Joan of Arc without making her look like a martyr. They knew the peasants loved her and considered her a saint because her prophecies all came true, so the English court conspired to discredit her in the people's eyes by trying her for heresy. Her heresy trial was rigged from the beginning, but it showed how incredibly wise she was. The judges who were trying her so marveled at her intelligence that the court closed the proceedings to the public.

The most famous lines of her trial's transcript show Joan's brilliance: "Asked if she knew she was in God's grace, she answered: 'If I am not, may God put me there; and if I am, may God so keep me.'"[7] The question was a trap since church doctrine was that no one could be certain of being in God's grace. If Joan answered yes, they could have convicted her of heresy. If she had answered no, she would have been confessing her guilt.

Everyone who heard Joan's response was dumbfounded, yet in spite of her intelligence, she was found guilty of heresy and sentenced to death. She was burned at the stake at the young age of nineteen, yet her legend lives on.

Despite Joan's exploits, the French made no effort to save her. Why did France leave her in an English dungeon instead of rescuing her? There are many theories. Some believe that once Joan cleared the way for Charles VII to take the throne, he no longer had any need of the impetuous warrior. Others think it was just a case of "out of sight, out of mind." Although the king of France refused to support Joan, influential women in his government did. Several of them financed her battles, supported her during her captivity and testified on her behalf at her trial. Women believed in Joan even when men turned their back on her.

If Joan of Arc had believed that women could not fight in a war or lead an army, France most likely would have lost the war and been overtaken by the English. But Joan listened to God's voice and saved a country from extinction. She believed that anyone could receive a divine calling from God—rich or poor, man or woman, educated or uneducated. Joan of Arc was a force of nature. Strong-willed, fierce and determined, she was an inspiring leader and a fearless warrior. She never doubted her divine call to lead France to victory, and she paved the way for women warriors for centuries to come.

4

I Believe Every Word of the Bible

I love to post statements on Facebook and see how people respond. There are always those who feel as though it is their job to police the cloud. Like secret agents, they hide their identities and conceal their faces while they scour the Internet, diligently searching for those they deem as violators of truth, false teachers or false prophets. (It does seem a little odd to be on Facebook and not show your face, but I guess that is normal for secret agents.)

Disguising themselves as friends or fans, these people try to hijack their foes' Facebook train to undermine the engineer and derail the cars. Of course, they ignore the fact that they have violated their own code of ethics by lying to get on board this train in the first place. But the end justifies the means—after all, they are self-appointed to defend truth, justice and the American way. Once they board the train, next comes their zealous stand for truth as they dogmatically rush headfirst into the fray, waving their swords and shouting their disapproval. "We believe the Bible!" they contend. "We stand for the Word of God!" they protest.

Their implication is that I do not. From their perspective, anyone who disagrees with them is part of the end-time, apocalyptic army of antichrist warriors. And because these self-appointed Scripture Police label "violators of truth" as deceivers, they set aside—for the greater sake of the "Kingdom"—the principles of sisterhood and brotherhood so firmly rooted in the Book they strive to protect.

I have come to enjoy messing with such people. I will post something on my Facebook page just to stir them up and make them think. It is actually kind of fun to throw out an idea and watch how the "Theological Police Department" deals with the crime. Empowering women is definitely on these people's Most Wanted List. When I post something like, "*Women are to be equally powerful and yet distinctly different,*" you can see the red lights coming on and hear the sirens screaming toward the scene of the crime.

Deeming themselves experts in the law, these folks show up with guns drawn and shields up, flashing their badges. They scrutinize the Scriptures much as an attorney would argue over legal documents or a biologist would dissect a frog. It is a violation of ethics for the Scripture Police to even consider the contextual or situational expression of the truth—unless, of course, it helps perpetuate their own agenda. They make arrests and take prisoners when you try to point out to them any obvious flaws in their arguments. In their court of law, evidence that the Bible often shares two *opposing* ideas, *both* in a favorable light, is inadmissible. They refuse to listen to reason because *thinking* is strictly forbidden; it is considered rationalizing away the truth and compromising the Word of God.

The Keystone Cops

A few years ago when we flew out of a tiny airport in a small town in California, a situation came up that reminded me so much of the Scripture Police mentality. Kathy and I arrived at this airport two hours early, relaxed and in a good mood. As we entered the airport, I surveyed the inside of the small building and noticed there was only one counter situated about twenty feet from the front door. Behind the counter stood a tall, skinny, rather naïve-looking young man. His company uniform was a few sizes too big, which made me wonder if he was a new employee. A couple of portable tables were set up a few feet in front of the counter, with two airport security guards standing behind them to search people's luggage. This placed the security tables right in the middle of the waiting area.

Both the guards were large, middle-aged men with their bellies hanging over their belts. They seemed like the kind of guys who had watched a lot of cop movies as kids and could not wait to strap a gun to their belts. Each passenger they dealt with would look on in horror as the security guards unpacked every single article of clothing from every single bag, spreading things out on the tables in front of them and searching through them as if each person who approached were on the FBI's Most Wanted List. Bras and underwear were separated into piles, as were other personal articles that I will not mention here.

Thankfully, only two other passengers were in the airport at the time, one sitting in the waiting area and the other standing at the counter in front of us. We stood in line for twenty minutes as the young, obviously inexperienced airline representative fumbled around nervously, trying to get a ticket to print for the passenger ahead of us.

I could feel the frustration rising in me. "What a bozo," I whispered to Kathy.

She glared at me in disapproval and encouraged me to sit down in the waiting area just a few feet from the counter, while she held our place in line. I sat down with a groan and stared on angrily. Another fifteen minutes passed, and finally it was our turn at the counter. I got up to join Kathy in the crucible.

The airline representative looked up at us from behind the counter and said sheepishly, "You have to have your bags searched before you can come to the counter."

I could not believe it! We had waited 35 minutes in line, only to be told that our bags had to be searched first. There was no sign instructing us on that procedure, and with only three customers in the entire *tiny* airport, no one bothered to say a thing to us. I was just about to come unglued when Kathy reached over, touched me and said to the young man, "Okay, sir, we'll be right back." (I knew her touch meant, "Be quiet. I've got this handled!")

We wheeled our luggage a few feet over to the tables where the two security guards were standing there looking like sergeants in a boot camp drill. One of the guards instructed us in a serious tone to lift our bags onto the table. I reached over to unzip my bag and was sternly reprimanded: "Stand back and take a seat until we're done!"

Wow, I thought to myself, *give a guy a badge and he thinks he's Dirty Harry!*

Kathy and I sat there with the two other passengers as the Keystone Cops searched our bags. They slowly pulled every single thing out of our luggage (including our underwear), inspecting everything meticulously and setting it all on the table as we watched in utter embarrassment. Twenty more minutes passed, and by now Kathy had joined me in righteous indignation. Finally, just as I stood up ready to march to the tables and give them a piece of my mind, the security guards handed our two suitcases to the airline representative through an opening in the counter.

The young rep motioned for us to come to the counter. We handed him our IDs and travel information. Then I stood there waiting impatiently as he stared intently at the computer screen for nearly twenty minutes without looking up. Every once in a while, he would type something on the keyboard and then let out a "hmm . . . whoa . . . yikes . . ."

Kathy could sense that the volcano in me was about to blow, so she started rubbing my arm to calm me down. "This is ridiculous!" I said to her loudly enough for him to hear.

Finally, the printer came to life behind the guy, and I began to feel some relief. For some reason, he printed the bag tags first and then carefully installed them on the handles. Without looking up, he nervously retreated back to the monitor, staring at it as if some horror movie were playing on the screen. Several more minutes ticked off the clock as I grew intensely more impatient. He kept pressing buttons on the keyboard and looking at the ticket printer. Finally, in what seemed like a last-ditch effort, he called the janitor over to help.

Without making eye contact with us, the young rep mumbled, "Something's wrong with the ticket printer—the stupid thing won't print!" The two of them ducked down behind the counter, whispering to one another while they pressed different keys on the keyboard.

By now nearly an hour and a half had passed, and our plane was waiting at the gate. The representative looked up from behind the counter and said in a tone of voice that revealed his anxiety, "I guess we have no choice. We'll have to call the tech support line." He fumbled around for a little while trying to find the phone number and finally made the call. It took several minutes for someone to answer, and then they immediately put him on hold. He stood there behind the counter and stared at the printer some more.

Several more minutes passed, during which I felt like climbing the walls. Finally somebody answered the phone on the other end, and he began to describe the problem. "Yup . . . that's right. I can't get the stupid thing to print! Yeah, I tried that. . . . Okay, let me see if that works."

He held the phone in one hand, and with the other he pressed a couple more buttons on the keyboard. "Nope, that didn't do it! Oh no! Seriously! There's no other way to handle this? Wow, okay then, I guess it's come to that . . . all right, good-bye," he said as he hung up the phone. He stuck his head up from the counter and made eye contact with me at last. He looked as if he had seen a ghost. "Well," he said, sounding as if he were going to tell me I had cancer, "we have to shut the entire system down and bring her back up again to fix this."

"You're kidding," I said sarcastically.

"No, sir, there's no other way to fix it," he said as serious as a heart attack. He ducked down behind the counter again and located the switch on the back of the computer. He carefully turned it off, as if it might trigger some bomb. He counted slowly to thirty out loud and then flipped it back on. The screen beeped, and the printers rattled as they came to life. He timidly stared at the screen as the computer slowly rebooted. His eyes brightened as if he saw some good news there. He reentered our information into the computer, asking us the same questions we had answered forty minutes earlier. He hesitantly pushed the button and the printer burst to life, printing our boarding passes. He carefully scrutinized our tickets and turned to match them to our luggage.

"Oh no!" he said with a shocked look on his face.

"What is it?" I responded in an angry voice.

"The boarding pass times don't match the luggage tickets," he moaned. "The luggage must be searched within twenty minutes of the ticket time," he continued.

"Are you out of your mind? You must be crazy!" I shouted. "You've had the luggage in your possession since it was searched!"

"I'm sorry, sir, that's the rule. I don't make 'em—I just follow 'em," he snapped as he handed the bags back to the security guards.

The security guards took our bags back through the passage in the counter and set them on the tables. I could not believe my eyes as they unzipped our luggage and began to pull everything out of our suitcases again. By now the other passengers were on the plane waiting for us. My anger meter was pegged.

"You guys *cannot* be serious," I said in a stern voice to the Keystone Cops. "You just searched my luggage *thirty* minutes ago! *What's going on in this place?*"

By now Kathy was doing her best to calm me down, but I did not want to hear it.

"Stand back from the table, sir! Homeland Security laws dictate that we search your luggage again," one cop insisted as they continued to meticulously inspect every piece of clothing in our bags.

The airline representative peered at us with stress written all over his face and said, "You have to get on the plane right now or the flight will leave without you. I don't think we'll have time to get your bags on the plane. We'll send them to you on the next flight out."

"This plane is *not* leaving without us, and I am *not* leaving without my luggage!" I insisted (loudly). "We've been here for *two hours* while you guys messed around with our baggage and tickets. Now give me my luggage and put us on that plane!" I demanded.

The airline rep and both security guards were staring intently at me. I was not about to give an inch. They whispered something to one another and then threw our stuff back in our bags and rushed them out to the plane, with us in tow. I have a feeling that none of those guys wanted to call the police and let us tell them our story.

Looking back now, the story is rather comical, yet it reminds me so much of how those with a religious spirit relate to the Bible. The religious spirit exposes weakness, unpacks our vulnerabilities, assumes the worst, trusts nobody and looks for evil in every suitcase. This pharisaical spirit protects rules above relationships. People under its spell adopt a slave mentality that inhibits them from thinking through the ramifications of the way they apply the truth. They view the concepts of situational relevance and contextual application as degrading to the Word of God. Much like my friends at the airport who refused to question the spirit of the law, but instead insisted on searching our luggage again by the letter of the law (even though the bags were under their control the entire time), the Scripture Police scorn anyone who believes that context dictates the definition of the Bible.

The fact is that without understanding the heart of God and believing in the cultural context of Scripture, only one other option exists to explain many contrasting passages—that the Bible contradicts itself. Yet these Theological Police Department types who are running around shouting, "We believe the entire Bible! We believe every word of the Bible!" have never really thought through the ramifications of their proclamations all the way to the end. They are under the delusion that applying every word of the Bible *literally* to all situations *universally* is what it takes to practice the apostle Paul's exhortation to Timothy when he said, "Be diligent to present yourself approved to God as a workman who does not need to be ashamed, accurately handling the word of truth" (2 Timothy 2:15).

Actually, it is impossible to literally apply every Scripture universally. (This is particularly important when it comes to empowering women to be all that God has created them to be.) Before you throw this book away, however, let me explain. God wrote the Bible through forty inspired authors with the intention that the Spirit would lead those who read it. The Word of God without the Spirit of God causes death. Paul put it this way: "But our adequacy is from God, who also made us adequate as servants of a new covenant, not of the letter but of the Spirit; for the letter kills, but the Spirit gives life" (2 Corinthians 3:5–6). The Bible is written in such a way that you need the Spirit of God to give you wisdom about how to apply the Word of God. Let me give you several examples so that you can understand my hypothesis.

Truth Held in Tension

The apostle Paul wrote to the Galatians, "Behold I, Paul, say to you that if you receive circumcision, Christ will be of no benefit to you" (Galatians 5:2). Yet look what happened when Paul wanted to take Timothy with him on a missionary journey. Dr. Luke records the situation:

> Paul came also to Derbe and to Lystra. And a disciple was there, named Timothy, the son of a Jewish woman who was a believer, but his father was a Greek, and he was well spoken of by the brethren who were in Lystra and Iconium. Paul wanted this man to go with him; and he took him and circumcised him because of the Jews who were in those parts, for they all knew that his father was a Greek.
>
> Acts 16:1–3

Okay, folks, which is it? Did Paul teach them to be circumcised or not? Which Scripture would you apply universally and literally?

Here is another good one. You will like this. The Pharisees were upset with Jesus again because His disciples were not washing their hands before eating, so they asked Jesus to explain to them their interpretation of the Old Testament laws about body cleansing. Jesus answered,

> Why do you yourselves transgress the commandment of God for the sake of your tradition? For God said, "Honor your father and mother," and, "He who speaks evil of father or mother is to be put to death." But you say, "Whoever says to his father or mother, 'Whatever I have that would help you has been given to God,' he is not to honor his father or

his mother." And by this you invalidated the word of God for the sake of your tradition.

Matthew 15:3–6

Now, let's contrast this passage in Matthew with what Jesus said in the book of Luke. Luke 14:26 records Jesus preaching, "If anyone comes to Me, and does not hate his own father and mother and wife and children and brothers and sisters, yes, and even his own life, he cannot be My disciple."

I hope you are getting my point. Jesus tells the Pharisees that they are invalidating the Word of God because they do not honor their mother and father, but He also tells other people that they need to hate their mother and father if they want to be His disciples. I understand clearly that we all have explanations for these verses, but in a practical sense, which of these verses would you apply literally to your situation?

For instance, if you were counseling a young man and he said, "I hate my mom and dad," would you think that he is fulfilling the Word of God? If you decided to confront him about his attitude concerning his parents, would your counsel be antibiblical? Why does the answer seem so obvious in this situation, yet when we talk about empowering half of the earth's population who have been reduced simply because of their sex, we find ourselves immersed in complex arguments about the interpretation of Scripture?

Let's examine the truth held in tension between a few more Scriptures. The Bible says that God "desires *all* men to be saved and to come to the knowledge of the truth" (1 Timothy 2:4, emphasis added). Contrast this with what Luke wrote in the book of Acts: "When the Gentiles heard this, they began rejoicing and glorifying the word of the Lord; and *as many as had been appointed to eternal life believed*," (Acts 13:48, emphasis added).

Obviously, one verse says God wants everyone to be saved, and the other says certain people are appointed to eternal life. Which verse depicts God's heart for the unsaved? Are there some people who are not "appointed to life"? Does this mean God does *not* want everyone to go to heaven? Of course He does, but why do a few verses seem to indicate that some people have been written off to hell? And what about when God said, "I have loved Jacob; but I have hated Esau" (Malachi 1:2–3)?

It is funny that I have never heard anyone preach these verses to crowds of unsaved people, yet many leaders think nothing of preaching a few seemingly disempowering verses against women to their congregations. We will get back to this point later, but first let's also look at a couple of verses related to eschatology, or the study of the end times. When the disciples asked Jesus what the signs of the end of the age would be, He said,

> You will be hearing of wars and rumors of wars. See that you are not frightened, for those things must take place, but that is not yet the end. For nation will rise against nation, and kingdom against kingdom, and in various places there will be famines and earthquakes.
>
> Matthew 24:6–7

But now look at what the prophet Isaiah, more than five hundred years before Christ, predicted concerning the last days:

> Now it will come about that
> In the last days
> The mountain of the house of the LORD
> Will be established as the chief of the mountains,
> And will be raised above the hills;
> And all the nations will stream to it. . . .
> And He will judge between the nations,
> And will render decisions for many peoples;
> And they will hammer their swords into plowshares and their
>   spears into pruning hooks.
> *Nation will not lift up sword against nation,*
> *And never again will they learn war.*
>
> Isaiah 2:2, 4, emphasis added

We all have different ways of deciding which of these Scriptures we are believing for in our lifetime or which we apply to our day or to our circumstances. The intention of this chapter is not to unveil my theological opinions about these verses, although I certainly have some. My purpose in exposing these contrasts—and by the way, Scripture contains literally hundreds of them—is simply to highlight the fact that "believing every word of the Bible" requires a relationship with the Spirit of God so that we can discern how to apply the Scriptures in a way that leads to the outcome the Author intended. Thousands of years ago, the wisest man in the world wrote, "Knowledge is easy to one who has understanding" (Proverbs 14:6). It is only when we understand the heart of God that we can apply the knowledge of the Scriptures in a way that embraces His purposes.

This point was driven home to me several years ago when I walked by our recording studio at Bethel Church. A sign on the door used to read, "*Stop Nursing Mothers Only.*" In those days, the music studio doubled on Sundays as a room for nursing mothers, and out of the blue I got this revelation: If you were unaware that the studio was also a room for nursing mothers, you could misunderstand the sign. I began to think about all the possible messages the sign could imply to those ignorant of the room's multiple uses. Could it mean, "Stop only nursing mothers—everyone else can go beyond this point"? Or how about this one: "We must stop mothers from nursing." Or could it indicate something like, "Everyone can nurse except for mothers"? Of course, these meanings sound silly to everyone who understands what is going on in that room on the weekends. We know the sign is actually not for nursing mothers at all; it is written to everyone else. It is obviously supposed to mean, "Don't come in here because there are mothers nursing their babies."

I am convinced that many people do not understand God's heart for women, so they read the signs in Scripture through the lens of restrictions. After all, the sign on the studio door clearly restricts nursing mothers from entering the room, correct? It is often from the place of restriction that leaders wrangle over Greek or Hebrew word definitions in Scripture and therefore completely miss God's original intention for women and men, whom He designed to co-reign together.

Can you imagine trying to decide what that sign on the studio door meant by dissecting each individual English word? The argument would go something like this: "According to the English dictionary, the word *stop* means 'to cease moving, to end, to prevent something from happening.' Therefore, in my expert opinion as someone who holds a literary doctorate, women specifically are prohibited from entering this room." It may sound crazy, but this is the hand that women have been dealt "based on Scripture" for thousands of years. It is time to set the record straight and bring freedom to God's most beautiful creation.

Documentary or Commentary?

For many people, it is hard to understand that not only are there hundreds of contrasting Scriptures in the Bible, but also that much of the Bible is God's documentary on man and not God's commentary on how to live life. When people say, "I live by every word in the Bible," it is not really true. The fact is, there are many words in the Bible you are *not* supposed to live by because God is simply recounting a story and not validating someone's behavior.

I think it is important to stop here and say that just because God recounts someone's story, that does not in any way mean He agrees with that person, or with his or her behavior. That much is obvious when God is sharing a documentary in which bad people do something bad (Judas is an example of this). The challenge comes when good people in the Book do something bad. Because we do not know what to do when good people act unrighteously in the Bible, we often retell the story in a way that sanitizes our hero.

Esther is one of my favorite Bible heroines. Her beauty, grace and courage helped rescue the Jewish people from terrible genocide. Yet the way we recount the story of Esther is often filled with fables and dishonesty. Despite popular opinion, Esther did not enter a beauty contest; she entered a sex contest. Each of the king's beautiful, virgin concubines were ordered to sleep with the king overnight. If he liked them, they would return to the second harem (the equivalent of qualifying for round two of the contest). Thankfully Esther took first place, or the story would have read much differently. The contest took place because Queen Vashti refused to dance before the drunken king and his powerful guests. She refused to compromise her values to entertain him or give in to the peer pressure of royalty. Queen Vashti was truly a woman of great character and strong convictions, but the king divorced her because he could not handle a woman who stood up to his debauchery. (Read Esther chapters 1 and 2 carefully.)

How does someone who says they live by every word in the Bible process the book of Esther? Do they teach their young people that Esther is a great example of how to win friends and influence people? If your daughter felt as though she were called to bring the Kingdom into the marketplace, could she pattern her strategy to influence megacorporations after Esther's exploits? Obviously, it would not be okay for her to pray that the leader of some huge corporation would dump his wife to date her so that she could influence the direction of the company toward the Kingdom, would it?

Let me point out a few things here. For one, we often read the Bible to validate what we already believe is true, and we recount the stories in our minds to satisfy some need we have to be right instead of being transformed.

Second, the Bible commonly recounts stories in which God does not give us His perspective on the characters who lack integrity or whose worldview is flawed. Remember when Abraham deceived King Abimelech by telling him that Sarah was his sister and not his wife—to save his own neck, no less? (See Genesis chapter 20.) God came to King Abimelech in a dream and reprimanded him for taking Sarah as his wife and nearly committing adultery with her. The funny thing is, we never see God talking to Abraham in the Bible about lying! In fact, God protected Abraham and prospered him. Years later, Abraham's son Isaac also lied to the same king about his wife, Rebekah. Isaac went on to name one of his two sons *Jacob*, which is the Hebrew word for deceiver or liar.

Does this mean that if you love the Lord, you can get away with sin? Of course not! It simply highlights the fact that we need the Holy Spirit to lead us into all truth and that the Bible's silence on a matter does not mean that God condones a person's behavior.

Proverbs and Ecclesiastes

Let's look at the "I live by every word of the Bible" idea from another perspective. (You had better buckle your seat belt for this next one.) Did you know that the book of Ecclesiastes was never meant to be taken as truth to live by? Rather, it was written to demonstrate what happened when Solomon, the wisest man on earth, lost relationship with his God. The book of Proverbs was Solomon's greatest contribution to mankind. It was written to reveal to us the wisdom of a man in right relationship with God. But Ecclesiastes shows us the thoughts of the wisest man in the world after he has lost relationship with God.

Let's ponder a few verses in Ecclesiastes to see if we can perceive a major flaw in the core values expressed through the aged king's thinking. Let me give you one hint: The word *vanity* is the Hebrew word *hebel,* which means "emptiness, fraud, delusion, futility" or "worthless."

In the book of Proverbs, wise King Solomon wrote (in his better days), "How much better it is to get wisdom than gold!" and that we should do everything in our power to "Get wisdom and instruction and understanding" (Proverbs 16:16; 23:23). As an aged, foolish king out of relationship with God, he contradicted that, saying,

> I saw that wisdom excels folly as light excels darkness. The wise man's eyes are in his head, but the fool walks in darkness. And yet I know that one fate befalls them both. Then I said to myself, "As is the fate of the fool, it will also befall me. Why then have I been extremely wise?" So I said to myself, "This too is vanity."
>
> Ecclesiastes 2:13–15

Here is another one. Solomon wrote in Proverbs 13:22, "A good man leaves an inheritance to his children's children." Notice in the verses below, however, that Solomon later thought leaving a legacy to your kids is vanity:

> When there is a man who has labored with wisdom, knowledge and skill, then he gives his legacy to one who has not labored with them. This too is vanity and a great evil. For what does a man get in all his labor and

in his striving with which he labors under the sun? Because all his days his task is painful and grievous; even at night his mind does not rest. This too is vanity.

Ecclesiastes 2:21–23

This next one should rattle your cage. We were made in the image and likeness of God, and He did something with us quite unlike anything He did when He created the animals—He breathed His very Spirit into us (see Genesis 1:26; 2:7). Yet the following verse that the aged king wrote could be one of the core values of evolutionists—except that it is not true: "The fate of the sons of men and the fate of beasts is the same. As one dies so dies the other; indeed, they all have the same breath and there is no advantage for man over beast, for all is vanity" (Ecclesiastes 3:19).

You have probably guessed it by now, but the common premise in these verses, and indeed the main theme of the book of Ecclesiastes, is that everything is "vanity." Although Solomon maintained the gift of wisdom throughout his life, in his latter years his broken relationship with God and his pursuit of false idols vexed his soul. His days, once full of life because of his relationship with God, were now meaningless. Depression overtook Solomon's wisdom, and his words became a complex mixture of right and wrong. In one breath, King Solomon would pen a profound truth like this:

Two are better than one because they have a good return for their labor. For if either of them falls, the one will lift up his companion. But woe to the one who falls when there is not another to lift him up. Furthermore, if two lie down together they keep warm, but how can one be warm alone? And if one can overpower him who is alone, two can resist him. A cord of three strands is not quickly torn apart.

Ecclesiastes 4:9–12

Yet in the next breath, the old king would write something dumb like this:

Do not be excessively righteous and do not be overly wise. Why should you ruin yourself? Do not be excessively wicked and do not be a fool.

Why should you die before your time? It is good that you grasp one thing and also not let go of the other; for the one who fears God comes forth with both of them.

Ecclesiastes 7:16–18

What is Solomon talking about? That it is okay to be a little wicked and a little foolish? And look at this one from Ecclesiastes 10:19: "Men prepare a meal for enjoyment, and wine makes life merry, and money is the answer to everything." Money is the answer to everything? *Really?* What ever happened to the wise words King Solomon had proclaimed in Proverbs 23:4–5, during the years when he walked with God? "Do not weary yourself to gain wealth, cease from your consideration of it. When you set your eyes on it, it is gone. For wealth certainly makes itself wings like an eagle that flies toward the heavens."

You may be thinking, *Okay, Kris, how do you know that these are contradicting verses, and not simply contrasting verses like those you pointed out previously?* That is a great question, and I am glad you asked. Contrasting verses must both be true in a certain context or in a specific situation (at the very least). But verses that contradict the message of the Scriptures and the character of God are *never* true no matter what the circumstances or context. Much (though not all) of what Solomon wrote in the book of Ecclesiastes is *never* true no matter the circumstances or context. Life in God is *never* vanity. It is *never* okay to be a little bit wicked. Money is *never* the answer to all things. The fate of animals and the fate of people are *never* the same.

You get the point. Reading the Bible without knowing the heart of God and being guided by the Holy Spirit can lead to deception, bondage and even death.

Slavery

It is vital that we understand *how* to relate to the Word of God, and it is imperative that we know the difference between God speaking narratively into a situation and God laying out His divine order for our lives. When God speaks narratively, He often gives instructions without correcting the glaringly dysfunctional culture that exists in the circumstances He is narrating. The point I made about Esther and Abraham in the previous pages illustrates this dynamic perfectly. On the other hand, when God gives us commands for life, we must fully embrace them and universally apply them if we want to receive the maximum benefit He intends.

Confusing God's narratives with God's commands can have deadly ramifications. For example, during the American Civil War, many devout Christians fought in favor of slavery. Those believers took Scriptures like Paul's letter to the Colossians to mean that they had the God-given right to enslave people. Such believers were protecting verses like these: "Slaves, in all things obey those who are your masters on earth, not with external service, as those who merely please men, but with sincerity of heart, fearing the Lord" (Colossians 3:22). "Masters, grant to your slaves justice and fairness, knowing that you too have a Master in heaven" (Colossians 4:1).

Sadly, the inability of these believers to understand *how* to relate to the Word of God enslaved an entire ethnic group. To make matters worse, 620,000 people died in the Civil War trying to set things right. Much like the story of Esther, in which the Bible seems to ignore the bigger picture of divorce and immorality to celebrate Esther's courage and resolve, the apostle Paul speaks to the Colossians about the slave/master relationship while seemingly ignoring the more profound truth, "It was for freedom that Christ set us free; therefore keep standing firm and do not be subject again to a yoke of slavery" (Galatians 5:1). The key is in knowing when God is speaking into our circumstances and when God is dictating our stances.

The Effect of Core Values

How do we tell when God is speaking into our circumstances and when God is dictating our stances? One of the defining factors in understanding how to approach the Scriptures is our core values. Core values are the principles, standards and virtues at the center of the way we live, love and think. Core values are also the lens through which we view the Bible. If our core values are flawed, so is our ability to see what Scripture is truly saying. Jesus made a powerful statement in Luke's gospel that helps clarify this point. He said, "So take care *how* you listen" (Luke 8:18, emphasis added). We often question *what* we hear, but we seldom question *how* we hear. This principle also applies to seeing. Many times we question *what* we see, but we hardly ever question *how* we see.

For example, all of us speak with an accent, though often we do not realize it until we are in the presence of someone who speaks with an accent different from ours. Of course, we all tend to think it is the other person who has the accent. What most of us do not realize is that we also *see* with an accent. This visual accent is a kind of processing prejudice—a lens—that shapes our view of the world, the Kingdom and the Bible by causing us to see things not *as they are* but *as we believe they are.* Thus, as we live out our faith and read the Bible, we look for and expect to see that which validates what we already believe. In other words, we tend to see only what we are *prepared* to see.

Dr. Lance Wallnau, a respected author and teacher, drove this point home for me at a conference recently. He brought a barrel of varicolored flags up on stage and gave us thirty seconds to count all the gold flags. Then he instructed us to close our eyes, and he asked us how many red flags were in the container. No one could answer the question because we had only counted the gold flags. This is such a great picture of our tendency to read our own core values, life experiences and doctrinal prejudices into what the Bible says. The danger is that by selective *seeing*, we sometimes make the Bible say something it does not say.

The story I told in the opening paragraphs of this chapter about the Keystone Cops and the airline representative illustrate the effect good and bad core values have on processing instructions. Those three gentlemen did not understand the heart of Homeland Security, so they clung to the letter of the law. Remember my *"Stop Nursing Mothers Only"* example of the studio sign and the flawed way people who were uninformed might interpret it? Those three airport men viewed the world through the letter of the law because they did not understand, metaphorically speaking, what was really happening in the studio. And because they did not understand the true purpose of the law and how it applied to their situation, they were reduced to protecting words that made up rules instead of people.

Son-Glasses

Going a little further with my studio sign metaphor, our understanding of *how* God views the room of womanhood determines *what* we think God is saying to us through the sign—His Word—on the door. If our core values about the empowerment of women are flawed, the lens through which we see the Scriptures that deal with women will be distorted. The result will be that none of us, male or female, will realize the maximum benefit of the powerful influence that God intends women to have on this world for the Kingdom. On the other hand, if we view Scriptures through the "Son-glasses" of Calvary's cross, which freed us all from every curse in the Garden, then we will view women as valuable and powerful.

What core values might have positively affected our experience at the tiny airport in California? First of all, the security guards would have had to ask themselves *why* they have been instructed to search people's luggage. Had they inquired, they would have discovered "Core Value #1"—their primary job was not to search luggage, but to secure the safety of the passengers. Homeland Security had charged these officers with the vital mission of rooting out and apprehending terrorists. Yet through ignorance, they were reduced to luggage inspectors. If "secure passenger safety" had been the lens through which they viewed their responsibility, it would have changed the way they read their employee handbook—and the way they dealt with us.

"Core Value #2" would be that the passengers whose safety they were securing were also the customers of the airline and the people whose income ultimately paid their salaries. If frustrated customers stopped flying out of that airport, there would be no need for security there and the airport employees would no longer have jobs. Ultimately, Homeland

Security works for the government, which represents the people those guards are searching. Being rude, irrational or harsh in the name of protecting passengers is not only stupid, it is self-destructive. Although I have been back to that city four more times since our crazy day at the airport, I have used other means to get there. I will never fly in or out of that airport again. If the employees had viewed things through the right core values, however, that would not be the case.

A New Operating System

Many years ago, I had a powerful, vivid dream that will help clarify how to correctly apply core values to biblical truth. In this dream, I saw written words begin to flow in front of my eyes on something like a ticker tape running across a television screen. Words like *holy*, *true*, *powerful*, *peaceful* and *godly* were moving from left to right across the screen. The words were flat and single dimensional, much like words typed on a piece of paper. Then suddenly, a loud voice thundering from eternity shouted, "I am releasing a *new operating system* upon My people!"

This proclamation created its own picture, a kind of living PowerPoint. The scene changed, and the words were now falling like rain all around me. But this time the words were multidimensional, like 3-D, yet alive. Some words were larger than others. It was as if I could see diverse aspects and perspectives on each word as I viewed it from different sides, sort of like looking at a car from the front, back, sides and underneath. I stepped into the vision and began to breathe in the words as if they were oxygen. They were flowing in and out of me, forming the very attributes that each individual word contained. For example, when I breathed in the word *peace*, I suddenly became a peaceful man. When I inhaled the word *courage*, it assimilated into my being and became cellular in my soul.

The words were alive with revelation. Everything I knew about each word now seemed elementary, hardly capturing the full essence of its meaning and the impact of the real truth. The revelation and implications of the words were not so much in their definition as in their experience.

Let me try to describe it like this. I could define the word *Corvette* for you intellectually, but if I gave you a ride at 180 miles an hour in the car instead, the word *Corvette* would suddenly take on a whole new meaning for you. The original definitions of the words I saw were not wrong, but they seemed almost irrelevant in light of experiencing each word itself. In this dream, every word became a vehicle traveling at the speed of light, illuminating celestial realities and casting shadows on my finite understanding.

The Lord said to me in that dream, "I am creating a new operating system that can contain My revelation, for the former wineskin will rip under the weight of My Kingdom. The stagnant mind-sets of religious structures must give way to a living organism that can embrace My dreams and empower My people."

All Truth Is Not Created Equal

In my dream, I saw that some words were larger than other words, and those carried more weight. I realized that part of God's new operating system is the revelation that all truth is *not* created equal—there are actually levels of truth. For example, Paul writes, "But now faith, hope, love, abide these three; but the *greatest* of these is love" (1 Corinthians 13:13, emphasis added). Did you notice that although faith is truth, hope is truth and love is truth, God assigns the word *greatest* to love? Jesus gave us another great example in Matthew's gospel:

> Woe to you, scribes and Pharisees, hypocrites! For you tithe mint and dill and cummin, and have neglected the weightier provisions of the law: justice and mercy and faithfulness; but these are the things you should have done without neglecting the others.
>
> Matthew 23:23

Jesus said that tithing was an important truth and that they should continue to do it, but that they were neglecting the *weightier* things of the law. Justice, mercy and faithfulness are *heavier* truths than tithing!

These greater and weightier truths create a kind of system of order. As I pondered my dream, I began to understand that truth out of order, out of context and out of proper timing is *perversion* (the wrong version). Isaiah explained it like this: "For precept must be upon precept, precept upon precept; line upon line, line upon line; here a little, and there a little" (Isaiah 28:10 KJV).

Let me give you another example. God created sex and said it was "very good." But if you take sex out of its designed context, it suddenly becomes perversion and is no longer good, but evil. What I am saying is that a "word" must be in its proper context to be true. If you do not realize that the word *love* carries more weight than the word *justice*, you will be prone to destroy your relationships for the sake of creating justice. The result is that you will be "dead right," just like Noah's son, Ham, who was cursed for telling his brothers the truth about his father's sin (see Genesis 9:20–27).

This revelation is exploding in me. I now can see that because we do not understand the dimensions of truth, we have limited our application of Scripture to its historical context. Even in this, we have often created perversions that destroy people. What happens when we lose sight of the fact that the word *love* is greater (carries more weight) than the word *submit*? We produce a family environment where wives are told to submit to their hateful, abusive husbands, often in the worst possible hell you can imagine living in.

I am not advocating divorce here (though that may be necessary in extreme cases); I am simply saying that Tarzan should have to live with the animals if he is going to act like one. I cannot count the number of times I have talked to women who are in dangerous situations with their children because a husband is brutalizing his family. Oftentimes, the wife has been counseled by her pastor to stay in the situation in the name of "submission."

I am sorry, but pastors who give people this kind of advice need to get their heads checked! Nobody should have to willingly submit to someone who abuses him or her. *Love* is weightier and therefore takes precedence over *submission* every time. Truth must have order or it becomes a destructive perversion, a dangerous counterfeit or a devious delusion.

The Devil Knows the Bible

The devil is the ultimate pervert. He is a master at twisting Scriptures to imprison, disempower, deceive and destroy people. The most destructive weapon in the world is the Word of God in the hands of the devil. The Bible misapplied is worse than a lie—it is religion. Religion starts wars, divides believers and oppresses people. The devil even used the Bible to tempt Jesus in the wilderness. Carefully read the dialogue they had:

> He led Him to Jerusalem and had Him stand on the pinnacle of the temple, and said to Him, "If You are the Son of God, throw Yourself down from here; for it is written,
>
> > "He will command His angels concerning You to guard You,"
>
> and,
>
> > "On their hands they will bear You up,
> > So that You will not strike Your foot against a stone."
>
> And Jesus answered and said to him, "It is said, 'You shall not put the LORD your GOD to the test.'"
>
> Luke 4:9–12

The devil actually picked specific Bible verses that were written about Jesus to hurl against Him (see Psalm 91:11–12). But the Bible in the hands of the devil is not true. It takes the Word of God plus the Spirit of God to equal the Truth of God. The Word of God in the hands of anyone besides the Holy Spirit always leads to religion, bondage and death. "For the letter kills," as Paul said, "but the Spirit gives life" (2 Corinthians 3:6).

Rescuing the King's Princesses

In this chapter, we talked about the different ways in which God wrote the Scriptures. Some verses are a documentary on the way people in the Bible lived, while other verses are a commentary about God's perspective on our lives. We shared the importance of having Kingdom core values that act as a lens to guide the way we see life and to help us accurately handle the Word of Truth. We talked about the need for order and the danger of perversion in applying the Scriptures. And finally, we discussed how Satan loves to use the Bible to kill, steal and destroy people's lives.

The truths we have learned here will become our drawbridge over the dangerous moat of religion that encircles the walls of the evil fortress of deception. These truths will become the thick climbing rope we will use to scale the castle tower of tradition and the sharp, double-edged sword we will wield to defeat the enemy. Our ultimate mission is to rescue God's princesses from decades of captivity and powerlessness, and to restore them to their rightful throne next to their King.

Harriet Tubman

Leader of the Underground Railroad

*H*arriet Tubman was the most famous leader of the Underground Railroad. Born as a slave in the nineteenth century and transformed into a freedom fighter, Harriet escaped the chains of bondage and became an agent for social justice. She faced insurmountable challenges in her life. She was a dirt-poor, completely uneducated, illiterate female slave. Yet in spite of her circumstances, hundreds of slaves were liberated from captivity because of her outrageous courage and self-sacrifice.

Harriet was born in 1820, 43 years before President Lincoln signed the Emancipation Proclamation. Her grandparents survived the treacherous journey of the slave trade ships from Africa, making Harriet a third-generation slave. It is hard for us to imagine what it must have been like to be owned and traded like a piece of property, the way Harriet and her family were.

Harriet suffered unthinkable pain during her childhood. Her owners whipped her multiple times, and she carried the scars from these beatings all of her life. When she refused to assist a slave owner in capturing his runaway slave, the owner threw a large rock that struck Harriet in the head. The rock knocked her unconscious for two days. When she regained consciousness, her master ruthlessly forced her back into the fields to labor in the scorching heat, though her wound was still open and bleeding. The attack caused brain damage, and she suffered from seizures the rest of her life.[1]

When Harriet heard rumors that she would be sold to a chain gang, she knew it was time to escape. The thought of being shackled in leg irons to a group of prisoners and digging ditches in the hot sun was more than she could bear. With the help of God she walked more than a hundred miles, until she reached a free state, Pennsylvania. She later said, "I looked at my hands to see if I was the same person, now that I was free. There was such a glory over everything . . . and I felt like I was in heaven."[2]

Yet it was difficult for Harriet to be alone in an unfamiliar land while trying to come to terms with her newfound independence. In spite of the great joy freedom brought, she missed her family and longed to see them liberated. This passion ultimately drove her to abandon a life of peace and risk her life to help set others free.

The consequences for escaping from slavery were harsh. Bounty hunters operated in both the South and the North, and a black could be arrested as a runaway simply on the accusation of any white person.[3] If runaways were caught, they were returned to their owners and tortured for running away. Anyone who helped a slave escape also faced severe punishment. Slave owners would stop at nothing to get their property back, posting rewards in the paper and putting bounties out on their slaves' heads. Harriet's illiteracy almost cost her freedom when she fell asleep under her own Wanted poster![4]

After her own escape, Harriet began covertly traveling back to the South and leading slaves to the free American states and Canada in the North, using the Underground Railroad. The Underground Railroad was a network of secret routes and safe houses slaves used to escape to freedom.[5] In more than twenty treacherous journeys, Harriet never was caught. She warned her travelers with the threat of death if any of them even considered turning back and surrendering. One fugitive she was traveling with lost his courage and insisted he was returning to his owner. She pointed a gun at his head and said, "You go on or die." Evidently she was pretty intimidating; he continued his journey to safety. She was later quoted as saying, "I was the conductor of the Underground Railroad for eight years, and I can say what most conductors can't say—I never ran my train off the track and I never lost a passenger."[6]

Harriet was called the Moses of her people for leading them to freedom. Could it be that part of her success was due to the fact that she was a woman performing a role as a spy that normally a man would fulfill? She was hidden in plain sight!

Harriet's methods of escape were ingenious. She would only travel in the winter, where the nights were long and people stayed inside, which lessened the chances of detection. The escapes were planned for Saturday nights, giving the escapees an extra day of travel before the newspapers would print runaway notices on Monday mornings. And Harriet used songs with coded messages to give directions or warnings to fellow travelers.[7]

Harriet Tubman's life involved so much more than just the Underground Railroad. When the Civil War began in 1861, she took on several roles. She began as a cook and a nurse, but then she served as an armed scout and a spy. She knew the territory better than anyone else, having hidden and traveled in the woods and swamps for years. She was the first woman to lead an armed mission in the Civil War, and she guided the troops in the Combahee River Raid that freed over seven hundred slaves.[8]

Later in life, Harriet was a leader in the fight for women's rights. She traveled to many cities, including Washington, D.C., to speak in favor of voting rights for women. She was the keynote speaker at the first meeting of the National Federation of Afro-American Women in 1896. In the early 1900s, she started a home for "aged and indigent colored people."[9] She spent her last days in that rest home, which was named after her, and she passed away from pneumonia in 1913.

Deeply devoted to the Lord, Harriet fervently believed in the goodness of God. She believed God had called her to set the slaves free, and she trusted Him to lead her and keep her safe. Someone once told her that he had never met anyone who had more confidence in the voice of God.[10] Harriet also refused to hold hatred and unforgiveness in her heart toward those who abused her, believing that God was the author of justice. Her unconditional love for all people defined her life.[11]

Harriet Tubman was an American patriot and a devoted humanitarian, and she was named one of the most famous civilians in American history before the Civil War. She imparted hope to people enslaved in hopeless situations. She was a warrior and a champion for civil rights.

5

Jesus: Founder of the First Women's Liberation Movement

When most Christians think of Jesus, they envision a mild-mannered, soft-spoken gentleman walking the streets of Jerusalem, meekly sharing His wisdom while kissing the foreheads of children. Sadly, many believers have very little idea about the real nature of the Christ they are following. For the most part, the Church has domesticated the Lion of the tribe of Judah, relegating Him to a household pet or imprisoning Him behind the bars of some religious zoo. But the truth is that when Jesus walked the earth, He was a countercultural radical who not only healed the sick and raised the dead, but also liberated the oppressed and set the captives free. Women were at the top of His list!

The four gospels, Matthew, Mark, Luke and John, were written to give us an account of Christ's life and teaching. Pastor Bill Johnson of Bethel Church in Redding, California, says, "Jesus is perfect theology." Bill is right. In fact, the apostle John put it this way: Jesus is the Word who "became flesh, and dwelt among us" (John 1:14). We are called to be Christlike because we were made in His image and likeness. When we act like God, we are being ourselves. That is why the apostle Paul wrote, "Be imitators of God, as beloved children" (Ephesians 5:1). In other words, the Son of God became the Son of Man so that the sons of men could become the sons (and daughters) of God.

Since Jesus is perfect theology, the million-dollar question is, how did He relate to women? Before we tackle this question, it is important that we understand what was going on that pertained to women during the days when Christ walked the earth.

First-Century Gentile Women

I guess we should not be surprised that most Gentile women were much more powerful and respected in their cultures than women in Judaism were. In Macedonia, women built temples, founded cities, engaged armies and held fortresses. They served as regents and co-rulers. Men admired their wives and even named cities after them. Thessalonica was such a city, and there women were given inheritable civic rights. It was the Macedonian businesswoman Lydia who founded the church at Philippi after Paul led her to Christ (see Acts 16:14–15).

In Egypt, women were legally equal to men. They could buy, sell, borrow and lend money. They could petition the government for support or help and initiate a divorce, and they paid taxes. The oldest daughter could also be a legitimate heir.

Roman women were more restricted than Macedonians or Egyptians. The authority of the father was paramount. A Roman girl was "sold" in name into the hands of her future husband. Both daughters and sons were educated, boys until seventeen and girls until thirteen (when they were expected to marry). A Roman woman could not conduct business in her own name, but could enlist the help of a male relative or friend who served as her agent. Women did have inheritance rights and the right to divorce. Roman women were not permitted to vote or hold public office. Nevertheless, Roman matrons had power and influence because they were the acting heads of households and business managers while their spouses were off fighting in Caesar's army. Early Christianity spread rapidly in the Roman world due largely to the influence of these wealthy Roman matrons.

As a rule, women had greater socioeconomic status in Gentile cultures that worshiped strong female deities such as Aphrodite in Corinth, Artemis (also called Diana) in Ephesus and Isis in Egypt. In virtually all first-century Gentile cultures, both women and men exercised leadership equally in religious worship.[1]

First-Century Judaism

In first-century Israel, no people group was more oppressed than women. They were considered second-class citizens akin to slaves. They had virtually no rights, no respect and no voice. They were the property of men. They were allowed little or no formal education. If a family had young boys and girls, the boys would go off to school, while the girls stayed home with their mother.

Like the women of Afghanistan before the American invasion, Jewish women were forbidden to speak to men in public and were required to veil their faces whenever they left their homes. If a woman was caught unveiled in public, it was grounds for divorce. They kept house, took care of the children and served at the will of their husbands. If a male guest came over to the house for dinner, the women had to eat in another room. Their fathers arranged most of their marriages, so they rarely married the man of their dreams. The best they could hope for was someone who treated them better than their fathers did. To make matters worse, polygamy was legal for men but not for women, so most women shared their husbands with other wives. And if their husbands got tired of them for most any reason, they divorced them, discarding them like used rags. Jewish women also could not vote and had no political influence whatsoever. A woman could not even be a witness in a court case!

Judaism was stricter than the Old Testament Law with respect to women. Women were relegated to the outer court of the synagogue and most often were not even allowed to read the Scriptures (Torah). One first-century rabbi named Eliezer said, "Rather should the words of the Torah be burned than entrusted to a woman. . . . Whoever teaches his daughter the Torah is like one who teaches her lasciviousness."[2] His comments depict the religious community's attitude toward women at that time. Women were not even allowed to recite the Shema or the Morning Prayer, nor pray at meals.[3]

Jesus' Many Girlfriends

When I say Jesus had many girlfriends, I obviously am not saying that Jesus had romantic or intimate relationships with women—that would be crazy. I am simply saying that in spite of the first-century Jewish culture, many of Jesus' close friends were women. Lazarus's sisters, Mary and Martha, were two of His closest friends. They were often with Him when He traveled, and He seemed to spend quite a bit of time at their house. Dr. Luke records one time when Jesus entered their village and Martha invited Him into her home. Like most of us when we ask a special or famous guest to our house, Martha was pretty freaked out about making sure the meal went well and the house was clean. But her sister, Mary, was hanging out in the front room with Jesus instead of helping. Mary seemed more concerned about building a relationship with Jesus than preparing a meal for Him. Martha stomped into the front room where Mary was sitting at Jesus' feet, raised her voice and said to Jesus in front of Mary, "Lord, do You not care that my sister has left me to do all the serving alone? Then tell her to help me" (Luke 10:40).

I am sure Martha expected Jesus to reprimand Mary sternly for several reasons. First, Martha was doing what Jewish tradition and culture required of a woman; she was working in the kitchen to prepare a meal for a man. Martha was playing the subservient role that Judaism required. Second, Mary was spending her time talking to and learning from Jesus, a man. As we pointed out earlier, Judaism strictly forbade men to teach women. Not only that, but it was taboo for a man to hang out and converse with a woman. Yet Jesus' answer to Martha was shocking: "Martha, Martha, you are worried and bothered about so many things; but only one thing is necessary, for Mary has chosen the good part, which shall not be taken away from her" (Luke 10:41–42).

What is Jesus saying to Martha? Is He saying, "Martha, I place no value on your gift of hospitality or hard work; I like hanging around with people who are lazy and irresponsible, so get a life"? By observing Jesus' work ethic, we know that cannot be true. So what is the Lord saying to Martha? Most likely He's saying, "Martha, you and Mary are both welcome to sit and talk with Me. I didn't come to your house to get a free meal or to have you serve Me. I really value your friendship and enjoy your company. You're accustomed to men using you and requiring you to serve them. Mary is more familiar with My heart than you are. Why don't you come sit and talk with us? We can eat later."

Lazarus Is Dead

John, the beloved apostle, reports another encounter Jesus had with Mary and Martha. Their brother, Lazarus, was deathly ill, so they sent word to Jesus to come and help him. When Jesus received the report of Lazarus's situation, John records, "Now Jesus loved Martha and her sister and Lazarus" (John 11:5).

It is interesting to me that John mentions Martha first here even after the kitchen incident. We know Jesus loves everybody, so John is not saying, "Jesus doesn't love most people, but He sure does love them." John is letting us know that Jesus had a special fondness for His three friends, two of whom are women. In fact, there are only four people that the Bible specifically says Jesus loved: John, Lazarus, Martha and Mary. John also wants us to know that in spite of the fact that Jesus loves His friends, He purposely delays His visit two more days so that Lazarus would die (see verse 6).

When Martha hears that Jesus is finally on His way to help her brother, she marches out a couple of miles to meet Him, while Mary stays back at the house. Martha is upset with Jesus' delayed response and says so: "If You had been here, my brother would not have died!" (verse 21).

I personally love Martha. I really understand her. She was strong, opinionated and confrontational. Martha was also an external processor; people always knew right where they stood with her. She was a black-and-white thinker who needed justice. To Martha, the world was divided into two categories: right and wrong. Her thinking went something like, *Mary isn't helping in the kitchen—that's not right!* and *Jesus took His sweet time getting to our house, turned a two-day walk into a four-day journey and cost Lazarus his life—that's wrong!* But then Martha basically says to Jesus, "You got here late, but You can still fix this." She declares, "Even now I know that whatever You ask of God, God will give You" (verse 22).

Jesus is not put off by Martha's strong personality, her need for justice or her insinuations. He understands her pain, and He actually had her in mind when He waited until Lazarus died before coming to help. He needs Martha and Mary to understand the resurrection. He needs them to grasp that not everyone who dies stays dead. He needs them to know that some people rise from the dead and that *He* will rise from the dead.

Now comes the teaching. Jesus is about to release the deepest revelation of God's resurrection power to a *woman*—someone forbidden to read the Torah, relegated to the outer court of the Temple, despised by the religious hierarchy, the property of men, a second-class citizen—and God's most beautiful creation. Look at their exchange. Jesus says to Martha, "Your brother will rise again." Martha replies, "I know that he will rise again in the resurrection on the last day" (John 11:23–24).

Jesus, probably thinking *Martha, you're not getting this*, puts it another way: "I am the resurrection and the life; he who believes in Me will live even if he dies, and everyone who lives and believes in Me will never die. Do you believe this?" (verses 25–26).

Martha answers him, "Yes, Lord; I have believed that You are the Christ, the Son of God, even He who comes into the world" (verse 27).

Did you notice that Martha answered in the past tense? "I have believed." In other words, "I know You told me this before, Jesus—*I have believed!*" Faith begins to rise in her heart, so she runs back home to get Mary and tells her, "The Teacher is here and is calling for you" (verse 28).

It may seem like a minor point to us, but in light of Jewish culture, a powerful truth begins to emerge here. Martha calls Jesus *Teacher*, not Master or Lord. She says *Teacher*. Jesus is teaching *women*, who had been God-starved for generations.

Mary finally musters up the courage to meet Jesus outside the village. But unlike Martha, Mary is weeping, broken with despair and full of emotion. In anguish she falls down at His feet, and through her tears she utters, "If You had been here, my brother would not have died" (verse 32). Jesus has no revelatory statement for Mary. He understands that Mary's struggle does not involve theological incongruity or intellectual betrayal like Martha's. Mary is simply grieving over the loss of her brother. She is not angry or disappointed with Jesus. She just wants her brother back.

Jesus is not afraid of her pain. Instead, He embraces Mary in the midst of her grief and weeps with her: "When Jesus therefore saw her weeping . . . He was deeply moved in spirit and was troubled, and said, 'Where have you laid him?' They said to Him, 'Lord, come and see.' Jesus wept. So the Jews were saying, 'See how He loved him!'" (verses 33–36).

Mourning was women's work; it exposed weakness and was not the macho thing to do. Still, *Jesus wept.* His weeping sent a message to Mary, to women everywhere and to the watching crowd. He was saying, "I value emotion, I feel your pain and I understand your sorrow."

Finally, deeply moved within, Jesus arrives at the tomb and says, "Remove the stone." True to form, Martha feels responsible for warning Jesus of the risks involved. She says, "Lord, by this time there will be a stench, for he has been dead four days" (verse 39).

Jesus answers, "Did I not say to you that if you believe, you will see the glory of God?" (verse 40). Jesus knew Martha was not really concerned about the smell; she feared the disappointment of broken prophecy and a lifeless brother. The rest is His-story.

A few months later, it is Passover and Jesus is hanging out at Mary and Martha's house. Of course, Martha is serving everyone, Lazarus is sitting at the table eating dinner, and you guessed it, Mary, the ever-so-passionate one, steps into the room with perfume worth a year's wages. With all the disciples watching, she gets down on the floor and begins to pour this expensive perfume over Jesus' feet, wiping them with her hair.

This passionate moment is almost lost in the testosterone-filled environment as the men begin to complain about the poor stewardship of wasting expensive perfume when it could have been sold to help the poor. Judas wants to sell the stuff and steal the money.

But Jesus says, "Why do you bother the woman? For she has done a good deed to Me. For you always have the poor with you; but you do not always have Me. . . . Wherever this gospel is preached in the whole world, what this woman has done will also be spoken of in memory of her" (Matthew 26:10–11, 13).

There Jesus goes, protecting the feelings of a woman, valuing Mary's passion, validating a $60,000 experience over meeting the practical needs of the poor that pressed against their souls.

Now I Get It

It is all starting to make sense to me, things like the reason the Pharisees brought a woman caught in adultery to Jesus but did not bring the man. If the Pharisees were simply trying to see if Jesus would extend grace to a person who broke the Law, they could have just as easily grabbed the guy. But they were not only upset about Jesus forgiving the guilty; they were angry that He was honoring and empowering women. They were hoping they could catch Him making a heretical statement to protect a woman. Or worse yet, they hoped He would be forced to defend His Godhood by stoning the woman, thus destroying the honor He had been exhibiting toward women throughout His entire ministry. (See John 8:3–11.)

Women saw Jesus as their deliverer from cultural oppression, their liberator from religious bondage and their knight in shining armor. He came to deliver the oppressed and to set the captives free. Women loved Him because He valued them, protected them and taught them. He treated women as equals and refused to bow down to the male-dominated, religious boys' club that had ruled the Jewish world for centuries.

Luke 7:36–49 records a powerful story of a woman loving on Jesus at a religious leader's house. I understand now what was really going on at Simon the Pharisee's place when the woman broke into his home and disturbed his dinner party. Remember, by all rights a woman should not have been in the same room where men were talking and eating. To make matters worse, this woman is a lady of the night, a woman of ill repute, the scum of the earth.

As the events unfold, Simon thinks to himself, *Some prophet this guy is—He can't even figure out this woman is a prostitute.* But suddenly the tables are turned when Jesus looks deep into Simon's soul and addresses him:

> "Simon, I have something to say to you." And he replied, "Say it, Teacher."
> "A moneylender had two debtors: one owed five hundred denarii, and the other fifty. When they were unable to repay, he graciously forgave them both. So which of them will love him more?" Simon answered and said, "I suppose the one whom he forgave more." And He said to him, "You have judged correctly." Turning toward the woman, He said to Simon, "Do you see this woman?"
>
> Luke 7:40–44

Note here that the Pharisees refused even to acknowledge women, much less do the unthinkable—acknowledge prostitutes. But Jesus said to Simon, "Do you *see* this woman?" The connotation was that Simon should look at her, recognize her and acknowledge her. Then Jesus went on:

Simon, "I entered your house; you gave Me no water for My feet, but she has wet My feet with her tears and wiped them with her hair" (verse 44).

Simon, "you gave Me no kiss; but she, since the time I came in, has not ceased to kiss My feet" (verse 45).

And, Simon, "you did not anoint My head with oil, but she anointed My feet with perfume" (verse 46).

Simon, "for this reason I say to you, her sins, which are many, have been forgiven, for she loved much; but he who is forgiven little, loves little" (verse 47).

Then Jesus spoke to the woman: "Your sins have been forgiven. . . . Your faith has saved you; go in peace" (verses 48, 50).

There He goes again, rescuing a woman from the clutches of another religious leader. Jesus defended a woman who obviously broke protocol by inviting herself to the dinner party of a powerful leader. As if that were not bad enough, instead of quietly blending into the crowd, she makes a huge scene and becomes the center of attention.

What does it look like when a woman of ill repute is hanging all over Jesus, kissing His feet and wiping them with her hair? Why does He let her do it when He should be protecting His reputation? After all, He is supposed to be the righteous Son of God who will die for the sins of the world. Why not make a clear statement to the religious community that nothing is going on between Him and these women? And maybe the most profound question is, why are these women attracted to Jesus? What is the draw? Why all the fanfare?

Wells of Compassion

I have to admit that before I wrote this book, I never understood the radical message of gender equality that the gospel writers were trying to convey through the life of Jesus. Yes, I knew that Jesus hated religion. I was aware that He was a countercultural radical who overturned the deceptive tables of hypocrisy and drove the moneychangers out of the Temple. Having read the Bible every day for thirty-plus years, I understood that quite a few women hung around Jesus. Yet because I did not have a real grasp on the oppressive culture of first-century Judaism and the massive mistreatment of women during the days of Christ, I totally missed one of the most profound messages of the gospels—that Jesus championed the equality of women. It is all through the four gospels; it is almost impossible to miss His message. Like *Wanted* posters in a train station or *Warning* signs at a nuclear site, the gospel writers etched their surprising decrees with alarming frequency throughout their manuscripts. But somehow I managed to stumble blindly through the hallways of freedom and step over the feminine treasures of womanhood.

In John's gospel, we see Jesus tired and thirsty from a long day's journey. He is sitting at the edge of a well in the hot noonday sun, with no way to draw water from the deep spring. His disciples have gone to town to get some lunch, so He is all alone, but not for long. By divine coincidence, a Samaritan woman emerges on the scene with a waterpot in her hand, just in time to quench His thirst.

Jesus says to her, "Give Me a drink" (John 4:7). I love the way Jesus gets right to the point and does not waste words.

The Samaritan woman says back to Him, "How is it that You, being a Jew, ask me for a drink since I am a Samaritan woman?" (verse 9).

I am sure she was being a little sarcastic here because she knew very well that the Jews had no dealings with Samaritans and looked down their noses at both Samaritans *and* women. She was obviously both. The Jewish people held a deep-rooted prejudice against her race and her sex. At one point, James and John even wanted to call fire down on the Samaritans, yet Jesus is asking this Samaritan woman for some help.

Jesus answers her, "If you knew the gift of God, and who it is who says to you, 'Give Me a drink,' you would have asked Him, and He would have given you living water" (verse 10).

Stop and think about what is really happening here. Step back in time with me once again, all the way back to the first century. Jesus is offering a woman—a Samaritan woman—living water. Remember, men do not talk to women; women are possessions. They are not taught, not valued and not celebrated. Their heads are covered, and they definitely are not spiritual.

The woman says to Jesus, "Sir, You have nothing to draw with and the well is deep; where then do You get that living water? You are not greater than our father Jacob, are You, who gave us the well, and drank of it himself and his sons and his cattle?" (verses 11–12).

This girl is smart and intuitive. When she met Jesus a few minutes earlier, she emphasized to Him that He was a Jew and she was a Samaritan.

But suddenly the tables have turned. The thirsty Man is honoring her. He is treating her as though she is a person, so she rushes to find common ground. Even though she is a half-breed, she claims Jacob as her father. She knows how to make a connection with a Jewish man; she reminds Him of their common roots.

Jesus tells her, "Everyone who drinks of this water will thirst again; but whoever drinks of the water that I will give him shall never thirst; but the water that I will give him will become in him a well of water springing up to eternal life" (verses 13–14).

The woman replies, "Sir, give me this water, so I will not be thirsty nor come all the way here to draw" (verse 15).

We can see that the woman is hungry and that Jesus is eager to give her a river of life. But now the story gets a little sticky. Jesus is about to uncover a painful cycle of dysfunction in her life. Will she lie to cover up the fact that she is a fornicator, or will she trust Him enough with her heart to let Him unearth decades of abandonment, divorce and betrayal? She chooses honesty:

> He said to her, "Go, call your husband and come here." The woman answered and said, "I have no husband." Jesus said to her, "You have correctly said, 'I have no husband'; for you have had five husbands, and the one whom you now have is not your husband; this you have said truly." The woman said to Him, "Sir, I perceive that You are a prophet. Our fathers worshiped in this mountain, and you people say that in Jerusalem is the place where men ought to worship."
>
> John 4:16–20

On His part, Jesus shows her respect in the midst of her sin and compliments her for being honest. On her part, she may have a messed-up personal life, but she also has a deep hunger for the things of God. In a culture that refuses to educate women, this Samaritan girl is well-read and obviously has been exposed to the Scriptures. Her story reminds me of so many people I have met throughout life. When you view their stories from a distance (in her case, five husbands and living with her boyfriend), they seem to have no interest in God whatsoever. The religious world often writes these people off, speaks piously about them from the podium and uses their stories to illustrate wickedness. But much like the story of Rahab of old (see Joshua 2), underneath years of dysfunction and a mountain of pain in such people, there lies a hungry heart . . . a passion to know God.

What happens next is amazing. The most profound teaching on worship ever revealed is taught to a Samaritan woman who is living with her boyfriend! Jesus says to her,

> Woman, believe Me, an hour is coming when neither in this mountain nor in Jerusalem will you worship the Father. You worship what you do not know; we worship what we know, for salvation is from the Jews. But an hour is coming, and now is, when the true worshipers will worship the Father in spirit and truth; for such people the Father seeks to be His worshipers. God is spirit, and those who worship Him must worship in spirit and truth.

> John 4:21–24

And five husbands and one boyfriend later, the woman is still looking for the Messiah, the anointed one, who will release the oppressed and set the captives free. She tells Jesus, "I know that Messiah is coming (He who is called Christ); when that One comes, He will declare all things to us" (verse 25).

Jesus answers her, "I who speak to you am He" (verse 26).

Did you get that? Jesus just revealed Himself personally as the Messiah for the first time in recorded history—and it was to a Samaritan who was a woman!

At this point, the disciples show up and are amazed to see Jesus speaking with a woman. Yet as shocked as they are that He is talking to a Samaritan who is a woman, they are not about to confront Him about His inappropriate behavior. They have seen this movie too many times before. Then things get even more interesting:

> The woman left her waterpot, and went into the city and said to the men, "Come, see a man who told me all the things that I have done;

this is not the Christ, is it?" They went out of the city, and were coming to Him. . . .

From that city many of the Samaritans believed in Him because of the word of the woman who testified, "He told me all the things that I have done." So when the Samaritans came to Jesus, they were asking Him to stay with them; and He stayed there two days. Many more believed because of His word; and they were saying to the woman, "It is no longer because of what you said that we believe, for we have heard for ourselves and know that this One is indeed the Savior of the world."

John 4:28–30, 39–42

Look at what is happening here. A Samaritan, a woman who has been married five times and is now living with her boyfriend, whom the religious world would not even allow to step foot in the synagogue, just became the first evangelist in history. This woman, who would never qualify as an elder in anyone's church, has just turned a Samaritan city upside down after one encounter with her Messiah. I am telling you that disqualifying women from leadership is costing us our cities!

You think, *She wasn't a leader.* You are right; she did not have a title. But she led people, and they followed her to Christ. Leadership is more than a title, a plaque on a desk or name on some flowchart. Leadership means people follow you, they listen when you speak, they value your words, they emulate your experience. A lot of people are running around who have a plaque on their desk, their name on some flowchart or who hold a lofty title, but nobody is following them. John Maxwell puts it like this: "He who thinks he leads, but has no followers, is only taking a walk."

Not only were those Samaritan people following this woman; they also learned about Jesus from her. She taught people that Jesus was the Messiah. If Paul's words in 1 Timothy 2:12, "I do not allow a woman to teach," were universally applied in this case, many Samaritans would not have found Christ. (We will talk more about this statement of Paul's in chapter 7.)

Some may argue about whether or not a woman should carry the title of leader, elder, apostle, prophet or the like, but true leaders are acknowledged by titles, not created by them. Calling people elders does not make them elders any more than calling people engineers makes them engineers. A builder is someone who builds. A skydiver is someone who jumps out of a plane with a parachute. A dancer is someone who dances, a leader is someone whom people follow and a teacher is someone whom people learn from.

You get the picture. You can choose to redefine these spiritual roles to protect your understanding of the Scripture, but you are refusing to acknowledge that when a man is learning from a woman, she is teaching him, and when people follow a woman, she is leading them—period.

My Mother Made Me Do It!

Where did Jesus learn to place such a high value on women? When you grow up as Jesus did, in a culture that devalues women, treats them like slaves or possessions and throws them away like dirty rags, how in the world do you embrace a completely different paradigm?

Part of the secret is revealed at a party. Let's step back a couple of thousand years and sneak into a wedding celebration at Cana. Jesus is there with His family and friends, so let's stand in the corner and watch how the guests behave to see what we can learn. Everybody seems to be having a great time, dancing, singing and drinking. It is a real shindig—until they run out of wine. Mary, the mother of Jesus, makes her way through the crowd and says to Him, "They have no wine" (John 2:3).

I find this interesting for a number of reasons. First of all, how did Mary know that Jesus could make wine unless He was doing it at home? Seriously, what would cause her to think that Jesus could do anything about the wine supply? But it is the next part of the dialogue that really intrigues me. Jesus says to His mother, "Woman, what does that have to do with us? My hour has not yet come" (verse 4).

In other words, He is saying, "It's not time for Me to launch My public ministry, do miracles or let the cat out of the bag that I'm the Son of God." After all, as Jesus said more than once, "I can only do what I see My Father doing and say what I see the Father saying" (see John 5:19–20).

Mary ignores His decree, turns to the servants and says, "Whatever He says to you, do it" (verse 5).

Think about it: Jesus' mother tells Him to make wine. He lets her know that it feels premature to launch His miracle ministry, and therefore He does not want to make wine. That is the only dialogue recorded at Cana between them. But I think she must have given Him one of those Jewish mother looks that said, "I'm your Mother—make wine, Son!"

Let's face it, folks. On a practical level, the guy is thirty years old, not to mention the fact that He just happens to be the Son of God. Yet Jesus submits to His mother against His initial judgment, turns to the waiter and says, "Fill the waterpots with water. . . . Draw some out now and take it to the headwaiter" (verses 7–8). This results in the headwaiter tasting the water, which has become wine, but having no idea where it came from.

What was the outcome of Mary's daring request? John recorded it like this: "This beginning of His signs Jesus did in Cana of Galilee, and manifested His glory, and His disciples believed in Him" (verse 11).

This entire incident flies in the face of the kind of thinking that says the Church should universally apply Paul's exhortation to Timothy: "A woman must quietly receive instruction with entire submissiveness. But I do not allow a woman to teach or exercise authority over a man, but to remain quiet" (1 Timothy 2:11–12). It is ridiculous to argue that Mary (a woman) did not instruct and influence the Son of God. This quick peek into the life of Jesus and His mother is a clear indication of the way in which He allowed Mary to influence His life.

Mary, the Mother of God

I find it interesting that Jesus grew up with a mother who supposedly got pregnant with Him out of wedlock. When Joseph found out his fiancée was pregnant, he tried to break off the relationship privately. The Lord finally had to send an angel to explain to Joseph that Mary really was pregnant by immaculate conception. I think it is amusing that Mary asked the angel Gabriel how she could possibly get pregnant since she was a virgin. Gabriel said, "The Holy Spirit will come upon you, and the power of the Most High will overshadow you; and for that reason the holy Child shall be called the Son of God" (Luke 1:35).

But then Gabriel went to see Zacharias. He told Zacharias that his wife, Elizabeth, who was beyond menopause, was going to have a son (John the Baptist). Zacharias said to the angel, "How will I know this for certain? For I am an old man and my wife is advanced in years" (Luke 1:18). The angel became really stern with him and said, "I am Gabriel, who stands in the presence of God . . . behold, you shall be silent and unable to speak until the day when these things take place" (verses 19–20). I find it funny that Mary and Zacharias both asked Gabriel the same basic question, yet the angel gives the woman an answer and strikes the man mute!

Now, if Joseph had a hard time believing Mary (and he knew her well), I can only imagine what the rest of the community thought about her. We have to keep in mind that this did not involve a twenty-first-century American family where people commonly live together without being married. This was in a first-century Jewish culture where adultery and fornication were dealt with by stoning. I can just imagine Mary, about six months pregnant, saying to her neighbors, "Joseph and I have never had sex. The Holy Spirit impregnated me with the seed of God!" I am sure everybody in the neighborhood had a good laugh when they heard that story.

Although Mary and Joseph were righteous and were of impeccable character, their reputation was still questionable thanks to these events. Then along comes Jesus about six months too early. Try to put yourself in His first-century shoes. Think about the scorn and ridicule He must have been exposed to because of His mother's supposed illicit behavior. It certainly would not have been uncommon for Jesus to overhear His neighbors talking badly about His mother. I imagine that even the kids whom He played with mocked His mother's character and maybe called her dirty names.

Growing up in a situation like that must have given Jesus an inside perspective into the intense shame that immoral women experienced in their lives. It is very likely that Mary, with her questionable reputation, felt extraordinary compassion for women who were sexually promiscuous. Perhaps she built friendships with them. This could be the reason why Jesus connected so well with sinners and why He was invited to their parties. It also could explain why so many women of questionable character bonded so easily with Him.

Even the Pharisees harassed Jesus by accusing Him of being born out of wedlock. When Jesus told the Pharisees in John 8:41, "You are doing the deeds of your father," they answered back, "We were not born of fornication; we have one Father: God." Their implication was that Jesus is an illegitimate son born of an affair. He was no stranger to the scorn such situations brought on. The gospels are filled with stories of immoral women who loved Jesus and whom He often set free. There was the prostitute named Mary Magdalene who had seven demons. There was the woman caught in the act of adultery whom the Pharisees wanted to stone. There was the woman of ill repute who showed up at Simon the Pharisee's house. And let's not forget the Samaritan woman at the well who was married five times and had a live-in boyfriend.

The mere frequency of Jesus' encounters with such women and the fact that the gospel writers specifically mention them is intriguing. In fact, the way Jesus deals with immorality in the New Testament is the polar opposite of the Old Testament's emphasis. Proverbs chapter 2 and chapter 7 both give clear examples of the Old Testament view of sexual sin. Let's take a look:

> My son, if you will receive my words
> And treasure my commandments within you,
> Make your ear attentive to wisdom,
> Incline your heart to understanding . . .
> Discretion will guard you,
> Understanding will watch over you . . .
> To deliver you from the strange woman,
> From the adulteress who flatters with her words;
> That leaves the companion of her youth
> And forgets the covenant of her God;

For her house sinks down to death
And her tracks lead to the dead;
None who go to her return again,
Nor do they reach the paths of life.

Proverbs 2:1–2, 11, 16–19

For at the window of my house
I looked out through my lattice,
And I saw among the naive,
And discerned among the youths
A young man lacking sense,
Passing through the street near her corner;
And he takes the way to her house,
In the twilight, in the evening,
In the middle of the night and in the darkness.
And behold, a woman comes to meet him,
Dressed as a harlot and cunning of heart.
She is boisterous and rebellious,
Her feet do not remain at home;
She is now in the streets, now in the squares,
And lurks by every corner.
So she seizes him and kisses him
And with a brazen face she says to him:
"I was due to offer peace offerings;
Today I have paid my vows.
Therefore I have come out to meet you,
To seek your presence earnestly, and I have found you.
I have spread my couch with coverings,
With colored linens of Egypt.
I have sprinkled my bed
With myrrh, aloes and cinnamon.
Come, let us drink our fill of love until morning;
Let us delight ourselves with caresses.
For my husband is not at home,
He has gone on a long journey;
He has taken a bag of money with him,
At the full moon he will come home."

With her many persuasions she entices him;
With her flattering lips she seduces him.
Suddenly he follows her
As an ox goes to the slaughter,
Or as one in fetters to the discipline of a fool,
Until an arrow pierces through his liver;
As a bird hastens to the snare,
So he does not know that it will cost him his life.

Now therefore, my sons, listen to me,
And pay attention to the words of my mouth.
Do not let your heart turn aside to her ways,
Do not stray into her paths.
For many are the victims she has cast down,
And numerous are all her slain.
Her house is the way to Sheol,
Descending to the chambers of death.

Proverbs 7:6–27

Did you notice anything obvious about these two passages from Proverbs? Right—they both warn men about seductive women. As a matter of fact, there are literally over a hundred verses in the book of Proverbs that warn men about loose women, but not a single proverb warns women about immoral men. In other words, Proverbs, along with most of the Old Testament, put the responsibility for immoral acts on women.

Now let's contrast the teachings of Jesus with the Old Testament's teachings on the issues of sexuality and divorce to see if we can discern any difference in their perspectives:

You have heard that it was said, "You shall not commit adultery"; but I say to you that everyone who looks at a woman with lust for her has already committed adultery with her in his heart.

Matthew 5:27–28

Some Pharisees came to Jesus, testing Him and asking, "Is it lawful for a man to divorce his wife for any reason at all?" And He answered and said, "Have you not read that He who created them from the beginning made them male and female, and said, 'For this reason a man shall leave his father and mother and be joined to his wife, and the two shall become one flesh'? So they are no longer two, but one flesh. What therefore God has joined together, let no man separate." They said to Him, "Why then did Moses command to give her a certificate of divorce and send her away?" He said to them, "Because of your hardness of heart Moses permitted you to divorce your wives; but from the beginning it has not been this way. And I say to you, whoever divorces his wife, except for immorality, and marries another woman commits adultery."

Matthew 19:3–9

Jesus' teaching on sexual immorality and divorce stands in stark contrast to Solomon and most of the writers of the Old Testament. Instead of warning men about seductive women, as Solomon did in Proverbs (where he basically blamed women for seducing men), Jesus warns men about looking at women with impure motives. Instead of blaming women, He puts the responsibility back on men for not watching over their hearts. And did you notice that not one time in the four gospels does Jesus ever specifically warn women about sensuality or immorality?

Of course, all of Jesus' teachings about immorality should apply to both men and women. I am simply pointing out that He directed His correction toward men and not women.

Now let's look at Jesus' view of divorce. Remember the cultural perspective on divorce that we talked about early on in this chapter? Women were throwaways, disposables. A Jewish man could have several wives and divorce any one of them without cause. Do you know why the Pharisees were the ones trying to test Jesus on the subject of divorce? Because the Pharisees and the religious community were the ones who oppressed women. Their test was not so much about divorce as it was about the value of womanhood.

I find it interesting that it is almost always the religious spirit that reduces and oppresses women. I love the way Jesus takes the Pharisees back to the Garden, before the fall of Adam, and reminds them of God's divine design for man and woman by saying, "So they are no longer two, but one flesh" (Matthew 19:6). Then in the same verse, He adds this little piece: "What therefore God has joined together, let no man separate." Jesus continues His radical dialogue by telling men that if they divorce their wives and marry someone else, they are committing adultery.

Make no mistake about it—Jesus just turned the Pharisees' test about divorce into a gender equality issue. In effect, He was stating, "You and your wife are one, inseparable, a divine unity, one flesh. Reducing her is reducing you; oppressing her is oppressing you. Pharisees, disciples, men, do you get it? She's part of you! She's not your slave, your possession or your mistress."

The disciples, many of whom were married, were so stunned by this radical idea of marriage that they responded, "If the relationship of the man with his wife is like this, it is better not to marry" (Matthew 19:10). Even Jesus' disciples did not value women and therefore did not marry with longevity in mind. Yikes!

Jesus Understood Womanly Issues

Two gospels repeat a powerful story about a woman who had been hemorrhaging for a long time. Her menstrual cycle was completely out of whack, resulting in her having a continual period for twelve long, agonizing, embarrassing years. In order to understand the significance of the story, you need to know two facts. First, when a woman was on her period, she was considered unclean. Jewish law required her to be quarantined during her cycle. Second, anyone who touched a woman on her menstrual cycle was also considered unclean for seven days and could not be out in public.

You can read the story in Mark 5:25–34 and Luke 8:43–48, but let me summarize it here. When this woman saw Jesus healing people, she said to herself, *If I touch the hem of His garment, I will be healed.* So she pressed her way through the crowd and touched His clothes. Immediately, she was healed and wanted to sneak away so that no one would know that an unclean woman was hanging out in public. But Jesus felt power leave His body and shouted over the crowd, "Who touched Me? Somebody touched Me!"

The disciples thought Jesus was being hypersensitive because lots of people in the large crowd were touching Him. They tried to tell Him that obviously the crowd would be touching Him and that it was no big deal (as if He did not know that already), but He knew better.

This woman realized she had been caught breaking Jewish protocol, and she was pretty freaked out about it. She confessed to Jesus in front of everyone that she had been hemorrhaging for twelve years and had been to every doctor for help. I am sure by that time you could have heard a pin drop as the noise of the crowd came to a sudden hush. Maybe people began whispering to one another, "What's this woman doing out of her house? . . . I don't know . . . Now Jesus is unclean . . . What's He going to do?"

But Jesus knew what was going on. He had created this turmoil on purpose to make an in-your-face statement to the religious leaders and the crowd. That was why He made such a big deal out of a touch in a jostling crowd. He wanted the woman to share her testimony. He wanted people to see that instead of Him becoming unclean when the woman on her cycle touched Him, she became clean. Jesus was telling women and people everywhere, "I don't care what the religious leaders tell you, as far as I'm concerned, women are clean. Women, you're welcome in My presence in any condition. Men don't have an advantage over you in spending time with Me just because you have a period and they don't."

God's Feminine Side

In Luke chapter 15, Jesus encounters His archenemies the Pharisees and scribes again. They are griping about Jesus receiving sinners and hanging out with them. Because they are complaining about how He accepts sinners, He tells them three parables. The first is about a shepherd who has a hundred sheep and loses one. You know the story. The shepherd goes out and finds the sheep that went astray, and he is more excited about the single sheep he found than about the 99 who did not stray.

Whom do the three characters represent in this parable? The shepherd is God. The lost sheep represents those sinners the religious leaders are complaining about. And the 99 sheep are the Pharisees and scribes, who see themselves as righteous.

The third story is the parable of the prodigal son. This is also a popular story, so I am sure you are familiar with it. (No, I am not forgetting the second story. We will get back to it.) The third story begins with a father who has two sons. The youngest son asks for his inheritance, and then he spends it all on prostitutes and winds up eating out of a pig trough. He finally works up the courage to go home, where his father runs out into the field to greet him. When the dad throws a party for the boy, however, the older brother refuses to come to the celebration because he thinks his brother should be punished and not celebrated.

Here we go again—whom do the three characters in this parable represent? The prodigal son represents the sinners Jesus is hanging out with. The father who runs out to meet him represents God. And the elder son who wants his brother punished instead of pardoned represents the religious leaders who want everyone to pay for their sins.

Now let's go back and look at the second parable. It is about a woman who had ten silver coins and loses one of them. She lights a lamp, sweeps the entire house and finally finds the expensive coin. She gets so excited that she invites all of her friends over her house to celebrate finding the lost coin.

Let's do this one more time—whom do the characters in the parable represent? The lost coin represents the sinners whom Jesus is looking for and whom the Pharisees are complaining about. The nine coins represent the Pharisees and scribes that view themselves as righteous. And whom does the woman represent? You guessed it—she represents God.

The connotation is obvious to the religious onlookers who were familiar with the Creation story. I have quoted this verse several times already, but here it goes again: "God created man in His own image, in the image of God He created him; *male* and *female* He created them" (Genesis 1:27, emphasis added). Jesus is clearly saying to the Pharisees and scribes that it takes both the femininity of women, whom they oppressed, and the masculinity of men to represent God. In oppressing women fashioned in the image of God, religion blinds people to the feminine side of God. This relegates people to a one-dimensional relationship with their Creator, and it robs them of seeing the full spectrum of the nature of God.

Making Disciples

Many people are quick to point out that when Jesus chose His twelve disciples and later promoted them to apostles, none of them were women. I think given the historic content of Judaism and Jewish culture in general, it is easy to see why it would have been impossible for Christ to commission women with leadership titles and formal positions. Not only would it have created a dangerous situation for the women in leadership, but practically speaking—taking into account the short time line of the three and a half years in which Jesus ministered—it would have been impossible for society to shift its mind-set to view women as leaders when for generations they had been valued only as possessions.

For example, can you imagine an African-American running for president of the United States three years after the Emancipation Proclamation? Or can you envision a black person leading a white church in 1950? Of course, any objection to these situations seems ridiculous now, but they perfectly illustrate why Jesus treated women equally but did not officially give them leadership titles in first-century Jewish culture.

Yet the fact is that many of Jesus' disciples were women! Luke points out that Jesus was ministering from city to city with the twelve disciples and some women, both married and single. Luke names three of these ladies: Mary Magdalene, Susanna and Joanna, the wife of Chuza (Herod's steward). He also mentions that there were "many others who were contributing to their support out of their private means" (Luke 8:3). The Greek word for contributing support is *diakoneo*. It is translated as "to serve, minister, care for," or as "deacons." This is the same Greek word used in Acts chapter 6, when the apostles chose seven men to *serve* (*diakoneo*) tables, which later became the foundation and qualification for *deacons* (*diakoneo*) who were leaders in the early Church. I am not saying that these women supporters were deacons in Jesus' ministry. I am simply pointing out that they were carrying out a similar role without the title.

I hope you can understand how the fact that gospel writers even acknowledged and documented that Jesus taught women, befriended women, traveled with women and ministered with women was a bold and countercultural statement. Remember that earlier in this chapter, I pointed out that when the disciples caught Jesus simply talking to the woman at the well, they were shocked? The gospels were written at least three decades after the Samaritan well incident, so by then their perspective on women had completely altered.

I used to think that when the gospel writers made statements like Jesus fed and taught five thousand men, *plus* women and children, they were degrading the women and children. But now I realize that the writers were trying to point out a radical dynamic taking place in the ministry of Jesus—He was teaching and thus equipping women and children, as well as men. This was an extreme departure from Judaism, which frankly viewed women as too unintelligent to be taught.

For Americans, the easiest way to grasp the huge gender gap that existed in first-century Jewish culture might be to envision our country before the civil rights movement and remember the great disparity between blacks and whites. Black people and white people did not use the same bathrooms, drink out of the same fountains or go to the same schools. White kids were not allowed to play with African-American children—period. *End of story*. It was taboo. It did not happen.

Now picture yourself reading a letter in that era from a friend who told you, "We went to the movies tonight with John and Henry, and some of our black friends." Or maybe something like, "We were at this great church, and the African-American people really got into the worship." Considering the cultural aspects of that era, the surprising part of the letter would not have been the movie or the church. The location would have been insignificant compared to the profound statement about the company being kept.

Given the time period in which He walked the earth, Jesus kept surprising company. I have spent this entire chapter uncovering Judaism's first-century oppression of women for you and contrasting it with Jesus' countercultural behavior and attitude toward women. My goal is that you would capture the true essence of those times and understand the intense love, honor and respect Jesus had for ladies.

72 Hours until Dawn

Does it strike you as odd that men were the *only* ones involved in the crucifixion of Christ? *Not a single woman* took part in His murder. It was a man who betrayed Him and male soldiers who arrested Him. It was Caiaphas the high priest, the scribes and the elders (all men) who accused Him. It was Pilate the governor and Herod the king who judged Him. It was Roman soldiers who beat Him and a Roman centurion who ordered Him nailed to the cross. It was a male prisoner who cursed Him and male soldiers who gambled for His garments. It was male guards who entombed Him and male disciples who denied Him.

On the other hand, it was a woman at Simon's house who poured expensive perfume on His body to prepare Him for burial. It was Pilate's wife who had a God-given dream and tried to convince her husband to release Christ. It was His mother, Mary, Mary Magdalene and Mary, the wife of Clopas, who stayed with Him through the dark night of His soul. Only two women were there the day of His burial, and there was just one faithful, grieving saint there to congratulate Him when He beat sin, death, hell and the grave; you guessed it—*a woman*.

With the great track record men have, it makes perfect sense to me that women should not be allowed to lead in the Church, for crying out loud! *Not!*

Where were the eleven world-changers who were supposed to rock the nations? When the two ladies discovered the empty tomb and the excited angels, they ran back to town to tell the disciples the good news, yet "the great spiritual leaders of the Church" still refused to believe in the resurrection. Although eleven apostles were left at the time, only Peter and John even bothered to check out the ladies' story. And remember, Jesus had been telling His disciples for months that He would die and rise again on the third day!

Thank God for women who believed Jesus and were not quiet about their experience. Christ pauses during His ascension to tell Mary Magdalene, a former prostitute who once was possessed by seven demons, to go tell His disciples that He was alive. Eight days later, the boys were still huddled up in a house, fearing for their lives. Thank God for women who refused to give up in dark times.

It certainly makes sense to me that women should not be allowed to teach in the Church—they might mess up the apostles' doctrine! The apostle Paul must have meant his restrictive principles to be universally applied to all women. But thank God that Paul's letters were not written until three decades after the resurrection; otherwise the apostles might still be trying to figure out what happened on that fateful day. (I am obviously being sarcastic here.)

It is my conviction that anyone (regardless of sex) who has an encounter with Jesus has something to say to the Church, and to the world, for that matter. Their words are recorded throughout Scripture. If you do not want to learn from women, you will have to cross a lot of verses out of your Bible (which I will discuss in greater depth in the next chapter). Not a single book of the Bible was written by a woman, but women are often quoted. (Some scholars believe the book of Hebrews was written by Priscilla, and that is why it remains unsigned. I think it is possible, though I am not sure how probable.) Thank God the authors were wise enough to know the Word of the Lord when they heard it. Thank God for women who visited empty tombs and believed in angels.

Bringing It Home

I grew up with men who oppressed women just because they could. They used their physical strength to bully their way through life. When I got saved and began reading the Bible, I was shocked that Jesus was so loving, empowering and protective of women. I can still remember coming to Church for the first time about a year after I was saved. I was surprised to realize that although the violence toward women was gone, the low value placed on them remained unchanged. I was also surprised that the Church was just another men's club that reduced women, assigning them all subservient roles. I am thankful that Kathy and I met Bill and Beni Johnson when we were still young believers. Bill loved and respected women, and he empowered them to teach, lead and minister. Kathy and I learned from the Johnsons the value of both sexes and the strength of their diversity.

As a country, we in America have asked Native Americans for forgiveness and have repented to African-Americans (as we should). Yet the most oppressed people group in the history of the world remains reduced within the Church. The world that Jesus died for empowers women. They can be mothers, doctors, astronauts, scientists, neurosurgeons, astrophysicists, teachers, sports analysts, athletes, firemen, police officers, soldiers, sailors, generals, entrepreneurs, detectives, artist, dancers, missionaries and so much more. Women can defend countries, start businesses, fight crime, create technology, rescue lives, put out fires and raise children. The Bible acknowledges women as queens, prophetesses, judges, teachers, mothers, leaders, apostles, coheirs, counselors, warriors, sons of God and much more. It is therefore confusing to me that somehow, in the Church that Jesus is the Head of, women are not considered qualified to talk, teach, shepherd or even help lead a congregation of thirty people. Something is wrong with this picture, and it is time that we got it right.

It is embarrassing that women in the world are more powerful than sisters in the Church. I cannot imagine what it must feel like for a woman who is the CEO of a large corporation to come to church and be treated like a second-class citizen. It is hard to fathom what a woman who is the mother of several children and the wife of an empowering husband must think when she goes to most churches for the first time.

I can tell you one thing—if Jesus had the opportunity to actually lead His Church, women would be powerful. Jesus refused to let the religious leaders of His day oppress women. It is about time that we become Christlike in this area today.

Rosa Parks

Founder of the Civil Rights Movement

*R*osa Parks was an ordinary woman who took an extraordinary stand against racism, becoming an American icon for civil rights for all African-Americans. Her single act of defiance against segregation laws inspired an entire movement. She is known as the Mother of Civil Rights, and she changed a nation with her courage. Her story is remarkable.

It was a dark, chilly evening on that historic day, December 1, 1955. In Montgomery, Alabama, Rosa Parks had just gotten off work after a long day working as a seamstress in a local department store. In the 1950s, it was not always easy for a black woman to find a job, so Rosa was thankful to have one. There was nothing particularly unusual about that day; nothing foreshadowed the life-changing events that were about to occur. As she stood on the street corner, waiting for the bus to pick her up, Rosa's thoughts were focused on getting home to her husband and enjoying the evening.

The bus rumbled to a stop and Rosa climbed aboard, taking a seat in the blacks-only section of the bus. Decades before, a Montgomery city ordinance had passed that mandated segregation for blacks and whites on buses. The law technically did not require any passenger to give up a seat if the bus was crowded. Yet over time, it became customary for blacks to be forced to give up their seats for white passengers if the bus was full. At times, they would even be told to get off the bus. Rosa had experienced this kind of discrimination firsthand before. In 1943, she had boarded the bus and paid her fare. The driver ordered her to get off the bus and use the back entrance so she could sit in the black section. Humiliated, she complied with his demand and exited the bus. Before she made it to the rear entrance, the bus driver roared away, leaving her stranded by the side of the road.

This time, however, Rosa was seated properly in the black section, but the bus was filling up quickly with commuters heading home. Three stops later several white passengers boarded the bus, and the driver (who happened to be the same man who had stranded her over a decade before) demanded that the four black people in her row stand up so the white passengers could sit down. At first, no one responded to the driver's request. Yet when he demanded a second time that they move, three of them complied. But this time was different for Rosa. After suffering decades of humiliation and abuse because of the color of her skin, something inside her rose up and she refused to leave her seat.

The bus driver threatened to call the police if Rosa did not move, but she held fast and would not leave her seat. Sure enough, the driver followed through and had her arrested. Later she said, "I would have to know, once and for all, what rights I had as a human being and a citizen."[4] She went on to say, "I only knew that, as I was being arrested, that it was the very last time that I would ever ride in humiliation of this kind . . ."[5]

In her autobiography, *My Story*, she said,

> People always say that I didn't give up my seat because I was tired, but that isn't true. I was not tired physically, or no more tired than I usually was at the end of a working day. I was not old, although some people have an image of me as being old then. I was forty-two. No, the only tired I was, was tired of giving in.[6]

Rosa Parks's arrest triggered a series of events that would become known as one of the most important challenges to segregation laws in history. Four days after she was arrested, she was found guilty of disorderly conduct. That same day, a small group of NAACP (National Association for the Advancement of Colored People) leaders gathered together to discuss Rosa's case and to organize a bus boycott by the black citizens of Montgomery. At that meeting, they elected a new leader, a young and unknown pastor from the Dexter Avenue Baptist Church. His name was Dr. Martin Luther King Jr.[7] The one-day boycott was so successful that they decided to continue. For 381 days, the black community, which comprised 75 percent of the ridership on the buses, refused to take public transportation. They found alternate methods to get to school, work and area shops. They taxied, carpooled, walked or biked in the pouring rain and scorching heat, for more than a year. Finally, the U.S. Supreme Court ruled that the city ordinance was unconstitutional and outlawed segregation on public transportation.[8] Their sacrifice had paid off, and the victory was theirs!

Even though Rosa's successful court case and the boycott brought worldwide attention to the cause of civil rights, it did not come without great personal sacrifice. She received regular death threats, she lost her job in the department store and her husband was forced to quit his job when his boss forbade him to talk about his wife or the court case. When they could not find work in Montgomery, the Parkses moved to Michigan to be near Rosa's sister. They started a new life in Detroit.

Rosa Parks was dedicated to the cause of civil rights throughout her life, founding the Rosa L. Parks Scholarship Foundation and the Rosa and Raymond Parks Institute for Self-Development. When she died, the nation paid its respects to Rosa as she lay in state in the rotunda of the United States Capitol in Washington, D.C. She was the only woman and only the second African-American in U.S. history to receive such an honor, which is usually reserved for presidents of the United States.[9] Rosa Parks was a catalyst for the civil rights movement, and her legacy lives on today.

6

The Misunderstood Apostles

For years I have read Paul's exhortation to the Corinthians that "women are to keep silent in the churches; for they are not permitted to speak . . . for it is improper for a woman to speak in church" (1 Corinthians 14:34–35) and have wondered how I could weasel my way out of these verses. My desire was to be relevant to the twenty-first century and still say that I honestly believe the Bible is the inherent Word of God. Most of the time I just ignored the verses, rationalizing that men who knew the Bible better than I did were allowing women to speak; therefore they must have some biblical reason why it is okay.

My wife, Kathy, never had a great passion to teach or preach (until recently), and she has always been more the quiet type, so in our younger years the issue of women being publically powerful in church was never in my face. But then our first two biological children were born, and they were both girls. I began to think of the consequences of raising my girls in church and having some Greek scholar or theological wizard reduce the destiny of my daughters. This created a passion in me to know the truth for the sake of the women I love so dearly. I am proud to say that both of my daughters co-lead churches as senior pastors of two local congregations. And in 2010, my wife became one of the twelve senior leaders at Bethel Church who give oversight to our church and movement. In the last few years, Kathy has also become much sought after as an international speaker and teacher. Watching the transformation in Kathy has been inspiring and exhilarating for me.

Let's get down to business and investigate the apostle Paul's perspective on women. In a previous chapter, I talked about how the context of a verse often determines its definition. I shared with you what King Solomon said: "Knowledge comes easy to him who has understanding" (Proverbs 14:6). I also demonstrated this principle to you in the story I told about the music studio at Bethel Church that was also used on Sundays as a nursing mothers' room. As you might remember, the sign on the door read "*Stop Nursing Mothers Only.*" We discussed some of the humorous ways the sign could be interpreted if the person reading it only viewed the room as a studio and did not understand that it was also a place where mothers nursed their infants. To a large extent, the apostle Paul shapes most of our understanding of the restrictions that seemingly should be imposed on women in ministry and/or leadership. But before we wrestle through specific verses, I want us to gain insight into what was going on behind the door in the studio of life in Paul's day. This will help us read the "sign on the door" through the clear lens of God's perspective.

Misunderstanding the Sign

The Bible is the bestselling book in the history of the world.[1] It is the only book ever written that is translated into every known language on the planet. God inspired 40 authors to write 66 books that comprise the Word of God. It took 14 centuries to complete the Divine Book. It was written in the depths of dungeons and on the porches of palaces . . . from the barley field to the battlefield . . . in times of great prosperity and under the curse of unimaginable poverty. It was penned in caves in the ground and from ships in the midst of storms. Its authors were kings, shepherds, priests, prophets, apostles, physicians, fishermen, farmers, generals, seers and even a former Pharisee—they all contributed to the Bible. (It is interesting to note here that Jesus, as a man, never wrote a single word of the Bible, although He was the Word of God who became flesh.)

To make our journey even more exciting, the Bible's authors often quoted many different sources, including God the Father, Jesus, the Holy Spirit, the devil, men, women, kings, queens, evil spirits, angels, believers, atheists, witches, diviners, prophets, prophetesses, enemies, friends, Pharisees, scribes, priests, wise men, fools, prostitutes, princesses, paupers, princes, secular books and even a donkey. Subsequently, all these quotes became part of the Word of God, which adds to the exhilarating adventure of navigating the whitewater of the truth in the Bible. We talked a little about this challenge in a previous chapter, but I want to look even more closely at it now.

The Bible is broken up into two sections, one entitled the Old Testament and the other called the New Testament. There are 252 commands and laws in the Old Testament, but in the New Testament even the Ten Commandments are reduced to two: Love the Lord your God with all your heart, with all your soul and with all your strength, and love your neighbor as yourself (see Luke 10:27). Remember in the last chapter, I told you that first-century Judaism was much more restrictive than the Old Testament Law? Here is a great example: Judaism had 613 commandments and laws!

Some people might be totally confused because I said that the Bible is divided up into the Old Testament and the New Testament, and then I mentioned Judaism as something different. I want to expand on that a little in case you are wondering what I meant. Although it is a little more complex than my explanation here, think of it this way: There were four hundred years of silence between the last Old Testament book, Malachi, and the first New Testament book, Matthew. In those years of silence, religious leaders called scribes and Pharisees began to reinterpret the Old Testament, adding their traditions, laws and opinions to the Bible (Torah). What they wound up with ultimately became known as Judaism.

You will shortly see what this has to do with empowering women. Consider that with 40 authors writing the Bible over a period of 1,450 years in several countries and multiple cultures, in various situations and in the Old and New Covenant, only one man seems to restrict women from leadership and teaching—the great apostle Paul. If God wanted to restrict half the population from leading or teaching men (kind of a big deal, I think), then why are 39 authors virtually silent on the issue, while Paul seems specifically to restrict women? And once more, why does Paul write to nine different churches or church leaders, but only restrict women in three locations? Why does Paul empower women in some places and limit them in others?

For example, Paul writes to Timothy, the leader of the church at Ephesus, and tells him that he does not allow women to teach or exercise authority over a man. But Paul writes sixteen chapters to the Romans and does not make a single restrictive comment about women. In fact, the first person Paul greets in the book of Romans is Prisca, along with her husband, Aquila. He calls them both "fellow workers," which is the exact phrase he used for the apostles Timothy and Titus, and Dr. Luke and Mark (author of the gospel of Mark.)

Here is another example of Paul's diverse instructions. Why does Paul tell the Corinthians that a woman is not allowed to speak in church, yet in his letter to the Galatians, he requires no restriction at all on women? As a matter of fact, he writes,

> For you are all *sons* of God through faith in Christ Jesus. For all of you who were baptized into Christ have clothed yourselves with Christ. There is neither Jew nor Greek, there is neither slave nor free man, there is *neither male nor female*; for you are all one in Christ Jesus.
>
> Galatians 3:26–28, emphasis added

Did you notice that he calls both men and women "sons" and then says there is no gender distinction in Christ?

What am I trying to say? If we want to have a biblical perspective on women in leadership, then we need to have a broader perspective on the

Scriptures and their context, broader than just the apostle Paul's few restrictive verses on women. Otherwise, metaphorically speaking, we misunderstand the sign on the door of the studio of life.

Relating to the Epistles

Most of the New Testament letters, called the epistles, were written to specific people or churches. The exceptions are the books of James, Jude and 1, 2 and 3 John, which are called "the general epistles" because they were not specifically addressed to a person or group. In 373 AD all these letters, along with the four gospels and the book of Revelation, were assembled into one book that we now call the New Testament. Therefore, a first-century congregation would have derived their doctrinal understanding of the Kingdom not from the New Testament as a whole, but from a combination of the Old Testament, a letter from an apostle (if they had received one) and anything taught by an apostle, prophet, pastor, elder or teacher who ministered to them.

It would have been common for letters addressed to one particular church to be copied and passed around to other churches, but it is important to understand that no first-century church would have possessed anything close to what we now term the New Testament. Nor would most of them have had the privilege of reading more than one or two letters from an apostle. The church at Thessalonica probably would not have read the letter to the Corinthians or the Galatians, and vice versa. Paul did not write a letter and tell the disciples to copy it five hundred times and send it to all the churches in the known world. Instead, his letters were written to address specific situations in specific locations.

When you contrast the epistles with the Pentateuch (the first five books of the Old Testament), an important truth begins to emerge. The Pentateuch, commonly attributed to Moses, was written with the broad audience of all God's people in mind. Much like the Constitution of the United States, the Pentateuch was originally penned to be corporately applied to an entire nation, Israel, the people of God at that time. A New Testament Christian cannot relate to the book of Corinthians in the same way that an Old Testament Jew would have been required to relate to the book of the Law.

Of course, both portions of Scripture should be revered as the inerrant Word of God. The Pentateuch was written to be a template for life, however, while the epistles are God's specific instruction to a particular person or church. From the epistles, we gain God's insight into how to deal with certain issues in a specific setting, but you cannot superimpose God's situational counsel over universal circumstances and have it be redemptive in every situation. The reality is that now, millions of copies of each individual letter, addressed to a particular person or church, have been distributed to most of the believers in the world. This has provided us with great insight into the way that God thinks about certain situations—in their context.

The problem is that oftentimes, the context of an epistle is either misunderstood or ignored, and then well-meaning people take God's situational counsel and try to enforce it universally. You would think people would realize that when they are applying Scripture in a way that is unredemptive, disempowering, oppressive or dishonoring, it somehow violates the nature of God. Yet people continue to make such applications, while ignoring the *full* counsel of the Word of God and undermining the purpose of the cross of Christ.

Ignoring the contextual settings of Scripture and applying the epistles universally has resulted in unimaginable consequences such as slavery and a preposterous gender prejudice toward women. For centuries, women were forced to take vows of silence when entering a church building and were reduced to being powerless citizens of the Kingdom. For too long, women have lived in a two-class environment most often promoted, perpetuated and propelled by misinformed believers.

Wrestling with Paul

You have waded through five chapters of this book, so by now you probably have had one of three responses: 1) You are angry and are taking notes to develop your own rebuttal. 2) You are open-minded and willing to listen, but you are really hoping there is a good argument for Paul's restrictive comments. 3) You already believe that empowering women is part of the Gospel, and you are excited that your faith is being reinforced. Whatever your response so far, I invite you to jump into the middle of things with me, take a closer look at the doctrinal debate and see if we can unravel some of the misunderstandings and misapplications of Paul's instructions.

As I mentioned previously, Paul wrote to nine people or cities, but he seemed to specifically restrict women in only three geographic locations. Those three involved the first book Paul wrote to the city of Corinth, the first letter he wrote to Timothy, the leader of the church at Ephesus, and finally his letter to Titus, who was the leader of the church on the island of Crete. We will examine each of these in a few minutes, but first I want to look at the historical context of women in those cities and see if we can gain any insight into Paul's concerns for these three locations.

The City of Corinth

When I studied the three places involved—Corinth, Ephesus and Crete—the first thing that jumped out at me is that all three cities worshiped female deities. In Corinth, you can still find the ruins of the temple of Aphrodite, the goddess of love. It had fallen into ruins by Paul's time, but the successors to its one thousand cult prostitutes continued to practice their profession in the city. Corinth was a harbor city that catered to sailors and traveling salesmen. Even in the Classical Age, it had earned an unsavory reputation for its immoral atmosphere. Calling a woman "a Corinthian lass" was like calling her a whore. The name *Corinth* therefore became synonymous with sexual immorality. It was specifically the temple of Aphrodite that gave Corinth its reputation for gross immorality because worshipers of the female deity incorporated orgies and outrageous sex into their worship services.[2]

The City of Ephesus

Ephesus was home to the Greek goddess Artemis, or Diana, as she is commonly called. The goddess Artemis was a combination of both the virgin goddess of the hunt and the Anatolian goddess Cybele. Sometimes known as the Great Mother, Cybele was associated with the earth and with fertility. (Yes, you heard it right. The Ephesian Artemis somehow combined the virginity of Artemis with Cybele, the fertile mother.) Artemis had a crown on her head, which could have signified female rulership. She also had eggs surrounding her midsection, which many think are a symbol of fertility.[3] Dr. Luke records the powerful influence of this Greek goddess in the days of Paul:

> A man named Demetrius, a silversmith, who made silver shrines of Artemis, was bringing no little business to the craftsmen; these he gathered together with the workmen of similar trades, and said, "Men, you know that our prosperity depends upon this business. You see and hear that not only in Ephesus, but in almost all of Asia, this Paul has persuaded and turned away a considerable number of people, saying that gods made with hands are no gods at all. Not only is there danger that this trade of ours fall into disrepute, but also that the temple of the great goddess Artemis be regarded as worthless and that she whom all of Asia and the world worship will even be dethroned from her magnificence."
>
> When they heard this and were filled with rage, they began crying out, saying, "Great is Artemis of the Ephesians!"
>
> Acts 19:24–28

The Island of Crete

In Greek mythology, Crete was the birthplace of Zeus, king of the gods. The Cretan goddess Diktynna also supposedly was born at Kaino, in the White Mountains of western Crete. The tiny island of Gavdos off the southern coast of Crete is where the nymph Calypso, a female deity, supposedly lived. According to a dramatic story in Greek mythology, Calypso took King Odysseus captive for seven years because she loved him. Finally Zeus stepped in and set the king free.[4] The story is much more complex than that, but for the sake of this book, suffice it to say that female deities were a major part of Cretan culture. The apostle Paul spent some time on Crete on his way to Rome (see Acts 27:7–8). Evidently, he was not impressed with the people of Crete. He wrote to Titus concerning them,

> For there are many rebellious men, empty talkers and deceivers, especially those of the circumcision, who must be silenced because they are upsetting whole families, teaching things they should not teach for the sake of sordid gain. One of themselves, a prophet of their own, said, "Cretans are always liars, evil beasts, lazy gluttons." This testimony is true. For this reason reprove them severely so that they may be sound in the faith.
>
> Titus 1:10–13

Apparently, the Cretans' appetite for Greek mythology skewed their core values and even affected the way the circumcised Jews approached the Gospel.

Journey Back to Corinth

Now that we have a little insight into the commonalities of the three cities where Paul seemingly restricts women, let's journey back to Corinth and see if we can unravel God's heart for women in ministry and leadership. The strongest restrictive exhortation in the entire Bible is found in the following passage penned by Paul to the Corinthians:

> The women are to keep silent in the churches; for they are not permitted to speak, but are to subject themselves, just as the Law also says. If they desire to learn anything, let them ask their own husbands at home; for it is improper for a woman to speak in church.
>
> 1 Corinthians 14:34–35

Some people lift this passage out of context and use it to reason that the Bible clearly does not allow women to speak in church. And if these were the only verses Paul wrote on the subject, then it would be hard to argue scripturally that these folks are wrong. We would be reduced to using human philosophy to justify the scriptural incongruence of allowing women to talk in church. Fortunately, that is not the case. It is very likely that Paul is actually quoting a question the Corinthians posed to him, and that he is answering their concerns in the pre-text and post-text surrounding these verses.

Let me explain the context of the letter to the Corinthians, along with its audience and intention. First of all, it is important to understand that Paul wrote the book of 1 Corinthians in response to a letter he had received from the Corinthians. This is evident throughout the book, for instance where Paul writes, "Now concerning the things about which you wrote, it is good for a man not to touch a woman" (1 Corinthians 7:1). The challenge with this book is that Paul does not always stick to the format of quoting the Corinthians' question before he gives them his answer, as you can see by reading the entire book. This leaves us with a couple of dilemmas: We are not always sure what question Paul is answering, and sometimes it is unclear which part of the text is the Corinthians' question and which part is his answer.

Second, it is important to note that 1 Corinthians is not written to men about women. It is a book written to a congregation of men and women. This makes a huge difference in the way we read this epistle, which I will explain further in a moment. But first let me demonstrate that Paul is instructing women about their issues, as well as men about their questions. Let me quote 1 Corinthians 7:1–7 and 12–16, which is a somewhat large section of Scripture, but we will extract several points from these passages. Here is Paul's exhortation to both men and women:

> Now concerning the things about which you wrote, it is good for a man not to touch a woman. But because of immoralities, each man is to have his own wife, and each woman is to have her own husband. The husband must fulfill his duty to his wife, and likewise also the wife to her husband. The wife does not have authority over her own body, but the husband does; and likewise also the husband does not have authority over his own body, but the wife does. Stop depriving one another, except

by agreement for a time, so that you may devote yourselves to prayer, and come together again so that Satan will not tempt you because of your lack of self-control. But this I say by way of concession, not of command. Yet I wish that all men were even as I myself am. However, each man has his own gift from God, one in this manner, and another in that. . . .

But to the rest I say, not the Lord, that if any brother has a wife who is an unbeliever, and she consents to live with him, he must not divorce her. And a woman who has an unbelieving husband, and he consents to live with her, she must not send her husband away. For the unbelieving husband is sanctified through his wife, and the unbelieving wife is sanctified through her believing husband; for otherwise your children are unclean, but now they are holy. Yet if the unbelieving one leaves, let him leave; the brother or the sister is not under bondage in such cases, but God has called us to peace. For how do you know, O wife, whether you will save your husband? Or how do you know, O husband, whether you will save your wife?

In light of everything we have learned so far in this book, these passages should jump off the page and grab you. The first thing that is obvious is that Paul is addressing both women and men. Therefore, this book is not written to men about women, as I stated earlier. But notice that the most radical statement ever written about wives in the first century was penned by this former Pharisee who, for most of his life, would have believed that women were possessions owned by their husbands and thought of as slaves. Yet this great apostle emphatically states that a wife has authority over her husband's body, just as a husband has authority over his wife's body! In fact, Paul specifically states that husbands do not have authority over their own bodies. Wow!

The next extreme idea that pops out of this passage is that a believing wife sanctifies an unbelieving husband. The Greek word *sanctified* is *hagiazo*, which means "to consecrate or make someone holy." A woman in relationship with God consecrates a man who does not know God. Another wow!

Would that mean that a believing wife would create a covering for an unbelieving husband? Would a born-again wife be under the covering of an unbelieving husband? Does a person's sex trump a relationship with God? In other words, would a man with no relationship with God—a man who refuses to walk with Jesus, who does not have the mind of Christ, who is void of the wisdom of God, who is devoid of the Spirit and is not Spirit led, but is in fact manipulated by the spirit of the power of the air that is working in the sons of disobedience (see Ephesians 2)—be expected to lead a woman who is a new creation possessed by the Spirit of God Himself? I will let you ponder these questions for now.

But wait, there is more. Did you notice what Paul says to women who have unbelieving husbands? "She must not send her husband away" (verse 13). Paul is talking to powerful women in the church whom he addresses as people who have authority, not as powerless slaves or mindless possessions. This is a radical departure from first-century culture, a new countercultural mind-set.

Let me make two more points from this passage. Paul writes to the wives of unsaved husbands, "How do you know, O wife, whether you will save your husband?" (verse 16). This flies in the face of the mind-set of 1 Corinthians 14:35, which states, "If they [wives] desire to learn anything, let them ask their own husbands at home; for it is improper for a woman to speak in church." This passage from chapter 14 seems to indicate that women are ignorant of spiritual things. But notice in chapter 7 that Paul tells Christian women they have power and influence over their husbands to lead them to Christ!

Also, we can see from these verses that the Corinthian congregation was obviously made up of many women who had unsaved husbands. Therefore, if Paul's solution for wives is to keep silent in the church and get their questions about the Kingdom answered by their husbands at home, then women with unsaved husbands would be relegated to a life of ignorance.

The last point I want to bring up concerning this passage is what the Corinthians' question reveals about their core values concerning women. Their inquiry reveals that they, not Paul, have a two-class core value system concerning men and women. It is important for us to keep the Corinthians' perspective about women in mind as we navigate our way through Paul's letter to them. Notice they do not ask, "Is it good for a woman not to touch a man and for a man to not touch a woman?" They only ask, "Is it good for a man to not touch a woman?" But Paul validates the sex drives of *both sexes* to the Corinthians when he says that a husband has a *duty* to fulfill his wife's passion for sex (not just for children) and vice versa.

Paul, what are you saying? Are you telling first-century husbands in the Church of Jesus Christ that they should care about their wife's sexual passions and fulfill them? You mean it is not all about men getting their needs met through wives who are all but sex slaves and servants in Judaism? Another wow!

Prophecy and Covering

Next I want to look at Paul's governmental strategy for empowering women to minister. (This is another longish portion of Scripture, but the context is vital to our understanding of God's perspective on life and ministry.) Paul writes:

Now I praise you because you remember me in everything and hold firmly to the traditions, just as I delivered them to you. But I want you to understand that Christ is the head of every man, and the man is the head of a woman, and God is the head of Christ. Every man who has something on his head while praying or prophesying disgraces his head. But every woman who has her head uncovered while praying or prophesying disgraces her head, for she is one and the same as the woman whose head is shaved. For if a woman does not cover her head, let her also have her hair cut off; but if it is disgraceful for a woman to have her hair cut off or her head shaved, let her cover her head. For a man ought not to have his head covered, since he is the image and glory of God; but the woman is the glory of man. For man does not originate from woman, but woman from man; for indeed man was not created for the woman's sake, but woman for the man's sake. Therefore the woman ought to have a symbol of authority on her head, because of the angels. However, in the

Lord, neither is woman independent of man, nor is man independent of woman. For as the woman originates from the man, so also the man has his birth through the woman; and all things originate from God. Judge for yourselves: is it proper for a woman to pray to God with her head uncovered? Does not even nature itself teach you that if a man has long hair, it is a dishonor to him, but if a woman has long hair, it is a glory to her? For her hair is given to her for a covering. But if one is inclined to be contentious, we have no other practice, nor have the churches of God.

1 Corinthians 11:2–16

The first thing we notice in this passage is that Paul is thanking the Corinthians for holding on to the *traditions* that he taught them. It is also important for us to understand that this portion of Scripture is a continuation of the conversation that began in the previous chapter of Corinthians about whether or not it is okay for them to eat meat sacrificed to idols when they are at someone's house who is not a believer. Paul is speaking to the Corinthian Christians in reference to the pagan cultural situations they were dealing with in their daily lives. As you will remember, Corinth was the home of Aphrodite, the goddess of love, and her one thousand cult prostitutes. The cult prostitutes shaved their heads as a sign of their devotion to Aphrodite and the power they had to seduce men. Women who were caught committing adultery in Corinth were also required to shave their heads, as their bald heads easily identified them as immoral women.[5]

Paul is saying to the Corinthian women that they can pray and prophesy in public, providing they are in right relationship with their leadership—which in the Corinthian culture was symbolized by having long hair. It has been common throughout history for the length of a person's hair or the way in which he or she dresses to be an outward expression of an inward stance. In the 1960s in America, if a man had long hair, he was considered a hippie associated with the countercultural, antiestablishment movement rooted in drug addiction and rebellion. Of course, today long hair is no longer a symbol of a countercultural movement, but is simply a style some men enjoy. The significance of a man wearing his hair in this fashion has changed, so people no longer view long-haired men as hippies.

Next, it is important to understand that men worshiped goddesses in the pagan city of Corinth. In paganism, the seduction of men was admired and celebrated as a positive attribute of these female deities and of womanhood. Paul takes the Corinthians through the governmental order of creation to show them the importance of being rightly related to one another.

This is where it gets a little complicated, and this is also the place where scholars disagree. In the Greek language (as in most languages), context often determines the definition of a word. In the case of the passage we just read, the Greek word for woman is *gune*, which is the identical word for wife. To make matters more complicated, the Greek word for man is *aner*, which is also the identical word for husband. Consequently, many translations of the Bible substitute the word *husband* for the word *man* and the word *wife* for the word *woman* in this passage.

Why is that important? Because it changes the scope of the influence and type of relationship that men and women have with one another. And the context that gives rise to your definition of the words in question will depend a great deal on the core values you hold about women. This is the reason Greek scholars disagree on this passage. For example, the scholars who believe *all* women should be in subjection to *all* men translate *gune* and *aner* as *woman* and *man* instead of *husband* and *wife*.

One way the passage can be read, then, is that God is the head of Christ, Christ is the head of every man, and every man is the head of every woman. The other way the passage can be read is that God is the head of Christ, Christ is the head of every husband, and every husband is the head of his wife. It goes without saying that there is a *huge* difference between every man having authority over every woman, and a husband (who is being called to lay down his life for his wife) having the authority to lead his bride.

Knowing Greek will not solve this issue since scholars disagree over the proper rendering of those two words, *gune* and *aner*. Consider that the New King James Version of the Bible, the New International Version and the New American Standard Version choose to render them as *women* and *men*. Several translations, however, render the same Greek words as *wife* and *husband*.[6] Here are a few:

> But I want you to understand that the head of every man is Christ, the head of a wife is her husband, and the head of Christ is God.
>
> 1 Corinthians 11:3 ESV

> In a marriage relationship, there is authority from Christ to husband, and from husband to wife.
>
> 1 Corinthians 11:3 MESSAGE

> But I want you to understand that the head of every man is the Messiah, and the head of a wife is her husband, and the head of the Messiah is God.
>
> 1 Corinthians 11:3 CJB

> However, I want you to realize that Christ has authority over every man, a husband has authority over his wife, and God has authority over Christ.
>
> 1 Corinthians 11:3 GOD'S WORD

Then, just to show how complex this can become, there is Young's Literal Translation and the Amplified Bible, which choose to mix the two words, translating *gune* as woman (not wife) and *aner* as husband. I love the way Paul concludes his thoughts concerning the levels of authority and covering. He says, "However, in the Lord, neither is woman independent of man, nor is man independent of woman. For as the woman originates from the man, so also the man *has his birth* through the woman; and all things originate from God" (verses 11–12). This seems to fit well with the exhortation he gives to the Galatians when he says, "There is neither male nor female; for you are all one in Christ Jesus" (Galatians 3:28).

I would like to suggest that Paul's ultimate goal in the passage we looked at from 1 Corinthians 11 is to exhort the believers at Corinth that men and women are not independent of one another. Corinthian men have reacted to the city's pagan, goddess Aphrodite culture by oppressing and reducing their women, but Paul is teaching these believers that despite the Corinthians' experience with pagan prostitutes, women should be empowered to pray and prophesy publicly, as long as their hearts are right.

Remember, Paul tells the Corinthians that a woman should cover her head specifically while praying and prophesying. He goes on to say that the covering is a symbol of authority worn for the sake of the angels. What did a woman's head covering have to do with angels? The angels honor women in right relationship with God by carrying out their prophecies and fulfilling the answers to their prayers. King David put it like this: "Bless the LORD, you His angels, mighty in strength, who perform His word, obeying the voice of His word!" (Psalm 103:20). When we prophesy, we are speaking for God, and it is often the angels who carry out these prophecies. They are also the ones who regularly fulfill our prayer requests. In fact, the book of Hebrews calls the angels "ministering spirits, sent out to render service for the sake of those who will inherit salvation" (Hebrews 1:14).

I personally have a struggle believing that a person's sex would inherently give him or her authority over another person. It makes no sense to me that a man who is living outside of a relationship with God would inherently have authority over a woman who is born again. It also seems wrong to me that a man who is a new believer would have authority over a woman who has known Christ all of her life. Of course, I am talking in general terms regarding the Church. A believing woman may go to work for a man in whatever spiritual condition he is in and properly submit to his authority because of their work-related positions (assuming that nothing he asks of her is contrary to Scripture, of course).

I like the way *The Message* deals with this entire topic in its translation of 1 Corinthians 11:1–16. Take a look:

> It pleases me that you continue to remember and honor me by keeping up the traditions of the faith I taught you. All actual authority stems from Christ.

In a marriage relationship, there is authority from Christ to husband, and from husband to wife. The authority of Christ is the authority of God. Any man who speaks with God or about God in a way that shows a lack of respect for the authority of Christ, dishonors Christ. In the same way, a wife who speaks with God in a way that shows a lack of respect for the authority of her husband, dishonors her husband. Worse, she dishonors herself—an ugly sight, like a woman with her head shaved. This is basically the origin of these customs we have of women wearing head coverings in worship, while men take their hats off. By these symbolic acts, men and women, who far too often butt heads with each other, submit their "heads" to the Head: God.

Don't, by the way, read too much into the differences here between men and women. Neither man nor woman can go it alone or claim priority. Man was created first, as a beautiful shining reflection of God—that is true. But the head on a woman's body clearly outshines in beauty the head of her "head," her husband. The first woman came from man, true—but ever since then, every man comes from a woman! And since virtually everything comes from God anyway, let's quit going through these "who's first" routines.

Don't you agree there is something naturally powerful in the symbolism—a woman, her beautiful hair reminiscent of angels, praying in adoration; a man, his head bared in reverence, praying in submission? I hope you're not going to be argumentative about this. All God's churches see it this way; I don't want you standing out as an exception.

The Originator of Authority

I would like to point out here that no matter how you view these Scriptures, headship and authority were never meant to be used to reduce a person. In 1 Corinthians 11:3, Paul says that "God is the head of Christ." Two things should stand out to us in this statement: First, the Father and Christ Jesus are both equally God, but they have different roles, one as the Father and the other as the Son. Second, and just as importantly, involves what God did as the head of Christ. Paul puts it like this in Ephesians 1:20–21: "He raised Him from the dead and seated Him at His right hand in the heavenly places, far above all rule and authority and power and dominion, and every name that is named, not only in this age but also in the one to come." Christ submitted to God, and God used His own authority to raise Christ up *even above Himself!*

But wait, it gets even better: God "raised us up with Him, and seated us with Him in the heavenly places in Christ Jesus" (Ephesians 2:6). Did you get that? God is the head of Christ. Christ is the head of man. Husband is the head of wife. God promoted Christ to the highest place in all of creation, and then He seated men and women with Christ in heavenly places!

My question to people who believe men have authority over women is this: Are you using your authority to empower, promote and exalt the women around you, or are you using your authority to reduce, oppress and suppress women? Jesus made it clear that the greatest among us is to be the servant of all (see Luke 22:26). In my opinion, the argument over where authority originates is dwarfed in light of the responsibility, servanthood and humility that true authority requires.

Danny Silk and I were doing a conference in England together. Danny, the family pastor at Bethel Church, is the author of the amazing book about empowering women entitled *Powerful and Free: Confronting the Glass Ceiling for Women in the Church* (Red Arrow, 2012). At the conference, Danny was speaking on the subject "Empowering Women." He closed his session with a question-and-answer time. Before anyone could ask a question, two women started shouting at him, "*Men don't give power to women! Women are not in submission to men, and therefore they don't access authority through a man! Men don't have the power to give to women. Women get authority directly from God!*"

The shouting continued for quite some time. I stepped in to try to rescue my friend from the angry women protesters, but it only served to make them more vigilant. I have to admit that at the time, I did not understand the root issues that troubled these two women. But now I understand that some people (especially women) view the concept of men empowering women as a slap in the face. They argue that this puts men between women and their relationship with Jesus. They insist that a woman's authority originates from God and does not flow through a man to her.

I do think that you can make a very good case for the fact that in marriage, there is a natural governmental flow in which a wife is required to submit to a loving husband who is laying down his life for her. Of course, for a husband, truly laying down his life is much more humbling and selfless than submission. This creates a marriage that has a great culture of service, sacrifice and mutual submission.

It is very difficult, however, to make a case that men, *as a sex*, have authority to give to women, *as a sex*. I do believe in all believers being in submission to spiritual authority. The author of Hebrews clearly points this out when he says, "Obey your leaders and submit to them, for they keep watch over your souls as those who will give an account" (Hebrews 13:17). But authority from God can flow from both a woman and a man, as it did in the Garden of Eden, or it can flow from one or the other—just from a man, *or* just from a woman, as it did in the days of Deborah the prophetess, who was Israel's judge (see Judges 4:4). We will talk more about this in the next chapter, but now let's get back to the Corinthian concern of women being silent in the Church.

Prophecy: Catalyst to Confusion

We have just established the fact that no matter how you view the origin of authority, women have power that even the angels recognize to pray and prophesy in public when they are in right relationship with God. (I would propose that men need to be in right relationship with God also to move in the gifts of the Spirit. Again, the apostle Paul is simply addressing women because of the cultural context in Corinth of female deities and temple prostitutes.) Yet the interesting thing about Paul's exhortation for women to be silent in the church is that it is in the context of public prophecy. So let's fast-forward to chapter 12 of 1 Corinthians and investigate the contextual setting of Paul's seeming restriction on women. Paul writes:

Now concerning spiritual gifts, brethren, I do not want you to be unaware. You know that when you were pagans, you were led astray to the mute idols, however you were led. Therefore I make known to you that no one speaking by the Spirit of God says, "Jesus is accursed"; and no one can say, "Jesus is Lord," except by the Holy Spirit.

Now there are varieties of gifts, but the *same Spirit*. And there are varieties of ministries, and the *same Lord*. There are varieties of effects, but the *same God* who works *all things in all persons*. But to each one is given the manifestation of the Spirit for the common good. For to one is given the word of wisdom through the Spirit, and to another the word of knowledge according to the *same Spirit*; to another faith by the *same Spirit*, and to another gifts of healing by the *one Spirit*, and to another the effecting of miracles, and to another prophecy, and to another the distinguishing of spirits, to another various kinds of tongues, and to another the interpretation of tongues. But *one and the same Spirit* works all these things, distributing to each one individually just as He wills.

1 Corinthians 12:1–11, emphasis added

I want to remind you again that Paul is not writing to men about women; his target audience is men and women. The passages above were written to both sexes to clarify the difference between the pagan view of the spirit realm and the Kingdom view. It is interesting to note that Paul is writing to a church that is moving powerfully in the gifts of the Spirit, yet their theological understanding of God is rooted in Greek mythology. When Paul says that no one speaking by the Spirit of God says, "Jesus is accursed," and no one says, "Jesus is Lord," except by the Holy Spirit, he is referencing their pagan gods who fought one another for spiritual dominance. Then he makes reference to the nine spiritual gifts the Corinthians are familiar with, and he tells them seven times that these gifts are coming from the same Spirit, the same Lord and the same God.

In other words, the Corinthian church had the right experience, but the wrong doctrine. They thought, for instance, that the gift of wisdom was one god, the gift of miracles was another god, the gift of prophecy was another god and so on. It may seem crazy to us that Christians would not understand that we are serving one God with many manifestations, but these were converted pagans who, unlike born-again Jews, had no understanding of the Bible (or Torah) whatsoever. They were raised in Greek mythology, not in Judaism.

Paul goes on to say, "There are varieties of effects, but the same God who works all things in *all persons*" (verse 6, emphasis added). Here again, Paul is telling the Corinthians that the gifts of the Spirit are available to everyone, which would include men and women. Years earlier, the apostle Peter had already established that God would use both men and women equally to prophesy. Peter, quoting the prophet Joel, proclaimed,

> "And it shall be in the last days," God says,
> "That I will pour forth of My Spirit on all mankind;
> And your sons and your daughters shall prophesy,
> And your young men shall see visions,
> And your old men shall dream dreams;
> Even on My bondslaves, both men and women,
> I will in those days pour forth of My Spirit
> And they shall prophesy."
>
> Acts 2:17–18

Let's fast-forward one more time to 1 Corinthians 14, where Paul writes, "Pursue love, yet desire earnestly spiritual gifts, but especially that you may prophesy. . . . Now I wish that you all spoke in tongues, but even more that you would prophesy; and greater is one who prophesies than one who speaks in tongues" (verses 1, 5). The obvious connotation is that they would *all* prophesy. Paul did not say all males or all men, so up to this point we still find no hint whatsoever of gender restriction on women ministering in public meetings. Then Paul goes on:

What is the outcome then, brethren? When you assemble, *each one* has a psalm, has a teaching, has a revelation, has a tongue, has an interpretation. Let all things be done for edification. If anyone speaks in a tongue, it should be by two or at the most three, and each in turn, and one must interpret; but if there is no interpreter, *he must keep silent* in the church; and let him speak to himself and to God. Let two or three prophets speak, and let the others pass judgment. But if a revelation is made to another who is seated, the *first one must keep silent.* For *you can all prophesy one by one,* so that all may learn and all may be exhorted; and the spirits of prophets are subject to prophets; for God is not a God of confusion but of peace, as in all the churches of the saints.

1 Corinthians 14:26–33, emphasis added

We see in this passage that Paul exhorts "each one" to have a teaching, a psalm, a revelation or the like, and the connotation is edifying one another within the church. It is important to note here *again* that women, along with men, are being empowered to teach and to move in the gifts of the Spirit. It is also vital to know that every Greek scholar (every one I could find) believes that the uses of the words *he, him* and *himself* in the passage above are generically applied to both sexes and are not meant to be taken as gender references, which the text makes clear anyway.

Now let's examine more closely the most restrictive verses regarding women in the entire 66 books of the Bible. Paul writes:

The women are to keep silent in the churches; for they are not permitted to speak, but are to subject themselves, just as the Law also says. If they desire to learn anything, let them ask their own husbands at home; for it is improper for a woman to speak in church. Was it from you that the word of God first went forth? Or has it come to you only?

1 Corinthians 14:34–36

And then Paul concludes with these thoughts:

If anyone thinks he is a prophet or spiritual, let him recognize that the things which I write to you are the Lord's commandment. But if anyone does not recognize this, he is not recognized.

1 Corinthians 14:37–38

Let's take a moment to recount what we already know. The first thing is that women were present in the public meetings in Corinth and were being taught alongside the men—unlike in Judaism, in which Paul was a leader during the time when he was a Pharisee. This in itself makes an extreme value statement to the women of Paul's day when taken in the context of first-century Judaism.

The next thing that we are sure of is that men and women both carried equal value in marriage, as we talked about when we looked at 1 Corinthians 7. Remember the passages where Paul said that the husband does not own his own body, but his wife does, and the wife does not own her own body, but the husband does? This indicates that the women at Corinth were thought of as powerful people, not as slaves or peasants.

Another thing we have learned is that women were commissioned to pray and to prophesy publicly, if they were in right relationship with God. In the cultural context of Corinth, this right standing was symbolized by their heads being covered.

Finally, we have learned that both women and men were taught to earnestly desire spiritual gifts, especially the gift of prophecy. Paul exhorts the entire Corinthian church to come to their public meetings with each believer having something spiritual to give to the others.

So, the million-dollar question is, how do Paul's seemingly restrictive words about women in the Corinthian church apply to us today?

The Process of Elimination

Greek scholars much more intelligent and qualified than I am have argued over these passages for more than a thousand years. Some of these scholars have concluded that women should be restricted in public meetings, while many other scholars feel quite the opposite. Let me offer you a little different approach to solving this complex issue. I propose that we process the information that is difficult to understand by eliminating the things we know for sure *cannot be true*. Then we can see what possibilities remain.

Here is an example of this approach. I have been married to Kathy for 38 amazing years. I have known her since she was twelve years old. If she were an hour late coming home from work and a person told me she had been seen engaging in an inappropriate relationship with a man, I would have to admit that I did not know where Kathy was at that particular moment—but I *did* know for sure where she was *not* because I know *her*! She was *not* involved in an inappropriate relationship.

We have spent a lot of time recounting the powerful ministry that these Corinthian women were engaged in. We know that they were included in Paul's exhortation for men and women to "earnestly desire" the nine spiritual gifts (see 1 Corinthians 12 1–11; 14:1). We must therefore conclude that these passages *cannot* mean that women are to be universally and unilaterally restricted from speaking in church.

Furthermore, we know without a shadow of a doubt that women in the Corinthian church were actually encouraged, taught and exhorted to pray and prophesy publicly. It would not make any sense, then, for Paul to use two verses to disqualify women from the ministry that he had already been equipping and commissioning them to do for fourteen previous chapters.

Probable Cause

Now that we know what these restrictive passages *cannot* be saying, what could they possibly mean? There are two prominent schools of thought on these verses, which frankly both make sense to me. The context of these verses is about creating order around the use of the gifts of the Spirit in public meetings. Remember that Paul has already told the people who speak in tongues with no interpreter to "keep silent," and he has also told someone who has a revelation while prophets are speaking publicly to "keep silent." Obviously, these two groups of people are not being told *never* to talk. They are simply being instructed—within the context of the disorder displayed in the Corinthian church—to follow protocol and not add to the confusion by talking out of turn.

Keep in mind that the Corinthian church was made up of former pagans who worshiped in the temple of Artemis, where women played a dominant role. In this context, it seems logical to me that if the women were behaving the way they commonly had back in the pagan temple and were being disruptive, Paul's "restrictive" correction would then make sense—especially if the women were trying to figure out the meaning of the preacher's message by discussing the sermon while the leader was still preaching, which seems to be the case. It is clear in this context that Paul could not be saying women unilaterally should be silent in church. He is saying that these women who are being disruptive need to "keep silent" in these particular services and get their questions answered privately later. The empowering part of this passage is that Paul still wants women to be taught by their husbands, which would have been a countercultural idea in Paul's upbringing.

True, there are a couple of holes in this theological perspective. First of all, many women in the Corinthian church were unmarried, so Paul's exhortation would not be a viable solution for them. Second, these passages seem to indicate that husbands understood the Scriptures and therefore could answer questions their wives asked. Judging from the target audience of 1 Corinthians, however, the men seemed just as ignorant as the women with reference to the things of the Spirit. For those reasons, I struggle with the idea that the ultimate solution to these restrictive passages is that women should always stay silent in church and husbands should always explain things to them at home.

The other commonly held view among some scholars is that these two verses in question are quotes from the Corinthian men themselves, in which they were in effect saying that the women should keep quiet and ask their husbands any questions they have. In this theory, Paul answers the men with the next verse by asking, "Was it from you that the word of God first went forth? Or has it come to you only?" (1 Corinthians 14:36). Or in other words, "Do you men think that the Word of God originated with you or that it only came to men?" Then Paul follows it up with, "If anyone thinks he is a prophet or spiritual, let him recognize that the things which I write to you are the Lord's commandment. But if anyone does not recognize this, he is not recognized" (verses 37–38). In other words, "I told you Corinthian men that you can *all* prophesy and that *everyone* should come with a teaching, a revelation. . . . If you were a prophet, you would recognize that this is the Word of the Lord!"

It's All Greek . . .

There is a good bit of evidence around this theory of the verses being an exchange between Paul and the men of Corinth. Some of the evidence is quite complex and involves the Greek language itself. I will try to simplify the argument, along with providing some references in the endnotes so that you can do your own research. The Greek language has something referred to as the "expletive of disassociation," denoted by the Greek word ἤ.[7] Though it is used in various ways, at times Paul uses it as an emotional rebuttal to express his disapproval of existing situations.

The closest equivalent to ἤ in the English language would mean "What?" or "Nonsense!" or "No way!" The following list is from the book entitled *Why Not Women* by Loren Cunningham and David Joel Hamilton. This list gives us an idea of how Paul uses this Greek symbol throughout 1 Corinthians. (The following are all from the NIV1984 translation.)

- 1 Corinthians 1:13 ἤ (No way!) Were you baptized into the name of Paul?
- 1 Corinthians 6:2 ἤ (What?) Do you not know that the saints will judge the world?
- 1 Corinthians 6:9 ἤ (Nonsense!) Do you not know that the wicked will not inherit the kingdom of God?
- 1 Corinthians 6:16 ἤ (No way!) Do you not know that he who unites himself with a prostitute is one with her in body?
- 1 Corinthians 6:19 ἤ (What?) Do you not know that your body is a temple of the Holy Spirit, who is in you, whom you have received from God?

- 1 Corinthians 7:16 Or ἤ (What?) how do you know, husband, whether you will save your wife?

- 1 Corinthians 9:6 Or ἤ (Nonsense!) is it only I and Barnabas who must work for a living?

- 1 Corinthians 9:7 ἤ (No way!) Who tends a flock and does not drink of the milk?

- 1 Corinthians 9:8 ἤ (What?) Doesn't the Law say the same thing?

- 1 Corinthians 9:10 ἤ (No way!) Surely he says this for us, doesn't he?

- 1 Corinthians 10:22 ἤ (Nonsense!) Are we trying to arouse the Lord's jealousy?

- 1 Corinthians 11:22 Or ἤ (What?) do you despise the church of God and humiliate those who have nothing?

- 1 Corinthians 14:36a ἤ (Nonsense!) Did the word of God originate with you?

- 1 Corinthians 14:36b Or ἤ (What?) are you the only people it has reached?[8]

As you can see, this Greek symbol changes the way we would read those restrictive verses in 1 Corinthians 14:34–36. When the men of Corinth say that their church's women should keep silent until they get home, Paul's rebuttal is, "(ἤ) *Nonsense!* Was it from you that the word of God first went forth? (ἤ) *What?* Has the word of God come to you only?"

I tend to agree with scholars who hold this position because it makes the most sense in the context of the entire book of 1 Corinthians. It also fits the flow of the question-and-answer format clearly laid out through much of the book. But one other interesting point leads me to believe that our restrictive passage is a question *to* Paul rather than Paul making a statement. Whoever is behind verse 34, which reads "for they are not permitted to speak, but are to subject themselves, just as the Law also says," did not know the Law. Nothing in the Law restricts women from speaking in any public setting.

Paul was an expert in the Law (Torah). He was a former Pharisee mentored by Gamaliel, the most famous Jewish Law instructor of all time. Without a doubt, Paul would have known that the Law did not validate any possible points taken from this passage. There were women prophetesses under Old Testament Law. I would therefore conclude that the apostle Paul is quoting the Corinthian men, who are not well versed in the Law and have somehow twisted it to meet their own need to reduce women, as we see throughout the book of First Corinthians.

This reminds me of my upbringing. When I was a boy, my mother tried to inspire me not to be lazy by saying, "God helps those who help themselves." I was shocked when I read through the Bible and realized that my mother's motto was not rooted in Scripture. I think this was the case with the Corinthian men also. I believe they simply struggled to understand how to treat powerful women who were saved out of a religious, immoral, pagan environment that empowered women.

Whatever conclusion you come to about these seemingly restrictive verses, one thing is for sure. Paul had no intention of silencing women in the church universally or unilaterally. There is no question that in spite of being raised in Judaism, Paul was a powerful promoter of women.

JOYCE MEYER

A Matriarchal Legacy

Joyce Meyer is one of the world's most profound Bible teachers of our time. She is well-known for her practical life applications and humorous delivery. Joyce, along with her husband, Dave, founded Joyce Meyer Ministries over three decades ago, which currently employs more than eight hundred people in fourteen offices around the world. Joyce's television and radio programs reach multitudes every day with the Word of God. She is also a *New York Times* bestselling author and has written more than a hundred books that have been translated into more than a hundred languages. One of the most interesting aspects about Joyce Meyer Ministries is that Joyce is the Bible teacher and public face of the ministry, while her husband supports her with his strengths in administration and finance.

Joyce was born in 1943 in St. Louis, Missouri. She had an extremely difficult childhood because her father sexually abused her for many years, while her mother refused to acknowledge the situation. By the time Joyce graduated from high school, she was a wreck. Desperate for love, she married the first man who showed any interest in her. Joyce suffered for five long years with her first husband's repeated infidelity, until her marriage finally ended in divorce.

Years later, Joyce met Dave Meyer, a godly and kind man, and they were married in January 1967. Even though they were in love, Joyce was not easy to live with. She was angry, rude and selfish. One day the Lord spoke to her and said, "Joyce, I really can't do anything else in your life until you do what I have told you to do concerning your husband." This was the beginning of a breakthrough in her heart and in their marriage.

In 1976, Joyce was driving to work when she heard the voice of the Lord tell her that she would go everywhere and teach His Word. She was still so emotionally broken at that time that she could not see how it would ever be possible for her to have a worldwide ministry. She was faithful to what the Lord had spoken to her, though, and she started with a tiny Bible study in her home. Four years later, she became an associate pastor of a small storefront church in St. Louis. The church grew into one of the leading charismatic churches in the area, largely because of Joyce's popularity as a Bible teacher.[9] Three years later, she left the comfort and security of her job at the church and started her own ministry.

Joyce and Dave never questioned the fact that she was called to teach. Joyce's personality is outgoing and passionate, while Dave's personality is steady and patient. Dave's wisdom and stewardship in finance and administration have led him to become the vice president of Joyce Meyer Ministries, and his strengths have helped build the ministry into what it is today. As a matter of fact, it was Dave's idea to branch out from radio into television ministry. Joyce credits Dave's stability and perseverance with bringing a lot of healing to her life. Joyce and Dave have an incredible marriage and partnership. They have learned to appreciate their differences and realize that they could not carry out the calling God has on their lives without their gifts and strengths working together in harmony.

Joyce Meyer is loved around the world because of her humorous, gently scolding style and her openness about her own shortcomings. Her women's conferences fill stadiums around the United States and beyond. Besides her conferences, television and radio ministries, she and Dave started the St. Louis Dream Center in 2000, reaching the inner city of

St. Louis. Their ministry also includes feeding programs with centers in more than 30 countries, providing food to over 70,000 children every day. Joyce Meyer Ministries has 39 children's homes around the world, and they provide free medical care to more than 270,000 people a year, disaster relief assistance, prison ministry, human trafficking ministry and water relief.

In 2005, *Time* magazine named Joyce Meyer one of the "25 Most Influential Evangelicals in America."[10] Much of Joyce's teaching comes from her journey out of pain and brokenness into wholeness. Her transparency has ministered to millions of people. Her success did not come overnight; it was a long, difficult and seemingly impossible road. But Joyce's life has become an incredible testimony of the dynamic, redeeming work of Jesus Christ.[11]

7

Excavating Restrictive Foundations

There I was in a foreign country, thousands of miles from home, lying on a bed in a tiny hotel room, preparing my heart to speak to a thousand leaders who had gathered from around the world to seek the Lord. While I lay there on the bed, I began to envision something like a large tsunami crashing over Latin America like a destructive storm wreaking havoc on the nations. As the tsunami moved swiftly across the countries, the winds grew stronger and more violent. Suddenly, this huge tsunami was transfigured into a massive, angry crowd of women all fighting for their rights! The countries were immersed in chaos as women left their families and took to the streets, shouting and carrying signs in a violent protest against generations of oppression.

Families were torn apart by the heavy winds of adversity as something like a civil war emerged from every city. Men everywhere took a stand in the streets to try to stop the winds of change from sweeping across the nations, but the massive crowds of women trampled them mercilessly, like frightened cattle stampeding across barren plains. My spirit wrenched within me as I wrestled to make sense of the vision. I kept hearing, "Warning! Warning! Warning!"

I personally avoid doom-and-gloom predictions like the plague. It takes no faith at all to make negative forecasts about the days ahead. We are called *believers*, therefore it is necessary that we live by faith. If God wanted us to live by sight instead of by faith, He would have called us *facters* and not *believers*. It is my conviction that God's divine truth overrides man's finite facts. I am convinced that God has an answer before we ever have a problem. After all, Jesus was crucified before the foundation of the world. With this in mind, I began to pray for God's supernatural intervention in this impending disaster.

In the midst of my intercession, the scene changed in the vision in my mind. I saw women all over Latin America groaning in prayer for release from generations of oppression, but what happened next was stunning—thousands of churches emerged out of the soil of the land, with their steeples shining brightly in the sun. Their bells began ringing, as if they were calling people to some divine gathering. Millions of women filled the streets, their heads hung in sadness, their clothes tattered and ragged, their faces filled with grief. They slowly and tentatively migrated toward the beautiful steeples, as if the bells were ringing out some kind of Morse code message of hope.

The camera in the movie of my mind peered inside the sanctuaries of the emerging chapels. I saw men sitting on thrones, and situated next to each of them was an empty, beautiful throne. Each vacant throne was decorated in majestic gold leaf but was covered with layers of dust, as if it had been unoccupied for centuries. Jesus was handing out spectacular royal scepters to the men sitting on these thrones. Each scepter was solid gold, with a huge red ruby positioned at the top. The women sheepishly made their way to the platforms as the men stood to welcome them with their scepters extended. Before the women had a chance to bow, the men knelt down in front of them as if to humble themselves . . .

Each man handed his scepter to a woman and invited her to sit on the vacant throne next to him. As the daughters of God took their rightful places, their tattered clothes were transformed into gorgeous, white satin gowns. Their countenances brightened, and their faces shone like the sun. Each man returned to his throne. Jesus handed each man another beautiful, golden scepter, but this time it had a large blue sapphire at the top.

As the vision emerged in my mind, I began to realize what God was saying to me. The enemy was trying to stir up a destructive, bitter and vile movement of women who would react to the oppression of their sex by rebelling against men. This would result in marriages and families being washed away in a tsunami of hurt, grief and pain.

But God also had a plan. In fact, I have come to understand that God's plan is not a reaction to the devil's scheme, but quite the opposite! God is not trying to thwart some evil ploy of the enemy; rather, the enemy is reacting to something God has already put in motion. The enemy is on the defense, having seen signs of an epic season change in Latin America as God begins to pour His Spirit out on *all* flesh. The enemy is trying to pervert this epic season in which God is empowering His beautiful daughters to sit beside the sons of God and bring wholeness to the nations. The result of this heavy rain will be that sons and *daughters*, fathers and *mothers* will take their rightful seats in heavenly places and begin to move powerfully in celestial unity to destroy the works of the devil.

I now understand that the Lord's plan was to answer the cries of the oppression from His daughters by using His Church to demonstrate how His noble men empower women to lead with them. It was only after the men gave away their ruby scepters to the women that they received the sapphire scepters from Jesus. I know now that men and women are both called to lead, but their scepters are different colors. These colors represent distinctive and divinely orchestrated roles in life and in the Kingdom. The vision in my mind ended, but my spirit was in turmoil within me as I wrestled with how to share this message with the leaders whom I was about to encounter.

Embracing Change

A couple of hours passed, and soon my friend and I were whisked away to the conference, where we would speak for the next three days.

As we neared the church, my stomach churned. I felt torn between honoring the leaders for allowing us to have influence in the life of their network, and being responsible to steward the vision that God had given me for their countries. The network of churches we were speaking to are having a massive impact on all of Latin America, yet they restrict women from most leadership roles in their churches. I determined that I would not share the vision at the conference unless the leadership of this movement asked if God had given me something specific for them.

Soon the morning session was over. The conference leaders asked us to join them for lunch and to share anything God had specifically shown us for them. *Yikes,* I thought, *I hope this doesn't get ugly!* About an hour passed as twelve of us sat eating and laughing together at a long table. Knowing where the conversation was heading, however, I personally was not very hungry. Finally, everyone quieted down and my translator leaned over to interpret the network leader's words: "Pastor Kris, the leaders are asking if you think God has anything specific to say to them," he repeated in a thick Spanish accent.

"Actually, John, I do," I said, trying to hide my anxiety. "But I'm a little concerned about how you might receive it."

The leaders all nodded in agreement toward me to go ahead, and the interpreter reassured me that they were open to hear whatever I felt that the Lord was saying to them.

Okay, here goes, I thought. "Men, I was lying on the bed in my hotel room a few hours ago, and I had this vision . . ."

Slowly and cautiously, I began to articulate the vision, toning it down as much as possible without losing the essence of its content. You could hear a pin drop in the room as my translator interpreted my words. His tone of voice and the countenance on the leaders' faces said it all. Within a few minutes, I could tell that we were in for a long week.

The tension thickened by the second as I finished describing the vision and shared a general overview of how I felt it applied to them. There was complete silence for what seemed like an eternity. Finally, one of the leaders spoke up in Spanish in an angry voice. The leader and I stared intently at one another as the translator hesitated over interpreting his words. I do not know a word of Spanish, but I understood clearly what he was saying without any interpretation. I have heard the arguments a hundred times before. I had hoped that my words could pierce through the veil of centuries of tradition and generations of oppression—but evidently I was wrong.

Within minutes the room was filled with passionate conversations going on between the leaders, while my translator struggled to sift through their arguments and give me an overview of what was being said. Before long, they turned their attention toward me and tried to ask several theological questions all at once. Before my translator could finish interpreting one question, they would fire another one at me. I was slowly growing impatient and angry. What began as an insightful vision to free the women of Latin America was quickly turning into a theological argument and a test of wills.

It was time for the afternoon session to begin, so the leaders decided to table our conversation until the next day. They informed me that their top theologian would join us in our discussion tomorrow. (I looked forward to that conversation about as much as having a root canal done without Novocain.) I reassured them that I would not share my vision or any part of its content publicly at the conference. That seemed to relieve some of the anxiety in the room.

Theological Warfare

Thinking about the coming dialogue with my friends, I did not sleep much that night. It was not that I was afraid of conflict or that I thought their theologian would pull some Greek or Hebrew rabbit out of his hat and destroy the foundation of my line of reasoning for empowering women. I had heard every case against women in leadership there is, and I had actually believed and taught some of it myself for many years. I knew that the theology was weak and the thinking was wrong. My concern was that I only had as much influence in these leaders' lives as they had value for me. I had learned the hard way that whenever I stepped beyond the boundaries of my favor with a person or organization in trying to persuade them of something, they could feel manipulated.

Keeping that in mind, I was struggling to find an honorable way to shift these leaders' paradigm through honest dialogue, not discussion. There is a huge difference! A dialogue is an exchange of ideas in which people interact to gain understanding. A discussion is a conversation in which the goal is to defend your position. The word *dialogue* is formed by the two Greek words *dia* and *logos*, which can literally be interpreted as a two-way flow or exchange of meaning. The word *discussion*, on the other hand, comes from the Latin word *discutere*, which means "strike asunder, break up."[1]

The next day, the conference began with a great morning session. My friend brought a powerful word to the Latin American people. I could tell his ministry was having an extraordinary impact on the leaders, and I hoped it would help bring us favor in the conversation we were about to have. As we entered the conference room, I told myself, *Stay calm! Don't be defensive!*

Within minutes the room was abuzz with network leaders greeting one another and finding their places. The translator turned to me and asked me to repeat the word that I had shared the day before, for the sake of those who were absent from the meeting. As I cautiously shared the vision, the mood in the room shifted from joyous celebration to an intensity you could cut with a knife. Their theologian wasted no time in introductions or idle chatter. He opened his Bible as if he were unsheathing a sword and began to read the apostle Paul's exhortation to Timothy. In an authoritative voice he thundered, "A woman must quietly receive instruction with entire submissiveness. But I do not allow a woman to teach or exercise authority over a man, but to remain quiet" (1 Timothy 2:11–12). Then he added, "Your vision is opposed to the Word of God and is therefore judged as being wrong!"

Everyone stared intently at me, as if I had just been dealt the death-blow by a great gladiator. I could feel the passion beginning to intensify in my heart. I refused to be intimidated by some theological bully—after all, the Latin American countries of the world were at stake here.

Meeting his intensity, I answered back, "What troubles me is that you don't hold fast to your own interpretation of Scripture." A question mark formed on his face as he waited for me to complete my response, and I went on, "The great apostle who penned that verse to Timothy also wrote to the Corinthians, 'The women are to keep silent in the churches; for they are not permitted to speak, but are to subject themselves, just as the Law also says. If they desire to learn anything, let them ask their own husbands at home; for it is improper for a woman to speak in church.' We've been in your church for two days, and I've listened to your women talking without being corrected. So I'm surprised by your confident exhortation, as if you take the Bible literally and I don't. So let me ask you a question as a theologian and an expert in the Scriptures: Why do you allow your women to speak in church?"

My translator's voice cracked slightly as he struggled to keep his composure. The theologian staggered, as if having me use a more restrictive Scripture against him surprised him.

"Well," he said in a condescending voice, as if I were ignorant, "The historical context of this Scripture dictated that women did not speak in church. In the first-century Corinthian church, men sat on one side of the church and women sat on the other side. Women were disrupting the service by asking their husbands questions across the aisle. This necessitated the rule you cited in your argument."

I fired back, "It's interesting to me that you're okay with using the historical context of the church at Corinth to define your position on women speaking in church, but you refuse to apply contextual circumstances to Paul's letter to Timothy at the church in Ephesus." (By now I had given up on having a dialogue and decided that I would bring my own sword to the discussion.)

His voice intensified as he answered back, "It's ridiculous to think that women shouldn't speak inside the church building today. It just doesn't make any sense."

I replied, "It doesn't make sense to you that women should be silent in church, but it makes perfect sense to you that Paul's specific exhortation to Timothy at Ephesus that women could not teach or exercise authority over men was meant to be universally applied, even though it was specifically written? Let me get this straight—God created man and woman in His image and gave them both authority to reign over the earth. God appointed a woman judge named Deborah to rule a country. The Lord commissioned Esther to rule as a queen and positively acknowledged the Queen of Sheba. At least ten women are recognized as prophetesses in the Bible, women such as Anna, Miriam, Deborah, Huldah and Philip's four daughters. Not to mention that there are several passages in which women teach men the Bible. Apollos, a man who was already mighty in the Scriptures, was more accurately taught by Priscilla and her husband, Aquila. Add to all this the fact that many of the Scriptures are quotes from women, such as Mary's exhortation in the first chapter of Luke. Or how about the book of Proverbs, which Solomon's *mother* and father taught him? If the apostle Paul's point was meant to be universally applied to everyone and women were never to teach men, then you'd have to remove a large portion of the Bible or only allow women to read it!"

By now the conversation had become adversarial, and the tension in the room continued to escalate. The theologian paused, as if he were again surprised by my argument. I think he had expected me to collapse with the first thrust of his sword. We stared at each other for several moments, I waiting for him to respond, and he seemingly reloading his weapon for another assault.

One thing was clear in my mind—the other leaders present that day had never been exposed to the idea that the Scriptures empowered women. Although they were obviously rooting for their great theologian to come out as victor in this contest, the look of surprise on their faces exposed their lack of understanding on the subject. It is not that they were not brilliant men or that they were poor leaders; it was simply that their cultural paradigms had blinded them to the biblical fact that God does not universally restrict women from leadership. But like all of us, they read the Bible through a lens that filtered out or redefined anything that was opposed to what they already believed.

We are all inclined to read the Bible in a way that validates what we already believe. Not only that, but we all tend to find what we are looking for, and we are blind to the unexpected. Most of us have had the experience of buying something that we thought was unique or different, only to see several people wearing it or driving it the day after our purchase. Sometimes our powers of observation are skewed and we do not know it.

The theologian gathered his thoughts and stepped into the arena for another round. The others watched with great anticipation as we wielded our swords, each looking to slay the other with the Word of God. As the hours passed, the intensity that initially marked our conversation evaporated for two reasons. First, it became obvious to the leadership that there are plenty of biblical reasons to empower women to lead. Balancing against that was their perspective that enough Scripture remained to restrict women from leadership.

Second, on my part I realized I had misjudged these leaders by thinking that they wanted all the power and were unwilling to humble themselves to empower women. Deep into our conversation, it became clear to me that these men were trying to honor God by being true to His Word to the best of their understanding. They did not want their movement to become culturally relevant at the expense of perverting the Word of God. Our respect grew for one another through the evening, and our discussion turned into a dialogue.

The leaders I spoke to are still today in the process of learning how to empower women in a way that does not violate their understanding of Scripture. I honor them for their integrity, and I look with anticipation for them to fulfill God's desire to see the women of Latin America living powerfully and freely. But I came away from that experience with a new resolve to help people understand through the *Scriptures* that it is God's intention for women and men to co-reign on the earth.

D-Day at Ground Zero

I wish I could say the Latin American Church was the final frontier, the place where the religious spirit that reduces half of the world's population is making its last stand. Unfortunately, this simply is not true. Most of the Christian world still uses the Scriptures to position women in a subservient role to men. But something happened to me that day at that table in Latin America. First, I found myself ill-prepared to answer the deep theological questions that plague the hearts of many leaders eager to empower women without violating their consciences. And second, I walked away from that conversation determined to understand the theological foundation that would undergird the prophetic revelation I had experienced in the Latin American vision.

For me, today is D-day, the time when I return to Ground Zero, the place where the most caustic case ever created against women in the history of the Christian church was born. It is here that I will excavate the breeding ground of the age-old restrictions on women in leadership. I will attempt to unearth the shackles buried deep within the foundation of the church at Ephesus to understand Paul's limitations on women. I want to invite you to join me in this archaeological dig through the Scriptures. Let's begin with Paul's challenging statements to Timothy:

> A woman must quietly receive instruction with entire submissiveness. But I do not allow a woman to teach or exercise authority over a man, but to remain quiet. For it was Adam who was first created, and then Eve. And it was not Adam who was deceived, but the woman being deceived, fell into transgression. But women will be preserved through the bearing of children if they continue in faith and love and sanctity with self-restraint.
>
> 1 Timothy 2:11–15

These verses stir up many difficult questions that we must honestly ponder as we navigate our way through this find, which can, if improperly excavated, be treacherously twisted to oppress women. Is Paul saying that a woman who has known the Lord for thirty years and has studied the Bible her entire life is not qualified to teach a brand-new male believer? Is Paul saying that there is no situation in which a woman should have authority over a man in a spiritual environment? Is Paul saying that because Eve was deceived, women should not be trusted with leadership ever again? What happened to the born-again experience that makes old things pass away and makes all things new? (See 2 Corinthians 5:17.)

Or is the great apostle saying that because Adam willingly disobeyed God but Eve was deceived, Adam is therefore inherently more qualified to lead? Are we to believe that the cross of Christ released men from the curse in the Garden, but that women are still under the curse's power? Why did women like Deborah, who led the nation of Israel, have authority over men and women before the redemptive nature of Calvary?

Review the Context

Let's review the context of Paul's epistle to Timothy, who was the leader of the church in Ephesus. Remember that we spent quite a bit of time in chapter 4 talking about the importance of the context of Scripture and how it determines the definition? Let's also revisit Ephesus and remind ourselves of the culture Paul was addressing. As I mentioned earlier, Ephesus was home to the Greek goddess Artemis, a combination of both the virgin goddess of the hunt and the Anatolian goddess Cybele. We saw that Cybele, associated with the earth and fertility, was sometimes known as the Great Mother, and that Artemis had a crown on her head, which could have been a sign of female rulership. Artemis also had eggs surrounding her midsection, which many think are a symbol of fertility.

Because Artemis was the goddess of fertility, the Ephesians believed that she protected a woman and her baby during childbirth. We can only imagine what a huge issue this must have been in the first century. The global infant mortality rate just a hundred years ago was 15 percent, not to mention the death rate of mothers during childbirth. Giving birth in first-century Ephesus had to be quite risky, which explains why women wanted a goddess who could protect their infants and save mother and baby from death. That is the reason why Paul told the church there, "But women will be preserved through the bearing of children if they continue in faith and love and sanctity with self-restraint" (1 Timothy 2:15).

The word *preserved* here is the Greek word *sozo*, which means "saved, restored, preserved and cured." Paul is reminding the Ephesian women that they no longer need the goddess Artemis to protect them because they gave their lives to Christ and He watches over (*sozo*) them and their children during childbearing. Of course, this verse does not mean that women are saved in the sense of the salvation of their souls by bearing children. Only faith in Christ saves us from hell and delivers us to heaven.

Instructing Women

Another encouraging word taken from this portion of Scripture is where Paul orders that women be instructed: "A woman must quietly receive instruction with entire submissiveness" (1 Timothy 2:11). We talked earlier about the fact that women were not taught spiritual things in Jewish culture, so this Scripture reinforces the value women had in the first-century Church. Ephesus women were instructed to receive teaching with a submissive attitude.

The Greek word for submissiveness is *hupotage*, and it means "to be in subjection." In this particular verse, the context dictates that the women should be in subjection to the *instruction*, not the *instructor*. No instructor is named or implied in the text, although some would insist that women are being told to submit to men. This is not substantiated in the text, however.

It is also interesting to note that the Greek word *hupotage* was also used with reference to both men and women in Paul's letter to the Corinthians. He wrote,

> For the ministry of this service is not only fully supplying the needs of the saints, but is also overflowing through many thanksgivings to God. Because of the proof given by this ministry, they will glorify God for your *obedience* to your confession of the gospel of Christ and for the liberality of your contribution to them and to all.
>
> 2 Corinthians 9:12–13, emphasis added

The word *obedience* in this text is that Greek word *hupotage*, so it was not only the women who were required to be submissive; it was all the saints.

Another interesting fact stands out from Paul's writings. Two verses before Paul instructs women, he corrects the Ephesian men Timothy pastored when he wrote, "Therefore I want the men in every place to pray, lifting up holy hands, without wrath and dissension" (1 Timothy 2:8). The Greek word for wrath is *orge*, which means "anger." The Greek word for dissension is *dialogismos*, which means "arguing or disputing." In effect, Paul is telling the women that they need to be submissive to the Word of God, and he is also telling the men that they need to stop being angry and argumentative.

Teaching and Authority

Let me repeat one of the most restrictive passages about women so it is fresh in our minds. I promised in an earlier chapter that we would come back to this one. Paul wrote, "I do not allow a woman to teach or exercise authority over a man, but to remain quiet. For it was Adam who was first created, and then Eve. And it was not Adam who was deceived, but the woman being deceived, fell into transgression" (1 Timothy 2:12–14). This Greek passage, translated into 45 English words (at least in the NASB), has become the cornerstone for the limitation of women in leadership in the Church for hundreds of years on every continent on the planet.

The key issue in this passage is that a woman may not "exercise authority over a man." This phrase forms the foundation for those who do not allow women to lead or teach in the Church. But is it accurate? The Greek word in question is *authentein* (translated as "exercise authority over" in the NASB). The word occurs only once in the entire Bible! Originally it meant "to murder with one's own hand" or "to commit suicide." As time passed, the word evolved to mean "to originate something with one's own hand." (This is where we get our terms *author* and *authentic*.) Two other definitions are "one who acts on his own authority" and "to govern or exercise dominion." Surprisingly, twelve other words in the Greek dictionary also deal with exercising authority, and a staggering 47 words relate to "rule" or "govern."[2] Yet Paul, under the guidance of the Holy Spirit, did not choose one of those. Instead he chose this unique word, *authentein*.

Linda Belleville does a fascinating study on the word *authentein* in her book *Discovering Biblical Equality*. In her chapter titled "Teaching and Usurping Authority," she reviews how this word has been interpreted down through the ages in various Bible translations. I will list just a few of her examples:

Old Latin (2nd-4th Century A.D.) "I permit not a woman to teach, neither to *dominate* a man (neque dominari viro)."

Vulgate (4th-5th) "I permit not a woman to teach, neither to *domineer over* a man (neque dominari in virum)."

Geneva (1560 edition) "I permit not a woman to teache, neither to *usurp* authoritie over the man."

KJV (1611) "I suffer not a woman to teach nor *usurp* authority over a man."[3]

Belleville argues persuasively, "There is a virtually unbroken tradition, stemming from the oldest versions of the Bible and running down to the twenty-first century, that translates *authentein* as 'to dominate' rather than 'to exercise authority over.'"[4] She concludes that if Paul had meant the routine exercise of authority, then he could have chosen any number of better terms to state that. He chose this word because it carried a nuance meaning "to hold sway over, to dominate or to gain the upper hand." Therefore, Belleville translates 1 Timothy 2:12, "I do not permit a woman to teach so as to gain mastery over a man," or "I do not permit a woman to teach with a view to dominating a man."[5]

Richard and Catherine Clark Kroeger take a different tack in their work entitled *I Suffer Not a Woman: Rethinking 1 Timothy 2:11–15 in Light of Ancient Evidence*. They do a detailed study of *authentein* and write,

"*Authentein*," when used with the genitive, as it is in 1 Timothy 2:12, could imply not only to claim sovereignty but also to claim authorship. In other words it would mean, "To represent oneself as the author, originator, or source of something." This is validated in various dictionaries, such as the *Thesaurus Linguae Graecae*.[6]

Kroeger and Kroeger conclude that 1 Timothy 2:12 therefore could be translated, "I do not allow a woman to teach nor to proclaim herself author of man,"[7] which makes sense given that in the next sentence of the passage Paul is reasserting the original order of creation.

With this backdrop in place, it is reasonable to assume that the Artemis cult had influence among the people Timothy was pastoring. (The evidence in Acts 19 alone supports this.) The practical results of this influence were that some in Ephesus elevated the feminine above the masculine, such that some women would try to assert their status as women to dominate the men. This is exactly what Paul writes should not happen. When Paul refers back to Adam and Eve, he is not building a doctrine for all male-female interactions. Rather, keeping in mind that those influenced by the Artemis cult believed that Artemis appeared first and then her male consort, Paul is simply correcting the myth with the truth found in the biblical record of Adam and Eve. He reasserts, "For it was Adam who was first created, and then Eve" (verse 13).

If Paul was not correcting a myth, then we have a serious problem with the next phrase: "And it was not Adam who was deceived, but the woman being deceived, fell into transgression" (verse 14). Essentially, Paul would be linking women's silence and submission to original sin. In effect, Paul would be arguing that forgiveness does not have the power to cover sin and restore us, both male and female. Yet the New Testament makes it abundantly clear that Christ's sacrifice has defeated sin and death itself. How, then, can Paul argue for a permanent, eternal subjection of women based upon the one sin of Eve? Did he forget about the cross and the blood? Of course not. Paul is offering further evidence from the biblical record to counter Greek mythology and its influence in the Ephesian church.[*]

The Contextual Dilemma

Before we leave the subject of women having authority and/or teaching in the Church, I want to prove to you beyond a shadow of a doubt that Paul's concerns about women were specific to three cities, as I mentioned in the previous chapter. His restrictions were never meant to be universally applied or unilaterally practiced as congregational rules. That is the reason he did not repeat his instructions to the other nine locations. Neither did he ask for letters to those three places to be copied and passed along to the other churches, as he did with a few of his letters. Here is one example of the apostle instructing that his letter be passed along to a specific church: "When this letter is read among you, have it also read in the church of the Laodiceans; and you, for your part read my letter that is coming from Laodicea" (Colossians 4:16). Yet when Paul wrote to the Corinthians the first time, he narrowed the scope of his letter to them personally. Check out his instructions: "Paul, called as an apostle of Jesus Christ by the will of God, and Sosthenes our brother, to the church of God which is at Corinth . . ." (1 Corinthians 1:1–2). That would be the book we have been investigating that seems to instruct women not to speak in church.

When Paul wrote his second letter to the Corinthians, though, he expanded the audience to include Achaia. Here it is in black and white: "Paul, an apostle of Christ Jesus by the will of God . . . to the church of God which is at Corinth with all the saints who are throughout Achaia" (2 Corinthians 1:1).

When he wrote his first letter to Timothy, which included the restrictions on women we just talked about, he directed it to the Ephesians who were teaching strange doctrine. Here is his opening statement: "Paul, an apostle of Christ Jesus . . . to Timothy, my true child in the faith. . . . As I urged you upon my departure for Macedonia, remain on at Ephesus so that you may instruct certain men not to teach strange doctrines"(1 Timothy 1:1–3). Unlike the epistle Paul wrote to the Colossians or the letter that he apparently wrote to the Laodiceans (which we have no copy of), he did not instruct Timothy to pass this letter on to any other church. Nor did he broaden the scope of his letter to other regions or cities beyond Ephesus, as he did in his second letter to the Corinthians.

The same principle holds true in Paul's letter to Titus. He instructed Titus to set in order what remained in Crete: "Paul, a bond-servant of God and an apostle of Jesus Christ . . . To Titus, my true child in a common faith . . . For this reason I left you in Crete, that you would set in order what remains" (Titus 1:1, 4–5).

I am simply trying to reinforce the point I made in previous chapters—that the epistles were written to specific people and churches to address issues relevant to their specific culture and circumstances. We can glean a lot from these God-ordained epistles, but we need to proceed with divine wisdom when we expand the application of these letters beyond the scope of the author's intention and the cultural context in which they were addressed.

Women in the Ministry

One of the other ways we know for sure that most women in the first-century Church were not restricted from having authority or teaching in Paul's day is that the Bible makes several other references to women teaching men and having authority in the Kingdom. Priscilla is one of these gifted women who exhibited a significant amount of authority in the early Church. She is frequently listed before her husband in the Bible (a sign of importance), and she taught Apollos, who was one of the most powerful leaders in the Church. Read it for yourself:

> Now a Jew named Apollos, an Alexandrian by birth, an eloquent man, came to Ephesus; and he was mighty in the Scriptures. This man had been instructed in the way of the Lord; and being fervent in spirit, he was speaking and teaching accurately the things concerning Jesus, being acquainted only with the baptism of John; and he began to speak out boldly in the synagogue. But when Priscilla and Aquila heard him, they took him aside and explained to him the way of God more accurately.
>
> Acts 18:24–26

Then there is Junia, whom Paul calls "outstanding among the apostles" (Romans 16:7). Some translations have altered this to make it a man's name, Junias, because she is called an apostle, but there is no evidence grammatically or historically for this change. We can only conclude that Junia was indeed an apostle in the Roman church. This must have ramifications for our study of women in ministerial roles.

Phoebe is listed as a "servant" of the church in Cenchrea in Romans 16:1. Interestingly, the word used here to refer to Phoebe, *diakonon*, can mean servant, deacon or minister. In other passages from Paul (Philippians 1:1; 1 Timothy 3:8, 12), the exact same word is translated "deacon" when it is referring to a man, yet when referring to a woman, it is translated "servant." (Origen believed that women were official church deacons, and John Chrysostom interpreted *diakonos* as a term of rank.[8]) The scriptural evidence suggests that Phoebe was an official minister in her church. We can also conclude from Romans 16:1–2 that Phoebe was so trustworthy that she carried the letter of Romans from Paul to the church in Rome and was therefore his ambassador.

Old and New Testament Prophetesses

Let's not forget Deborah. As a prophetess in the Old Testament, she led Israel through some tough times. Some have suggested that Deborah only led in the absence of male leadership, but that assessment does not agree with the biblical record. Deborah was a prophetess and judge who was "leading Israel at that time" (Judges 4:4 NIV). The book of Judges also says, "Village life in Israel ceased, ceased until I, Deborah, arose, arose a mother in Israel," (Judges 5:7 NIV1984).

Think about this: How is it possible that an "inferior covenant," the old covenant that Deborah lived under, provided superior benefits to half of the human race—women? The writer of Hebrews put it bluntly: "When He [God] said, 'A new covenant,' He has made the first obsolete. But whatever is becoming obsolete and growing old is ready to disappear" (Hebrews 8:13). If God did not want women to lead, why would He have appointed a woman, under the Law, to be the head of a nation—especially as a judge, which was the highest office in the land both spiritually and politically?

There were also many other prophetesses in the Old Testament. There was the sister of Moses and Aaron, "Miriam the prophetess" (Exodus 15:20). In the days of the kings, there was "Huldah the prophetess" (2 Kings 22:14). In the days of Nehemiah, there was "the prophetess Noadiah" (Nehemiah 6:14). Isaiah was married to an unnamed prophetess (see Isaiah 8:3).

Let's take a look at some New Testament prophetesses, too, and see if we can draw any parallels. The first prophetess named in the New Testament is Anna. She was very old when Jesus was born, and she prophesied over Him right after His birth (see Luke 2:36–38). Elizabeth, wife of Zacharias and mother of John the Baptist, prophesied, as did Mary, the mother of Jesus, though neither of them were specifically termed prophetesses (see Luke 1:41–55).

The most intriguing prophetesses in the New Testament were Philip's daughters. Dr. Luke recorded this: "On the next day we left and came to Caesarea, and entering the house of Philip the evangelist, who was one of the seven, we stayed with him. Now this man had four virgin daughters who were prophetesses" (Acts 21:8–9). A couple of Bible versions incorrectly say that Philip had daughters who prophesied. It is highly doubtful that Dr. Luke would even have mentioned that Philip's girls prophesied because as the apostle Peter pointed out, God was pouring out His Spirit on all flesh, resulting in *all* of our sons and daughters prophesying (see Acts 2:17). In other words, if Philip's daughters were not prophetesses, but only had the gift of prophecy, why would Luke even mention them? It would have been assumed in the book of Acts that every son and daughter would prophesy! It should also be noted that Luke specifically named Philip as an evangelist before he named Philip's daughters as prophetesses. Philip is the only evangelist named in the entire Bible. Luke, author of the book of Acts, knew what he was doing when he gave people titles.

Why am I making such a big deal out of there being prophetesses in the New Testament Church? I will tell you why—in the New Testament, a prophet or prophetess is a governmental office. Their specific job description is listed in the book of Ephesians. Let's take a look at the role of a prophet or prophetess. Paul wrote:

> He [Jesus] gave some as apostles, and some as prophets, and some as evangelists, and some as pastors and teachers, for the equipping of the saints for the work of service, to the building up of the body of Christ; until we all attain to the unity of the faith, and of the knowledge of the Son of God, to a mature man, to the measure of the stature which belongs to the fullness of Christ. As a result, we are no longer to be children, tossed here and there by waves and carried about by every wind of doctrine, by the trickery of men, by craftiness in deceitful scheming; but speaking the truth in love, we are to grow up in all aspects into Him who is the head, even Christ, from whom the whole body, being fitted and held together by what every joint supplies, according to the proper working of each individual part, causes the growth of the body for the building up of itself in love.
>
> Ephesians 4:11–16

I have written two books on the roles of the apostle and prophet/prophetess in the New Testament Church. Even if you do not believe that apostles and prophets are alive today in the Church, still the fact remains that they were the foundation of the first-century Church. New Covenant prophets and prophetess were commissioned by God (along with apostles, evangelists, pastors and teachers) to equip the saints so that they would become one mature Body in Christ. This was to result in them growing up into believers who were doctrinally sound, love-filled and Spirit-empowered. The Bible never makes any distinction in either the Old or New Testament between a prophet and a prophetess. Prophetesses therefore had to have governmental authority to equip both men and women so that they could perform the work of spiritual service.

Another interesting thing to note here is that the book of Ephesians was written to the same church that Timothy pastored when Paul wrote his letters to Timothy. Paul could not have been restricting women from public ministry in the book of 1 Timothy, while still acknowledging in the book of Ephesians—to the same church body—their role as prophetesses. This serves to reinforce our theological view of Paul's letter to Timothy that we covered earlier in this chapter. I want to point out one last thing concerning prophetesses and prophets in the Church. Paul wrote, "God has appointed in the church, first apostles, second prophets, third teachers, then miracles, then gifts of healings, helps, administrations, various kinds of tongues" (1 Corinthians 12:28). The Greek word *first* is *protos*, which is a military term meaning "first in rank." In other words, prophets and prophetesses would be second in rank in the Church of Jesus Christ!

Oh, and by the way, note that this passage of Scripture was written in the first letter to the Corinthians, which seemed to restrict women from talking in church. This again reinforces the theological case we made in the previous chapter, that first-century women were being empowered alongside men in the Church, in spite of some specific struggles the early Church was having with people struggling to break free of the influence of female deities and paganism in general.

It Takes Divine Wisdom . . .

Now we have excavated the foundation of the age-old restrictions on women in the Church, only to discover that it is a shaky foundation when exposed to the light of the cultural context in which Paul's words were written.

Again, although we can glean a lot from these Scriptures we have unearthed, we need to keep in mind that Paul's epistles were written to address specific issues in specific churches in specific circumstances. It takes divine wisdom to avoid going beyond Paul's intentions when applying these Scriptures to women today.

I want to invite you to join the revolution that frees women from the age-old captivity of servitude and restores them to their rightful place as coheirs of the same promises that men have in Christ.

AIMEE SEMPLE MCPHERSON

Founder of the Foursquare Movement

Aimee Semple McPherson was one of the most charismatic and influential women of all time. Not only was Aimee the first woman ever to preach on the radio, she also pioneered the first Christian radio station in 1924, making her a household name. Her radio station was heard around the world, and her sermons were reprinted in hundreds of newspapers and read by millions of people.

From the time Aimee was a little girl, she knew how to draw a crowd. She had a spunky, impetuous personality that was evident in every aspect of her ministry. When Aimee was four years old, she stood on street corners and drew crowds by reciting Bible stories.[9] As time passed, her God-given favor became stronger and the crowds grew larger. Aimee had an incredible ability to connect with the young and the old, the wealthy and the destitute, the healthy and the sick. She was an unstoppable force of divine creativity. Discouraged by fire-and-brimstone preaching that constantly portrayed God as angry and vengeful, she started a magazine called *The Bridal Call*. The magazine portrayed the bond between Christians and their Lord as a marriage relationship.

Aimee was a champion for women's rights in an era when women were not even allowed to vote. Her list of achievements would be astounding for anyone, much less for a woman in the 1920s and 1930s. She built Angelus Temple debt free in Los Angeles, California, in the midst of the Great Depression. The temple seated more than five thousand people, and it was filled to capacity seven days a week, three services a day. In 1923 she built L.I.F.E. Bible College, which to this day is the cornerstone of the Foursquare movement.

Aimee was famous for her world-class creativity. She wrote 175 songs and hymns, 13 screenplays and several operas. Her preaching drew such large crowds that in San Diego they had to call out the National Guard to assist with the crowds of thirty thousand people lined up to hear her preach. Not only could Aimee preach; she could also move in signs and wonders. So many people were healed miraculously through her ministry that the American Medical Association launched an investigation into her ministry. The investigators found that the healings were "genuine, beneficial and wonderful."[10]

Perhaps Aimee Semple McPherson's greatest legacy lies in the founding of the Foursquare denomination, which began in 1923. In a time when Americans still viewed women as second-class citizens and the religious world would not even allow them to be elders in the Church, Aimee planted a church fellowship that now stretches to every continent in the world. The Foursquare Fellowship currently has more than 66,000 churches in 140 countries. Aimee was a pioneer who was able to shatter the glass ceiling of women in ministry by using her God-given creativity and innovation in countless avenues. Aimee's courageous spirit helped her break through the masculine barrier of naysayers and doubters. Like Jesus, she was not afraid to be seen with sinners. She even baptized Marilyn Monroe! Though most of the religious world scorned and hated her, she refused to pay any attention to them.

Aimee's cutting-edge media presentations gave her influence with the rich and famous in the entertainment world, as well as with government officials and educational leaders. *Time* magazine named Aimee one of the most influential people of the twentieth century.[11] In the era before television, movies and theater were the primary entertainment. This created an atmosphere where Aimee's dramatic presentations were spellbinding. Not only was she entertaining, but thousands upon thousands of people found the Lord through her creative productions.

Aimee's intense compassion for the needy also helped break the gender barrier in ministry. Drawing on the experience of her mother, who worked for the Salvation Army, Aimee opened a commissary during the Depression where people could get food, clothing and blankets 24 hours a day, 7 days a week. When the city government closed their free school lunch program, Aimee stepped up and took it over. She created soup kitchens and free medical clinics, feeding an estimated 1.5 million people.[12] She tirelessly worked to improve her community, and she gained favor with her city because of it.

Aimee wanted as many people as possible to hear the Gospel, so she used every opportunity with the press to gain publicity and attract audiences. One time she chartered a plane so that she would be home in time to preach on Sunday. She arranged for more than two thousand people, along with members of the press, to be at the airport when she was leaving. The plane had a mechanical failure, so she boarded another plane and used the story as an example in a Sunday message called "The Heavenly Airplane." Another time, she was pulled over for speeding and created a message entitled "Arrested for Speeding."[13] She was constantly in the news, and her audiences loved hearing her messages and reading articles about her in the newspapers.

In spite of Aimee's natural abilities and the incredible favor that she carried, her life was filled with difficulty and pain. Her first husband died soon after they moved to China to be missionaries, leaving her eight months pregnant. She subsequently married again, and her second husband filed for divorce. A third marriage also ended in divorce. She received many death threats and was kidnapped for ransom three times. Aimee suffered from sickness most of her life, and died at the young age of 54 from an accidental overdose of pain pills. Despite the heartache and physical pain she endured, she did not allow these setbacks to minimize her impact. Aimee was a princess warrior, a history maker and a forerunner for women all over the world.

8

Women, Take Your Places

*I*n 2008, a terrible tragedy struck our family. Our youngest son, Jason, uncovered an adulterous affair that his wife of ten years was having with another man. As if that were not hard enough to swallow, it soon was revealed that she was pregnant by this man and did not want to be our son's wife anymore. Over the next couple of years, we stumbled through life like drunken sailors, trying to find stability on a storm-tossed ship. Yet the most painful part of this hellish situation was watching my three young grandchildren stagger through months of deep grief, disillusionment, insecurity and fear. I was raised in a very violent and dysfunctional home, but I had never experienced pain so deep in my soul that I literally despaired of life itself—until now. In the midst of Jason's darkest days, I would take my son's face in my hands and say, "You will live again! You will love again!" He would reply, "I hope so."

It has been nearly five years since Jason's wife walked out on him. I am happy to say that those dark days are behind us, and I was right about my family living and loving again. Last year Jason remarried, and his wife is a beautiful woman who is a great mother. The storm has finally passed, and laughter has returned to our homes.

Gender Cloning

We can learn so many lessons from the storms of life. One of the most powerful insights I gained through this trial came from watching my son parent his children. What I observed surprised me, although looking back, I realize now that it should not have. Jason, a fantastic father, was now saddled with trying to fill the role of both dad and mom to his three children. (Jason and his ex-wife had joint custody of the children, but the children lived with him most of the time.) Jason's role as father suffered dramatically in those years as he struggled under the pressure of both mothering and fathering his kids when they were with him. His love for his children never wavered and he made huge efforts to care for them, but the dualistic role of mother/father resulted in Jason being only mildly effective at either. Thankfully those years have passed, and Jason has put the superdad cape back on.

Through this dark season in our family, I came to understand one of the most unique social dynamics that is at work in our world today—in the absence of women taking their proper place in society, men have unsuccessfully tried to fulfill both the masculine and feminine roles. In America, women were considered second-class citizens from our country's inception. It was not until 1848 that women in the United States began to agitate for equality. Women struggled for 72 years before they even gained the right to vote. But what many people fail to understand is that with the advent of women's rights came the redefinition of feminine roles.

Let me explain *how* women gained authority in our country and what the long-term ramifications of that process are. First of all, *men* determined which virtues were held in honor and which were disdained. Men alone held every seat of authority in the country, so they controlled the value systems of our society. This resulted in society esteeming masculine virtues, while degrading feminine qualities. Women gained equal rights, but it was only because they submitted themselves to male gender cloning. Basically, men said, "If you want to have the same rights as we have, then you need to be like us."

I often wonder what would have happened if our women had said to their husbands, "I'll make you a deal. You stay home with the kids for one month, and I'll go to work and do your job." I have a feeling that at the end of one month, the men would have gladly given our women equal rights *with* gender distinctions.

To this day, most leadership positions have a big old invisible sign over the doorway that says, *Only Masculine Distinctions Are Welcome Here*. All this resulted in women leading in the same *way* as men lead. Let me make it clear that while gender distinctions should not determine *where* men and women lead, they should make a difference in *how* men and women lead.

Gender Differences

In chapter 2 we discussed the fact that it takes a supernatural gift from God to live singly. The reason it takes a supernatural gift to live a healthy single life is because men and women are both equally important, but in distinctly different ways, and they need each other. A man cannot give birth to a child or breastfeed an infant, yet it takes a man to impregnate a woman. No matter how strong, talented, educated or experienced two men are, they are incapable of producing a child without a woman. The same is true of two women; they cannot produce a child without the assistance of a man.

Someone might argue that Peter's exhortation to husbands in 1 Peter 3:7 to "live with your wives in an understanding way, as with someone weaker, since she is a woman" means that women are not as capable as men. It is *generally* true that men are physically stronger than women when it comes to football, boxing, mud wrestling and the like, which is the point Peter is trying to make here. He is simply saying, "Husbands, you may be capable of beating up your wife, but if you do not show her honor as a fellow heir of the grace of life, God won't answer your prayers." Yet it is both intellectually irresponsible and scientifically refutable to say that women are inferior to men. It is equally imprudent to refuse to acknowledge that men are better at some things and women are better at others.

In most of the world, it is politically incorrect to gender profile people or in any way acknowledge strengths, weaknesses or distinctions related to gender outside of the obvious physical reproductive differences (men have a penis and women have a vagina). But in spite of what you may have been taught, men and women are not the same. When God creates physical distinctions, He also fashions attributes that synergistically enhance the strength of those characteristics. God did not simply give women breasts so they could physically feed their infants; He also planted a nurturing characteristic in their personhood. In other words, women's physical capability to breastfeed is a manifestation of their God-given ability and assignment as nurturers.

On the other hand, men are generally physically stronger, but with their physical strength God also created in men a sense of responsibility to protect and provide for their environment. God never gives a physical characteristic to one of His creations without it affecting the created one's divinely appointed role in life. As a matter of fact, I believe that God first determines a person's divine purpose, and then He designs the person with all of the characteristics needed to successfully apprehend his or her divine destiny.

I have struggled to forge this chapter while avoiding the land mines of giving offense, knowing that people could react by feeling pressured to defend their lifestyles and perspectives. For example, physically strong women who are not instinctively nurturing want to argue that I am stereotyping them. Nurturing, stay-at-home dads are about to throw this book in the garbage because they are insulted by my insinuation that I assign a feminine role to their responsibility. I want to acknowledge right now that no two people in the world are the same. God has created us uniquely and individually different. I have no desire to force anyone into a mold or to make anyone feel bad or dysfunctional because he or she has a passion, responsibility and/or call that is different from the way in which I express gender distinctions in this chapter.

I also know that I am painting the world with a wide brush in my attempt to bring clarity to this highly volatile subject. I want to state clearly that I am not saying that men and women cannot play the same role. I am trying to point out that they will approach the same role differently because of *who* they are. Sometimes men and women take on certain *ways* of carrying out their roles that do not play to their sex's strengths, and they do so because society insists on those ways. Many such people, although forced into operating differently than they were designed, have become quite proficient at it. They have adapted to this new approach toward their roles, responsibilities and duties.

Other people such as Jason, who are left with no choice but to take on the duty of a different sex because they have no other option, struggle with proficiency. They do the best they can in the situations they face, yet they are well aware that they are not always operating in their strengths.

The G.I. Jane Syndrome

A dynamic that I call the "G.I. Jane syndrome" is trying to distort the role of women in society. In my opinion, it is just another way that men manipulate women into playing the "same role, equal value" game. One of the greatest challenges the syndrome creates is that some women see it as a compliment and choose to embrace a masculine role to inherit an equivalent place in society. Sometimes this happens as a reaction to someone important in their lives who placed no value on the feminine role, yet highly valued the male role.

Suppose an army sergeant is blessed with two sons and a daughter. His daughter loves him and wants to please him. It does not take her long to figure out that her dad loves to play army with the boys but is not too interested in playing dolls with her. She therefore embraces the role her father values in exchange for his admiration and affection.

Another common way the G.I. Jane syndrome perpetuates is when women react to being oppressed by men. This results in them feeling as if they have something to prove, and they fall into the trap of playing the masculine game to make the point that they are equally valuable. The problem is that very few women can be as good at the masculine role as men are because they were "taken out of the man" at creation. The man is not in the woman, and the woman is not in the man.

Before you get mad and react to what I am saying, think about this: Isn't there a reason why the NBA, NFL, MLB, UFC and every other professional sport are not coed? Do you really think, for example, that an all-female NFL team would be competitive against an all-male team? Are you aware that in every single physical game where men and women can be equally measured, women are slower and not nearly as strong as men? In the Olympics, for example, women are about 10 percent slower in speed events, and there is approximately a 15 percent difference in strength events.

"Kris, are you saying that men are better than women?" you ask.

No! These competitions are designed to display the strengths of *manhood* (not womanhood). *Typically*, women cannot compete at the same level at those things in life that are designed *for* and *by* men.

When I use the word *typically*, it does not denote an absolute attribute etched in stone or strengths that have no exceptions. I am using the word to mean "most often" or "more often than not."

"Kris, are you stereotyping the sexes?" you ask.

No, I am not! These are facts proven over centuries of competition. When women insist on competing *against* men in the games of life that were designed *for* and *by* men, they *typically* validate what chauvinistic men have been trying to prove for generations—that men are better and stronger than women at everything in life; therefore, placing a woman in leadership is like sending the "B" team into the game.

This is simply not true, but as long as women fall for the lie that they are the same as men, they will get sucked into these comparisons in which they *typically* cannot win. This fuels the competition between the sexes that results in women being assigned a second-class status. This second-class status is a lie and a curse on womanhood that must be broken.

Understand that I am certainly not saying women should not compete in sports or in any other arena. I am only pointing out that measuring a man against a woman in these types of physical contests and then summarizing that the difference in their performance is indicative of their personhood is wrong.

It is also important to clarify that "woman" is not a personality type. Having a strong personality or being a strong person is not taking on a masculine role. Like men, women come in a variety of personality types. Women with strong personalities are sometimes tagged with names like a "Jezebel." That is ridiculous, hurtful, unfounded and untrue. I have often observed men who are intimidated by strong women. They try to hide their fear by demonizing the women. This is just another way of forcing women into a mold that does not fit.

Many women love to hunt, fish or do other things that some cultures ascribe as male attributes. These women are sometimes labeled "tomboys." Why is it that people feel as though a woman is masculine simply because she likes the outdoors? To me, the G.I. Janes of the world are women who are *reacting* to some dysfunctional relationship or unhealthy culture. The problem is not their behavior—it is their motive. On the other hand, if people's actions are coming out of their personhood and they are whole and healthy, then their passions are pure and they should be celebrated as manifestations of who God made them to be.

My previous book *Outrageous Courage: What God Can Do with Raw Obedience and Radical Faith* (Chosen, 2013) might help you understand my value for strong women. This book follows the life story of Tracy Evans. Her life has had such an unbelievable influence on me, my family and my friends that I wanted to introduce her to the world. Her courage and exploits remind me of people like George Washington, Winston Churchill and Joan of Arc. Short of biblical characters, I struggle to find anyone with whom to compare Tracy's passion for God or her amazing courage. I threatened to tell her story for more than a decade before she agreed to a book. She has always resisted drawing attention to herself.

Tracy received Christ in the army, and now, some thirty years later, she leads a powerful and dangerous ministry in the jungles of Africa.

At a distance, some may think that Tracy is a perfect example of a G.I. Jane. She is not. She has no desire to compete with men, but instead leads in the strength of her womanhood. She is not reacting to gender oppression or hurts from her past. She is just being who God made her to be and walking in her high calling in Christ. I do more than just celebrate Tracy's life—I wrote her story so that the world could see what it looks like when grace and courage collide.

Wake Up, Sleeping Beauty

We need the G.I. Janes of the world to become healthy people living in response to their God-given call, like Tracy, instead of living in reaction to some dysfunctional situation. But we also need the sleeping beauties of the world to be kissed awake by their Prince. He died more than two thousand years ago to free the planet from the curse, yet women continue to be devalued, oppressed and assigned subservient roles in society. Most of this is the result of women's inability to defend their God-given high call in civilization because men are generally physically stronger (in the ways I just described). For centuries, many men have bullied their way through life, using their physical strength to dominate, dictate and force their will on society at the expense of any who cannot defend themselves. This sad situation has crushed the spirit of multiple millions of beautiful and capable women, robbing them of their destiny and undermining their authority. No wonder 60 percent more women are taking antidepressants than men. (One in four women in America takes psych meds.)

What many have failed to understand is that not only has the place of women been undermined in society, but this social dynamic has also sabotaged the destiny of men as they try to play both the patriarchal and matriarchal roles. As I pointed out in the example of my son Jason's single parenting, when people are put in situations that they are ill-equipped to handle and are not designed for, those circumstances siphon off the resources they need to fulfill their God-appointed role. Plainly stated, the oppression of women has resulted in the mutation of the masculine role. Men no longer lead in the strength of their masculine

God assignment, because they have taken on the dualistic responsibility of men and women. The world therefore has rarely seen or experienced men leading in the strength of their design and call.

The truth is that the absence of the feminine and matriarchal presence in leadership has come at an incalculable and sometimes cataclysmic expense to society. In the last thirty years, I have observed many women coming into their place in leadership, but as we have discussed, for multiple reasons they are often required to play the patriarchal role. This, of course, puts them at a disadvantage because it does not optimize their leadership abilities. It is all too tempting to observe this dynamic and conclude that men are better leaders than women. I would like to propose to you that men are better patriarchs than women and women are stronger matriarchs than men. Both roles are equally important and carry the same level of authority, but they require different skills, strengths and attributes.

We do not need women to lead like men. The world is starving for matriarchs who are compassion driven, intuitively gifted, nurturing leaders. These leaders foster the maternal instinct in society that gives birth to a much more loving, caring, patient and compassionate planet. It is my honest conviction that if women were commissioned to lead in their rightful *place* and *role* globally, the planet would be a much safer, more compassionate, nurturing place to live. Violence and war would dramatically decrease worldwide if women would co-lead *with* men, without feeling the pressure to lead *as* men.

Do you think I am crazy? Consider this: In America alone, men are ten times more likely to commit a violent crime than women. Furthermore, how many women do you know of in the history of the world who have caused or initiated a war, a coup, a violent revolution, a rebellion or a hostile takeover of any kind? I am not saying the answer is none; I am simply making the point that global violence is more often a symptom of male leadership. I also understand that other dynamics are at work in these statistics, but it is a fact that women are inherently more nurturing, more compassionate, less violent, less hostile and more prone to find a peaceful solution in conflicts.

Divine Design

Years ago, Bill Johnson and I were leading a men's retreat together. Before the first session began, the men were making their way around the room and visiting with one another. Bill came to the podium to open the meeting and said, "Men, please find your places." He meant for the men to take their seats so we could start the meeting, but in that moment, I was overwhelmed with the sense that the theme of the retreat was to be "Men, find your place in life."

I am once again struck with that same overwhelming sense, but this time I hear God saying, "Women, find your places." In order for women to take their rightful place and role in society, we need to define some terms and search deeper into the foundation of the Creator's divine intentions for women. Let's go back to the Garden and take another look at the formation of the prototype woman. Here is the account God shared through Moses:

> So the LORD God caused a deep sleep to fall upon the man, and he slept; then He took one of his ribs and closed up the flesh at that place. The LORD God fashioned into a woman the rib which He had taken from the man, and brought her to the man. The man said,
>
> > "This is now bone of my bones,
> > And flesh of my flesh;
> > She shall be called Woman,
> > Because she was taken out of Man."
>
> For this reason a man shall leave his father and his mother, and be joined to his wife; and they shall become one flesh.
>
> Genesis 2:21–24

We can gain so much insight from this short passage. God is the ultimate anesthesiologist—He put man to sleep before He performed the operation. Of course, there were "side" effects to the procedure. This is the only place in the Bible where the Hebrew word *tesla* is translated "rib." The word *tesla* is translated "side chamber" ten times in the Old Testament. Furthermore, when the Bible says God took *one* of the man's ribs, the word used for *one* often means "a certain one or specific one." I would like to suggest that God took a specific "side chamber" from Adam and *fashioned* a woman out of it. The Hebrew word for *fashioned* means "built." Adam said that the chamber removed from his side was the woman.

I think it is important to note here that the chamber was not extracted from man's foot, so that it would be intrinsic for woman to be walked on. Neither was it taken from his hand, so that she would spend her days in slavery. The chamber God used to fabricate the woman was probably removed from the cavity that encompassed Adam's heart. This was a prophetic statement that speaks to the fact that woman was made to stand along*side* of man, for it was from the *side chamber* that she was fashioned. That woman was taken from a chamber close to man's heart is indicative of her intuitive nature—the way she processes from the heart to the head, as opposed to man, who processes from the head to the heart.

Revelation Bumps

I learned about the heart chamber the hard way in my marriage. Kathy and I were married in 1975, when I was twenty and she was seventeen. Kathy graduated a year early from high school so that we could get married, yet she still had the highest GPA in her entire school. Kathy has a brilliant mind and an intuitive heart. I really loved her (still do), but I did not understand how to relate to her as my wife.

My biological father drowned when I was three years old, so his voice was absent when it came to my understanding of the opposite sex. My mother remarried twice. My first stepfather was a six-foot-four tyrant. He ruled "his kingdom" through intimidation and fear. He was convinced that women were slaves that men married to have sex available on demand. He believed that women should have no authority in life except over their own children. When my mother tried to take a stand on any issue, he would literally beat her into submission.

My second stepfather was also a rageaholic. His leadership style was similar, although he never laid a hand on my mother (he did not keep that rule with us kids). It is funny that my first stepfather was raised in a *very* religious family and my second stepfather was raised in a military home. The similarities in the way they related to their wife (as well as to other women in general) are stunning. Consequently, the only examples I had of the way a husband should relate to his wife were hierarchical at best and oppressive, cruel and abusive at worst.

Growing up in this environment affected me deeply. I love my mother, and I have a great relationship with her. I have a lot of respect for my mother's opinion, and as a teenager I often went to her for counsel. She intuitively understands people, which causes her to see life from a different perspective than I do. Yet I also saw the oppression she lived under, and I felt sorry for her. Even as a boy, I thought it was barbaric that the strength of a man's body gave him the right of rulership. This seemed cavemannish and stupid.

It was not only the injustice in our home that troubled me; it was the fact that my mother was a more capable leader in many ways than the men in my life. There is no question that she was always more capable of leading our family than my stepfathers were. Although my fathers were physically much stronger, I saw a kind of strength in her that I never observed in men. For example, I watched my mom create a caring and nurturing environment in the midst of terrible circumstances. She remained graceful in pain and kind, even when circumstances seemed to dictate the opposite response. Her determination was unwavering. Granted, she was not good at choosing men, but it was uncanny how insightful she was in other aspects of life.

I knew when I got married that I did not want to be a tyrant or a dictator, but frankly, when I married Kathy I did not know what it meant to be a husband. And as if my upbringing were not confusing the role enough, my early life in Christ proved to compound the problem. I received Jesus at eighteen, the year after I moved out of my parents' home. I was shocked to see that the oppression of women I had observed as a boy growing up in a dysfunctional home was being taught as a lifestyle in church. I do not mean that violence toward women was tolerated or encouraged, but the same low value for women that this behavior was rooted in was being spiritualized. It made me sick to think that so many Christians embraced this dualistic value system, and as a newlywed, it further muddled my understanding of how Kathy and I were to relate in marriage. I always wanted Kathy to be powerful, but I was not sure how to go about fostering that. I certainly had no desire to be married to a manly girl, yet for me, *strong* and *manly* were not the same thing.

We got engaged when Kathy was thirteen, and we courted for five long years! (I know you are thinking that getting engaged at thirteen is crazy, and I agree.) We talked a lot about marriage in those years—the roles we would play, the kids we would have and how we would make decisions. We agreed that we would make important decisions only as a couple. That was fine with me because I really trust Kathy, and I have no desire to act as a king making decrees for his family. But the storm clouds were gathering and trouble was brewing on the horizon. I just could not see it coming.

The challenge was not *who* got to make the important decisions (as I said, we had settled that before we got married); it was *how* we would make decisions that began to drive me nuts! For me, making decisions was simple. I researched all the *facts* to determine the most logical choice. Kathy, on the other hand, also wanted all the facts, but as far as she was concerned, knowing the facts did not necessarily mean that we had all the information we needed to make the right decision. Let me illustrate by letting you in on a common dialogue between us. Our conversations would go something like this:

Kris: I think we should buy a new car. We have the money, and our old car keeps breaking down all the time. My uncle Ray has a really nice Mercury Capri he wants to sell. I'm sure he would give us a great deal on it.

Kathy: I think we should wait awhile and pray about it. I'm not sure we need the car right now.

Kris: You don't want a new car?

Kathy: Yeah, I do, but I'm not sure about the timing.

Kris: Timing? What do you mean by "timing"? We have the money, and we need the car. My uncle will sell it to someone else if we don't buy it now. It's a great deal.

Kathy: I agree, but I just don't feel good about it.

Kris: Why don't you feel good about it?

Kathy: I don't know. Something just doesn't feel right.

Kris: You don't like the car?

Kathy: I love the car.

Kris: You don't think we need a new car?

Kathy: Actually, I think we do.

Kris: Maybe you don't like the price?

Kathy: I think the price is great.

Kris: [By now I've grown extremely frustrated.] So, what's the problem? What is it that's bothering you?

Kathy: [She's trying to appeal to my need for logical dialogue.] I just feel, ah, like, ah, something isn't good. . . . I'm not sure what it is. It could just be something we aren't supposed to do right now . . . maybe . . . ah . . . I'm not certain.

By the end of this kind of discourse, I would be so exasperated with Kathy that I wanted to climb out of my skin. It was not so much that I had to have my way (although I am sure that was true sometimes); it is just that there was no logical reason not to do what we both wanted to do. Of course, the fact that I am an extremely driven D personality in the DISC personality profile only served to intensify the process. That meant I was particularly prone to being dominant and forceful. I would usually wear Kathy out with my Spocklike, Vulcan need for logic and my relentless prodding. Exhausted from the dialogue and without any facts to defend her hesitation, she would usually give in to my desire.

What I did not understand until many years later was that the word *ah* that Kathy often uttered in our conversations had many definitions. Sometimes the word meant, "The wheels are going to fall off that new car for no logical reason at all." Other times it meant, "We don't know it yet, but I'm pregnant and that car isn't going to work for our family." To this day I have to admit that I do not completely understand it, but I know this for a fact: When God took the side chamber from the man, the *ah* was in it. But the *aha* stayed in the man chamber. It took dozens of *ahas* to help me learn to value Kathy's *ahs*. I finally realized that although Kathy's *ah* was not always rational, it was uncommonly insightful.

Intuitively Speaking

One of the greatest challenges I face in this book is trying to define the *ah* to people who have not experienced it. It is like attempting to explain love to somebody who has never been in love. When we pull out the dictionary, read the Bible or Google the word *love*, we find academic definitions that may satisfy the need for some intellectual dialogue. But for everyone who has experienced love, the mere attempt to define with words what was experienced in relationship seems futile at best. Yet when we observe two people passionately in love in a movie, or when we watch newlyweds gloating over one another, our heartstrings begin to vibrate with the instinctive sense of understanding something our brains cannot define.

Like love, *ah* is multidimensional in nature. It is much more easily understood by experience than it is defined by the intellect. Yet I will forge ahead in the pages that follow to try to explain the *ah* of womanhood and the creative advantage it gives them. I am acutely aware that every word I etch on paper in this context can be scrutinized, analyzed and argued, especially by those who are convinced that women are simply men who have a vagina and breasts instead of a penis. These people's intellectual arguments could easily neutralize my experience-oriented convictions. Nevertheless, this subject is important enough to risk sounding intellectually uninformed.

One of the advantages of the *ah* in women is that they tend to have this amazing ability to "feel" their way through circumstances and situations. This ability often transcends logic and reason. By this I do not mean that women's solutions are unreasonable or illogical; it is just that women process differently than men.

Women, for example, tend to respond to crisis out of compassion for people, while men are inclined to respond out of a need to protect someone or bring justice to a situation. Even our entertainment industry recognizes these gender preferences. This is why we semi-jokingly call certain movies "chick flicks." These movies appeal especially to the emotional or more "felt" side of life. Their themes inspire compassion, love, adoration, affection, devotion, care, sympathy, empathy, understanding, concern, loyalty and faithfulness. On the other hand, men tend to gravitate toward action movies with themes like justice, rescue, competition, winning, revenge, courage, heroism, vengeance, retribution, fighting, wars and rivalry. Metaphorically speaking, the felt needs of life and the intuitive sense of humanity most often are the right hand of women, yet they tend to be the left hand of men.

In a healthy culture, organization or family where men and women have the freedom to operate in their strengths, these gender distinctions bring great balance and synergistic insights that benefit people. For example, over the past fifteen years I have traveled much of the world to equip churches in prophetic ministry. One of the things I have observed—without a single exception—is that whenever we gather intercessors or prophetic people, 75 to 80 percent of them are women.

"Why?" you ask.

Because women are instinctively more intuitive. Men's need to have the facts, plus their bent toward logic and reason, frequently neutralize their spiritual connectivity, which often (though not always) operates outside the laws of physics. Women, by their very nature, are accustomed to valuing things that cannot necessarily be explained. Women therefore more easily embrace the higher realms of the Kingdom because those realms are entered into by faith, not by reason.

Leading the Church

Matriarchs have been absent from leadership in the Church for more than two thousand years. It is hard to imagine how much more profound an impact the Kingdom could have had on this planet if women had been empowered to take their proper place alongside men in the Church of Jesus Christ. But one thing is certain—the absence of the ones fashioned from the side chamber of man has caused there to be way too many *aha* moments in the Body of Christ.

We simply cannot continue to believe that we will fulfill the Great Commission with spiritually motherless families and spiritually dysfunctional fathers who are trying to carry out dualistic roles they were never designed to fulfill. It is past time for men to scoot over and allow our matriarchs to co-reign with us to help bring the Kingdom of God to a desperate and dying world.

SARAH EDWARDS

The Mother of a Legacy

Sarah Edwards's legacy is still having a profound impact on American society today, even though it has been centuries since she passed away. Many times, society views powerful people as those who are well-known, are public speakers or are strong personalities. Yet Sarah was none of these things. Instead, her life was spent behind the scenes, supporting her husband and his ministry while equipping her children to play a vital role in society. Sarah had a quiet disposition, but she changed history in a way that is often overlooked. Sarah mothered eleven children and shaped them into world changers.

Her story started in 1710, when she was born into a minister's home and grew up as the descendant of many generations of ministers. She was raised in one of the wealthiest and most distinguished families in Connecticut. It was rare for women to be educated in that era, but her father was one of the founders of Yale University, so he provided her with an excellent education.

Sarah was only seventeen when she married Jonathan Edwards. Jonathan was a preacher and a theologian, and he is now considered one of the most influential intellectuals in American history.[1] Even though Sarah was young, she was the personification of a Proverbs 31 woman:

practical, caring and wise in handling her family's affairs. And it goes without saying that with eleven children, Sarah was extremely organized.

Being a mother in the 1700s was not an easy task, especially with a large family to feed and clothe. Big families were common in those days because children helped with the family business. It is hard for us to imagine the multiple tasks wives performed every single day just to survive. Sarah had to chop ice in the winter to get water. She made all of her family's clothing, grew her own fruits and vegetables and hunted for their meat. To make matters even more difficult, there were no washers or dryers in those days, and Sarah had to cook all of their meals over an open fire. Sarah proved that it was not only possible to survive, but to thrive with her family in difficult circumstances. Once Sarah went out of town and left Jonathan to tend to the household. He wrote to her in desperation, "We've been without you almost as long as we know how to be."

In those days, it was commonly believed that a child was born on the day of the week on which he or she had been conceived. The funny thing is that six of Sarah and Jonathan's children were born on Sunday. Some pastors refused to baptize babies born on Sunday because apparently sex was an inappropriate Sabbath activity.[2]

Sarah Edwards poured her life into raising her children. Although Jonathan helped, Sarah did most of the parenting. She prayed constantly for her children, even before they were born, and regularly taught them the Word of God. Devotions were one of the Edwards family's top priorities. All throughout their childhood, Sarah cried out to the Lord on her children's behalf. Her diligence paid off. As the Edwards children grew into adulthood, all of them became known for their intelligence and strong character.

The Edwards children were also quite accomplished. Their résumés read like the who's who of the 1700s. Jonathan and Sarah's daughter Esther married Aaron Burr, Princeton's first president, and Esther's son Aaron Burr Jr. was the third vice president of the United States, under President Thomas Jefferson. Before becoming vice president, he was a successful lawyer and politician, and he served as attorney general and as a senator.[3]

Jonathan and Sarah's daughter Mary Edwards married Timothy Dwight, son of the famed educator Timothy Dwight Jr., the eighth president of Yale College. The Dwight family history includes a long list of professors, educators, authors and ministers.[4] The Edwardses' son Jonathan graduated from Princeton, where he studied theology. He was a tutor and a pastor; then he became president of Union College.[5] Pierrepont was their youngest son. He became a delegate to the American Continental Congress. He was also a United States federal judge and a senator.[6]

Sarah Edwards's legacy is astounding. By the year 1900, the descendants of Sarah and Jonathan included 13 college presidents, 65 professors, 100 lawyers, 30 judges, 66 physicians, 80 holders of public office, a publisher, 135 editors and more than 100 overseas missionaries. In 1900, a man named A. E. Winship studied the life of two contrasting families. One family had been a drain on society, and the other was the Edwards family. He wrote, "Whatever this family has done, it has done ably and nobly,"[7] and "Much of the capacity and talent, intelligence and character of the more than 1400 of the Edwards' family, much of those good qualities is due to Sarah Edwards."[8]

Have you heard the saying "The hand that rocks the cradle is the hand that rules the world"?[9] It comes from a poem written by William Ross Wallace. He was praising motherhood as the primary force for changing the world, and that was certainly true in Sarah's case. Her legacy is an inspiration to mothers all over the world, and her life proves that a powerful woman can leave a world-changing legacy through her lineage.

9

Empowering Strong Women

When Kathy read the first few chapters of this manuscript, she protested my analogies and reminded me that many women love to serve in other capacities besides preaching, teaching or some form of leadership that receives the applause of men. She felt I was actually cloning women after some D personality, extroverted female who was called to the limelight. Kathy said she would feel dishonored if this book did not give the same level of honor to women who possess a quiet strength and who love to serve their husbands or operate in the ministry of helps. Someone described this type of woman in a Facebook post to me:

> Some of the strongest women on earth are the ones who possess a quiet resolve of steel; she conquers the world one day at a time and is able to respond quickly to the Father's heart with complete abandonment. The world does not know her name . . . but it echoes in the halls of Eternity, causes chaos and confusion to flee in her presence, while the dominions of darkness bow to the King upon the throne of her heart.

Kathy reminded me of the words of Jesus, "If anyone wants to be first, he shall be last of all and servant of all" (Mark 9:35). Kathy understood that the purpose of this book is to remove the heavy oppression that the religious spirit has placed on many women, but she also felt that I could inadvertently introduce another type of bondage by making women feel as though they had to behave a certain way to be considered strong. It was a wise caution. I am reminded of Peter's exhortation to women: "Let it be the hidden person of the heart, with the imperishable quality of a gentle and quiet spirit, which is precious in the sight of God" (1 Peter 3:4). We need to value equally the full spectrum of honorable women and empower them to be all God has called them to be. Whether we are male or female, it is important to realize that reigning in this life often looks like serving those around us in a way that demonstrates the excellence of our humble King.

Given Kathy's wise observation, when we think about strong women, we should be careful not to define *strong* as extroverted, driven or possessing a dominant personality. Many women who are strong and noble leaders do not possess any of these qualities. There are also women (as well as men) who have dominant personalities but are neither honorable nor virtuous. No matter a person's sex, a dominant personality does not necessarily equal a strong leader, or a strong person for that matter. In many cases, a person's dominance is actually a smokescreen for insecurity, fear, resentment, anger and selfishness. Solomon wrote, "Like a city that is broken into and without walls is a man who has no control over his spirit" (Proverbs 25:28). When a dominating man or woman controls others with seduction, fear, manipulation or any other form of coercion, they have built a partnership with witchcraft, which ultimately leads to every form of evil.

I have led many competent women over the years in both business and in the ministry. As I shared with you in the previous chapter, leading women was complicated for me when I was younger because I did not understand the differences between women's strengths and my own. I was also brought up in a male-dominated environment that did not equip me with the skills I needed to lead women well. I have grown a lot in the last fifteen years in my ability to successfully lead strong women, no matter what their personality type.

I have run into a few situations, though, where strong women whom I was leading were being difficult or insubordinate. Sometimes when I confronted them on their attitude, they pulled the "woman card" on me and insisted that I was being chauvinistic because I would not accept their disrespectful behavior. It is important that we respect and honor one another, no matter our sexes. Being a woman with a dominant personality should not be a "get out of jail free" card. I do understand that women with strong personalities have been oppressed more often than men and have been treated disrespectfully for generations. But reacting to oppression by being rebellious, disrespectful or insubordinate only perpetuates the gender incongruity.

I have also discovered that some women are fighting a ghost from the past. For these women, any kind of conflict with a man is inflated, exaggerated and/or deemed discourteous. Whenever I have a disagreement with any woman who has the "ghost syndrome," I have learned to ask her to repeat back what she thinks I said. The difference between what I am trying to communicate and what she is hearing can be disheartening at times. Great communication requires both parties to take the time to listen to each other from the heart.

The "ghost syndrome" reared its ugly head many years ago when I was in Africa with some friends. Crossing from one country into another, we stood in line at the border crossing for about three hours in the hot African sun. Instead of being in well-organized lines, hundreds of us were herded together by the border guards into a kind of unorganized mob as they sort of drove us to the customs counter. Suddenly, out of nowhere, one of the ladies with us turned to the man in front of her and began screaming, *"Don't you ever touch my breasts! Do you understand me, mister?"*

With a stunned and embarrassed look on his face, the man said in a jittery voice, "Lady, I have no idea what you're talking about. I never turned around and touched you. I've kept my hands to myself!"

"You liar!" she shouted. *"You leaned backward and put your back on my breasts on purpose!"*

The man tried desperately to defend himself by reminding her that we were being herded like cattle and that everybody was being smashed together. She refused to listen to his plea and went on making a big scene for several minutes. I was just as shocked as the man she was accusing. I had been standing right next to both of them the entire time, and the crowd was often driven forward by the guards, which forced us into one another. There was no way the gentleman touched my friend inappropriately. I tried to calm her down, but she just waved me off. I wondered to myself, *What the heck is wrong with this lady?*

We were alone the next day for a couple of hours, so I decided to broach the subject. What I discovered was that my friend was the victim of several rapes and therefore had spent most of her life embittered toward men. Her bitterness, unforgiveness, betrayal and hurt were rewriting her reality. The man in line the day before had no chance of convincing her that he was moral because she had not actually been talking to *him*; she had been talking to a ghost from the past.

The "ghost syndrome" can be triggered for various reasons in different women, and also in men. I have often observed this syndrome at work when a woman with a strong personality is mislabeled a "Jezebel" in the Church or just is not tolerated in the marketplace. It is common for these women to feel as if they are in a constant state of warfare, which subsequently causes them to remain battle ready and on high alert. Interacting with anyone who, metaphorically speaking, is dressed for battle creates a defensive posture for those who are in relationship with that person, which ultimately leads the female soldier into feeling justified in her attitude.

This dysfunctional ecosystem can only be dismantled through trust, honor and respect. Hurting people inevitably hurt other people. It is not enough to be right; we must be redemptive if we are ever going to see a revolution that empowers both sexes equally and honorably.

My Best Friend

Kathy has never struggled with her identity as a woman and a leader. She is probably the most virtuous person I have ever known. We have always co-led our family and have made every important decision as a team. She has always done her best to make sure I succeed. I have never required this of her; it is just who she is in the depths of her soul. For instance, many years ago we decided to expand our business and open a couple more auto parts stores. This wound up having a treacherous effect on our cash flow to the point where we barely had enough money to feed our family. Instead of complaining, blaming or grumbling, Kathy jumped in with both feet to do what she could to help our situation. With three little children, it was nearly impossible for her to leave the house and come to work in our business, so she set up a desk at home and did all of our accounting from there, while simultaneously taking care of our kids. I have no idea how she managed both of those worlds so well.

I came home from work a little bit early one day during that tough financial season. As I navigated our snow-packed driveway on that dark, cold, winter day, I noticed that all the lights were out in the house. At first I thought my family was not home, until I walked up on the deck and heard the kids laughing. I opened the front door, and to my surprise there were three tents made out of blankets on the front-room floor. The only lights in the house were a couple of oil lamps. The woodstove warmed our small chalet situated in the mountains of the Trinity Alps. I did not realize it at the time, but Kathy had put herself on a tight budget that included rationing our electricity by determining how many kilowatts we could use a month. She would flip the main breaker off during the day to stay within her budget. When I walked in the house, the kids were excited because Kathy had told them that they were all "camping." Because Kathy had created a game out of our financial crisis, no one was complaining or upset that we were broke. Our children were learning from their mother how to lead a family through a financial calamity. To this very day, my children are excellent with money and are resourceful wealth managers. They did not learn this from their father; they were educated in their little tents as they watched their mother bring strength in a tough situation.

In those days, while I was away trying to generate as much income as possible, Kathy was taking all the hard calls from our suppliers who were being paid late. The whole thing never should have happened and it was my fault, but Kathy never grumbled. She answered all the angry phone calls and worked tirelessly to establish trust with our suppliers in a nearly impossible situation. When I would come home from a twelve-hour workday, exhausted from working so hard and stressed out because of our financial circumstances, Kathy never wavered. She was never afraid, and she refused to panic. Rarely would a day pass without Kathy encouraging me and reminding me that we were going to make it because God was with us.

In 37 years of marriage, I can count on one hand the times that Kathy has been upset or stressed out. For most of her life, her strength has not been seen behind a podium or preaching on big stages somewhere. Rather, her strength is reflected in the eyes of those she has stabilized in the storms of life and in the hearts of those she has served and empowered to capture their dreams. I often ask Kathy what her greatest vision is for her life. She always replies, "I was created to help other people fulfill their destiny." I thank God for Kathy every day of my life.

The Strength of Motherhood

To a large extent, we have lost the high value we should place on motherhood in society. I mentioned earlier that women were considered second-class citizens in this country from its inception. But with the advent of women's rights came the redefinition of feminine roles. Because men controlled the value systems of our society, they determined which virtues were held in honor and which were disdained. This resulted in masculine virtues being held in high esteem, while matriarchal roles were demeaned.

When society's value for maternal roles eroded, mothers who were at home raising children felt trapped while watching other women join men in the adventurous world of the workforce. It was not long before children became the stumbling stones of the great adventure, so they were sacrificed on the altar of materialism. To some men and women, being the head of a large corporation is more important than molding the hearts of tomorrow's leaders. I do not want to relegate the job of raising children solely to women, but children need the nurturing strength of a mother, just as they need the protection and virtue of a father. Our society is starving for both roles to be implemented in the hearts of our young people.

When the value society placed on motherhood eroded, gender confusion was the result. Gender confusion has become so prevalent that many states in America allow homosexuals to be adoptive parents and to call their union a marriage. I am opposed to homosexuality on several levels beyond the scope of this book, but for a start, the refusal to acknowledge the difference between the sexes is costing us a generation. It is impossible to call two women or two men a marriage. There is no way for two people of the same sex to become one flesh, because they are not corresponding or opposite of each other, as we talked about in chapter 2.

On the practical side of the family issue, children do not need two moms or two dads; they need a mother and a father. Cloning the sexes in the name of equality has caused untold sickness in our society and is one of the reasons for the exponential growth of homosexuality all over the world. (By the way, I am not a "hater" of homosexuals, but I am a strong "disagreer.")

I want to be clear that I am not in any way trying to relegate women to staying home and raising children while men "bring home the bacon." It is vital that you view this chapter in the context of the entire book, which was written to empower women to be all that God has called them to be. I have no desire to stereotype them or in any way reduce their God-given commission to co-reign alongside men. I do, however, want to elevate the call of motherhood. Motherhood belongs alongside the value and significance of running a multimillion-dollar corporation, being a doctor, a scientist, a soldier, an artist, a singer, a politician, a pastor or any other position that society holds in high esteem. I have often been in the presence of a mother with several children and have listened as someone asks her if she works. I understand that the questioner is most likely asking her if she works outside the home, but I cannot imagine someone walking up to a CEO of a company and asking if he or she works! Such a question asked of a mother might be just a slip of the tongue, but I am concerned that it is actually rooted in the low value our society places on one of the matriarch's most profound and powerful roles—that of motherhood.

Last year in our women's conference, Tiffany Williams stood behind a podium and read a poem that Christianna Maas, a mother of three children, wrote in the midst of her struggle with motherhood. Christianna is a gifted leader and could easily be the head of a large corporation. But by her own choice, she has decided to stay home and raise her children instead. Her poem created such a powerful stir in the conference that within minutes several people were in my office replaying the video for me. Most said it was the highlight of the entire conference. Here is the poem in black and white. I wish you could have heard Tiffany read Christianna's poem in the conference. Her incredible beauty, dramatic voice and body language were as powerful as the words.

Motherhood

By Christianna Maas

My willingness to carry life is the revenge, the antidote, the great rebuttal of every murder, every abortion, and every genocide. I sustain humanity. Deep inside of me, life grows. I am death's opposition.

I have pushed back the hand of darkness today. I have caused there to be a weakening tremor among the ranks of those set on earth's destruction. Today a vibration that calls angels to attention echoed throughout time. Our laughter threatened hell today.

I dined with the greats of God's army. I made their meals, and tied their shoes. Today, I walked with greatness, and when they were tired I carried them. I have poured myself out for the cause today.

It is finally quiet, but life stirs inside of me. Gaining strength, the pulse of life sends a constant reminder to both good and evil that I have yielded myself to Heaven and now carry its dream. No angel has ever had such a privilege, nor any man. I am humbled by the honor. I am great with destiny.

I birth the freedom fighters. In the great war, I am a leader of the underground resistance. I smile at the disguise of my troops, surrounded by a host of warriors, destiny swirling, invisible yet tangible, and the anointing to alter history. Our footsteps marking land for conquest, we move undetected through the common places.

Today I was the barrier between evil and innocence. I was the gatekeeper, watching over the hope of mankind, and no intruder trespassed. There is not an hour of day or night when I turn from my post. The fierceness of my love is unmatched on earth.

And because I smiled instead of frowned the world will know the power of grace. Hope has feet, and it will run to the corners of earth, because I stood up against destruction.

I am a woman. I am a mother. I am the keeper and sustainer of life here on earth. Heaven stands in honor of my mission. No one else can carry my call. I am the daughter of Eve. Eve has been redeemed. I am the opposition of death. I am a woman.

Molding Lives

Scientists and psychologists have discovered that most of our core beliefs about love and security are formed in the first four years of our upbringing. It is in these tender years that mothers, in their nurturing capacity, have the greatest influence in the lives of their children. Over twenty-five hundred years ago, King Solomon put it like this: "My son, observe the commandment of your father and do not forsake the teaching of your mother" (Proverbs 6:20).

King Lemuel's mother taught her son what is probably the most powerful and practical instruction on marriage ever given. It is recorded in Proverbs 31. The entire book of Proverbs opens with this statement:

"The proverbs of Solomon the son of David, king of Israel" (Proverbs 1:1), and the Hebrew name *Lemuel* means "belonging to God," so it is safe to assume that Lemuel is Solomon's symbolic name or nickname. That means Solomon's mother, Bathsheba, was the woman who gave him this profound marital instruction.

Here again, if you are a man and you are not convinced by now that women are commissioned to teach men, then you should not read this chapter. Although Solomon was taught this as a child, you are reading it as an adult, and if you read it, you will learn from it!

The words of King Lemuel, the oracle which his mother taught him:

> What, O my son?
> And what, O son of my womb?
> And what, O son of my vows?
> Do not give your strength to women,
> Or your ways to that which destroys kings.
> It is not for kings, O Lemuel,
> It is not for kings to drink wine,
> Or for rulers to desire strong drink,
> For they will drink and forget what is decreed,
> And pervert the rights of all the afflicted.
> Give strong drink to him who is perishing,
> And wine to him whose life is bitter.
> Let him drink and forget his poverty
> And remember his trouble no more.
> Open your mouth for the mute,
> For the rights of all the unfortunate.
> Open your mouth, judge righteously,
> And defend the rights of the afflicted and needy.
> An excellent wife who can find?
> For her worth is far above jewels
> The heart of her husband trusts in her,
> And he will have no lack of gain.
> She does him good and not evil
> All the days of her life.

She looks for wool and flax
And works with her hands in delight.
She is like merchant ships;
She brings her food from afar.
She rises also while it is still night
And gives food to her household
And portions to her maidens.
She considers a field and buys it;
From her earnings she plants a vineyard.
She girds herself with strength
And makes her arms strong.
She senses that her gain is good;
Her lamp does not go out at night.
She stretches out her hands to the distaff,
And her hands grasp the spindle.
She extends her hand to the poor,
And she stretches out her hands to the needy.
She is not afraid of the snow for her household,
For all her household are clothed with scarlet.
She makes coverings for herself;
Her clothing is fine linen and purple.
Her husband is known in the gates,
When he sits among the elders of the land.
She makes linen garments and sells them,
And supplies belts to the tradesmen.
Strength and dignity are her clothing,
And she smiles at the future.
She opens her mouth in wisdom,
And the teaching of kindness is on her tongue.
She looks well to the ways of her household,
And does not eat the bread of idleness.
Her children rise up and bless her;
Her husband also, and he praises her, saying:
"Many daughters have done nobly,
But you excel them all."
Charm is deceitful and beauty is vain,

But a woman who fears the Lord, she shall be praised.
Give her the product of her hands,
And let her works praise her in the gates.

Proverbs 31

When I read the first few verses of Proverbs 31, they caused me to wonder if Bathsheba blamed herself for the immoral relationship she had with King David before they were married, which ultimately cost her first husband his life. She said to her son, "Do not give your strength to women, or your ways to that which destroys kings" (verse 3). Bathsheba went on to teach Solomon that royalty should behave nobly and keep a clear head for making wise decisions. She exhorted him to use his authority to defend the rights of the helpless and poor. She had watched her husband misuse his power and forget his humble beginnings, especially in relation to the incident involving her first husband, Uriah, whom David had killed. I am sure she was trying to make sure that her son did not follow in his father's footsteps.

Finally, Solomon's mother taught him what to look for in a wife. Although Bathsheba was beautiful, she recounted to her son that charm and beauty are deceitful, vain qualities not worthy of consideration when searching for an excellent wife. She told him that instead of marrying a beauty queen, he should find a woman he could trust (not someone marrying him for his power or money). She wanted Solomon to find someone who would not lie around sunbathing on the roof in sight of the palace, sipping suds from the champagne fountain, but who would contribute nobly to the family and the kingdom. The girl must be hardworking, value excellence, love the poor and help make investments that would grow the family's wealth.

Unlike most queens who spend money like it is water, lavish themselves with the finest clothes and relegate their children to be raised by servants, Solomon's wife should be a lady who would make a great mother and have a vision for future generations. This was what Bathsheba taught her son, the richest man who ever lived. Bathsheba urged him to find a wife who would be wise, dignified and know how to teach.

She must not be a fragile, needy diva, but must be someone strong enough that he could lean on her in tough times because she would not be afraid of the winter seasons of life. And last but not least, she had to have a great relationship with God, a deep relationship full of conviction for righteousness.

These things Solomon was to look for in a wife are not personality traits; these are character qualities that need to be rooted in us all. It does not matter if we are introverted or extroverted, brilliant or average, assertive or passive—noble character is the natural outgrowth of a royal priesthood of which all believers are a part.

A Strong Woman

A strong woman is someone who is walking in her God-given identity, unaffected by the world's image of the feminine role or the religious pressure to conform to some reduced version of herself. There is so much peer pressure in the world for people to become a copy of someone else instead of being an original of themselves. This was reemphasized to me in 2012 when I was in Taiwan. I was speaking at several conferences with some friends, and one evening we went to a nice restaurant that happened to be in the middle of a giant mall. We walked a long way inside the mall to the restaurant, passing several women's clothing stores along the way. Suddenly it dawned on me that there was not a single Asian mannequin in any of the display windows. They were all white women with blond hair and, of course, perfect bodies.

Asian women do not have blond hair; they have black hair. And their faces have very distinctive features. I was stunned by the overt marketing strategy betrayed by the female mannequins. They were characterizing an image of what it (supposedly) looks like to be a beautiful woman. The only problem is that Asian women are not like those mannequins and never will be. I am sure that the subliminal message was, "If you wear these clothes, you will turn into a beautiful, blond-haired, blue-eyed, perfect-bodied white woman." By the time we got to the restaurant, I was infuriated by the blatant disrespect for the beauty of a different race.

Those mannequins personified the struggle that women (and men) have all over the world—everyone is pressured to be like someone else. Personally, I am sick of it on several levels. For the sake of this book, though, I will focus my frustration on the intense pressure women face every day to meet other people's expectations of who they should be and how they should behave.

Giving Up the Gavel

Many years ago, I counseled a woman who was really struggling with her unsaved husband. She received a lot of freedom in our sessions and asked me if I would be willing to meet with her husband. I told her, "Of course I am willing to talk with him, but he might not want to meet with a Christian counselor."

"I think he'll meet with you," she said with a smile. "He thinks you have already helped our marriage by counseling with me."

She was right, and about two weeks later they were both sitting in my office. He was a tall, thin man in his early forties, dressed in a pair of Levi's and a nice shirt. I could tell that he was really uncomfortable when he sat down in the chair next to his wife, but to my surprise, he brought an old, oversized King James Family Bible with him. We exchanged pleasantries as he nervously grasped the huge Bible to his chest.

I was not sure what to think. Was he trying to impress me or somehow send me a message that he believed in the Bible even though he admittedly was not Christian? After a few minutes I turned to him (thinking I would break the ice with a simple question) and asked, "So, Henry, where would you like to see improvement in your marriage?" (I have changed his name to protect his privacy, of course.)

"Well, Pastor," he began (looking like a frightened little boy in big trouble), "I think . . . well, Pastor, sir, . . . my wife is not listening to God's commands in the book of the Bible!"

"I'm sorry, Henry, you lost me completely. What is it exactly that you're trying to say?" I questioned with a curious look on my face.

He pulled the Bible down to his lap and opened it up to a page he had marked with a piece of cardboard. He was shaking so badly that he could barely hold the weight of the huge Bible. I could tell that his wife had been through this before; she began to get anxious, or maybe she was embarrassed.

"Pa . . . Pas . . . Pastor," he stuttered, "I would like to show you from the Bible that my wife is not . . . well, sir . . . she is not performing her duty in our marriage."

I chuckled in my heart as I kind of figured out where Henry was going with all this. "Okay, Henry, go ahead and read me the passage that you're concerned about."

"Yes, sir," he said, as if he were striking the final blow of a great gladiator. He began reading,

> Let every man have his own wife, and let every woman have her own husband. Let the husband render unto the wife due benevolence: and likewise also the wife unto the husband. The wife hath not power of her own body, but the husband: and likewise also the husband hath not power of his own body, but the wife. Defraud ye not one the other, except it be with consent for a time, that ye may give yourselves to fasting and prayer; and come together again, that Satan tempt you not for your incontinency.
>
> 1 Corinthians 7:2–5 KJV

Henry nervously stammered through the King James verses, but I knew this portion of Scripture well, so I simply waited for him to finish. It was quite comical; several minutes passed while Henry reread portions of Scripture that he got wrong. Finally, he looked up from the Bible and said as serious as a heart attack, "That's what I need her to do! She's not doing her godly duty for her husband, and it's got to change."

By now I was trying my best not to fall on the floor laughing. I worked hard to match his intensity and his serious look and said, "Henry, let me get this right—you're not a Christian and don't follow God. Is that true?"

"Well, yes, sir, yep . . . I do believe that's accurate," he said defensively.

"Okay, but you want to use the Bible to make your wife have sex with you. Is that what you're trying to tell me?"

"Pastor, the Good Book tells her that she has to have sex with me 'cause her body is not hers, it's mine," he insisted.

"Henry," I began.

"Yes, sir," he responded, with his wife about to faint from embarrassment.

"Henry, if you have to use the Bible to get your wife to have sex with you, then there's something else wrong in your marriage, sir," I said to him sternly. "The Bible was never written to use against one another or to manipulate someone into doing your will. The Word of God is not a list of rules to control someone; it is a set of values for wholeness," I said in fatherly exhortation.

Henry had never understood the true purpose of the Bible (which is true of many Christians as well). He was raised in a religious home where the Book was used to get him to behave, not to draw him into a relationship with Jesus. For Henry, the Scriptures were like the laws of a country, enforced by the courts and punished through prisons. Henry was taught to read the Bible like a lawyer, not a lover. I met with Henry and his wife several more times over the following months. Henry received Christ and wept his way to wholeness. His family life was radically altered as he gave up the gavel and embraced passion.

I am often taken aback by the way some leaders apply the Scriptures, not unlike the way Henry was doing. Jesus died to redeem mankind. The apostle Paul said it best: "It was for freedom that Christ set us free; therefore keep standing firm and do not be subject again to a yoke of slavery" (Galatians 5:1). Whenever we apply the Scriptures in a way that is unredemptive, creates hopelessness, reduces a person's destiny or enslaves them, we have missed one of the main points of the Gospel, which is supposed to be abundant life in Jesus Christ.

Paul Weighs In on Marriage

The first time I studied Paul's instructions to the Corinthians and Ephesians about women and marriage, I thought to myself, *Man, I know why this guy was single!* But as I began to go deeper into Paul's teaching, like a hologram a completely different picture began to emerge. Let's look at one of his marriage passages together and see what surfaces:

> Be subject to one another in the fear of Christ.
> Wives, be subject to your own husbands, as to the Lord. For the husband is the head of the wife, as Christ also is the head of the church, He Himself being the Savior of the body. But as the church is subject to Christ, so also the wives ought to be to their husbands in everything.
> Husbands, love your wives, just as Christ also loved the church and gave Himself up for her, so that He might sanctify her, having cleansed her by the washing of water with the word, that He might present to Himself the church in all her glory, having no spot or wrinkle or any such thing; but that she would be holy and blameless. So husbands ought also to love their own wives as their own bodies. He who loves his own wife loves himself; for no one ever hated his own flesh, but nourish and cherishes it, just as Christ also does the church, because we are members of His body.
>
> Ephesians 5:21–30

When I studied Paul's instructions to husbands and wives in the context of the first-century Church, several things began to jump out and grab me: First of all, Paul's teaching begins with husbands and wives both being "subject" to one another. This passage reminds me of the counterculture verses we studied earlier, in 1 Corinthians 7, where Paul says a man does not own his own body, but his wife does, and vice versa. This is radical stuff for a former Pharisee to teach. Let's remember that the Gentile cities of Corinth and Ephesus had a lot in common because men and women worshiped female goddesses in both places. The emphasis on the headship of husbands and the submission of wives therefore was obviously in the context of these cultic cultures (as we unraveled earlier when we looked closely at Paul's first letter to Timothy).

Whatever way you decide to read the context of the Ephesian culture into this passage is up to you, but it troubles me the way some people emphasize one part of the passage and deemphasize the other part. Some theologians, pastors and teachers tend to shout, "*Wives, be submissive to your own husbands,*" and then they whisper, "*Husbands, love your wives, just as Christ also loved the church and gave Himself up for her.*"

Note that a husband is commanded to die for his wife, while a wife is instructed to respect and submit to her husband. Yet somehow submission is taunted as some heavy weight dangled around the neck of a wife, while the death march of a godly husband who has laid down his life to protect the honor of his bride is played off as some joyride at Disney World. I do not know how people can read Paul's instructions to husbands and wives in the book of Ephesians and then walk away feeling as though submission and headship are the headlines of Paul's teaching. The guy just told husbands to lay down their lives for their wives!

In most marriage classes I have been in, they read this passage and then tell couples that it is the wife's duty to make her husband successful. I am sorry, but I think we just read that husbands and wives must submit themselves to one another. Let's remember that all of this instruction began with "be subject to *one another* in the fear of Christ." It was reemphasized to the wives, and then the men were told to give up their lives for the sake of their brides. How, then, did marriage get to be all about fulfilling the dreams of the husband while the wife keeps the house clean?

From the very first marriage in the Bible, Adam prophesied that a man would leave his father and mother and cleave to his wife. Obviously, the woman also would leave her mother and father when she married, but God is pointing out that the husband is the pursuer. He is in charge of cultivating his wife's destiny and sacrificing to see her dreams come true.

Paul said, "The husband is the head of the wife, *as* Christ also is the head of the church, He Himself being the Savior of the body" (Ephesians 5:23, emphasis added). Too often we leave that little word *as* out of the equation. Christ demonstrated that *headship* is servanthood in motion. Headship is not about demanding husbands who reduce daughters of God to sex slaves or housemaids.

I am not proud of the attitude I brought with me into my marriage. I met Kathy when she was twelve years old, and as I mentioned earlier, we got engaged when she was thirteen and were married by the time she was seventeen. On our honeymoon night, I laid a pair of my pants on the bed and said to Kathy, "Try these on."

She responded, "Your pants won't fit me."

"Don't ever forget that," I said with a sarcastic chuckle.

I was trying to be funny, but there is always a little truth in every glass of humor. As I mentioned earlier, I did not want to be a dictator or a tyrant, yet I was raised to believe that a man was the King of his Castle! Of course, there was no queen, nor any princes or princesses—only slaves "privileged" to serve at the will of His Majesty. Then Kathy and I met Bill and Beni Johnson in church a few years later. For the next fifteen years of our lives, our families were practically inseparable. We even lived with the Johnsons for six months. Kathy and I spent the next decade learning how noble people behave. We would lie in bed at night and discuss what we had learned from Bill and Beni that day about raising a family. We had three children who were the same ages as their three children, so consequently our kids grew up in a royal environment that cultivated princesses and princes. We made plenty of mistakes with our children, and our home was not the picture of perfection. Nevertheless, all of our children grew up loving God, and they are all in full-time ministry to this day (probably because of their deep respect for the Johnsons).

I learned how to treat my wife by watching Bill court Beni. I saw how he adored her, how he gave her freedom to be her own person and how he refused to let the church leaders dictate Beni's role in the church. After all, the apostle Paul said, "Wives, be subject to your *own* husbands." He did not say "Women, be subject to every man." As I have already stated, I do not think a theological case can be made that men as a sex have authority over women as a sex.

As time went on, I grew in my ability to lead my family and serve my wife. I began a tradition in those days that has served us well, even up through today. About three times a year, when Kathy and I are lying in bed, I ask her, "Are you happy?"

She always responds, "Of course I am."

Then I say, "Is there anything I could do to make you happier?"

"Well, not that I can think of," is her usual response.

That is when I begin to dig into the depths of her soul and look for treasures that are hidden in the secret recesses of her heart. Sometimes our conversations reveal things that she did not even know were there. Over the last thirty years, it has become kind of a game between us. It is a little bit like a hide-and-seek game of the soul. I love it when I find mysterious treasures, hidden desires, passions painted below the surface. These fine jewels are there, strategically placed by the King Himself, and they are just waiting for her prince to unearth them.

Peter's Instruction to Married Couples

Now let's discuss the apostle Peter's instruction to married couples:

> In the same way, you wives, be submissive to your own husbands so that even if any of them are disobedient to the word, they may be won without a word by the behavior of their wives, as they observe your chaste and respectful behavior. Your adornment must not be merely external— braiding the hair, and wearing gold jewelry, or putting on dresses; but let it be the hidden person of the heart, with the imperishable quality of a gentle and quiet spirit, which is precious in the sight of God. For in this way in former times the holy women also, who hoped in God, used to adorn themselves, being submissive to their own husbands; just as Sarah obeyed Abraham, calling him lord, and you have become her children if you do what is right without being frightened by any fear.
>
> 1 Peter 3:1–6

At first glance, Peter's exhortation to wives seems extremely harsh, especially when you take into consideration the pretext of the previous paragraph. Read these verses and cringe!

> Servants, be submissive to your masters with all respect, not only to those who are good and gentle, but also to those who are unreasonable.

For this finds favor, if for the sake of conscience toward God a person bears up under sorrows when suffering unjustly. For what credit is there if, when you sin and are harshly treated, you endure it with patience? But if when you do what is right and suffer for it you patiently endure it, this finds favor with God.

For you have been called for this purpose, since Christ also suffered for you, leaving you an example for you to follow in His steps, who committed no sin, nor was any deceit found in his mouth; and while being reviled, He did not revile in return; while suffering, He uttered no threats, but kept entrusting Himself to Him who judges righteously; and He Himself bore our sins in His body on the cross, so that we might die to sin and live to righteousness; for by His wounds you were healed. For you were continually straying like sheep, but now you have returned to the Shepherd and Guardian of your souls.

1 Peter 2:18–25

After I read these passages, I stopped and asked myself two questions: *Number one, to whom is Peter writing? And number two, why is he writing to them?* In other words, what is Peter's overlying message to his target audience?

The first question is answered in the first verse of the book. Peter is writing to Jewish Christians scattered throughout Rome who are under the persecution of Emperor Nero (see 1 Peter 1:1–2). The second question is answered in light of this; Peter's overarching message to these persecuted believers is that suffering has a purpose and will be rewarded. Eleven times in his short letter, Peter uses the Greek word *pascho*, which means "to suffer" or "to endure suffering." (It is interesting to note that Peter wrote a second letter to the same people and never mentioned suffering once.) The only book in the entire Bible that rivals Peter's exhortation on suffering is the gospel of Luke, which mentions suffering only six times, and five of those times are in the context of Christ suffering for us.

In the passage we just read, Peter tells these persecuted Christians that they will find favor with God when they *suffer* unjustly. He tells them Christ Himself *suffered*, giving them an example to follow in hard times, and when they are *suffering* they should not revile those who revile them, but instead should trust God to take care of them. He also tells them in later passages that if they *suffer* for righteousness they are blessed, and much like Christ who *suffered*, when they *suffer* in the flesh they cease from sin, but no one should *suffer* as an evildoer, and finally, when they have *suffered* for a little while, God will strengthen and establish them (see 1 Peter 3:14; 4:1, 15; 5:10).

Peter is instructing believers (not just married couples) about how to deal with suffering in the midst of intense persecution. These Christians were being impaled on stakes and burned in Nero's garden as human torches. They were slaughtered for entertainment—eaten by lions and cut to pieces by gladiators in the great Roman coliseums while the multitudes cheered. In light of their circumstances, it does not seem like a great sacrifice for Peter to ask Christian wives to put up with their husbands even if the men are being disrespectful or dishonoring. After all, thousands of believers are literally giving their lives for Christ all around them.

Sarah, the Submissive Wife

The next thing we see in this passage is that women are instructed to submit to their husbands, as Sarah did to Abraham. She even called him "lord" out of honor, not out of fear. I do not want to take away from Peter's exhortation for wives to honor and respect their husbands, but I do want to highlight Sarah's relationship with Abraham because Peter is using it as a model for holy women to follow. I am sure you noticed that Peter talks to women about the way they dress before he brings up Sarah. His point is that beauty should not be just skin-deep. I am sure it is at this point that Peter is reminded of Sarah because she was so beautiful that at 65 years old, she was abducted twice by two different kings who wanted to marry her. That is one beautiful woman! So let's be clear—Peter is not saying ugly is holy. He is simply pointing out that women need to be attractive inside and out.

Another thing important to note about Sarah's relationship with Abraham is that she only called Abraham lord one time, and even then she was not talking to Abraham; she was talking to God about Abraham. (At least that is the only instance recorded in the Bible.) Sarah called him lord in reference to God's insistence that she was going to bear a child after menopause, and therefore God wanted her to continue to have sex with Abraham. Genesis 18:12 tells us that Sarah laughed at the whole idea, saying to herself, "After I have grown old, shall I have pleasure, my lord being old also?" (You may take it another way, but if she is not talking about sex in this context, then I need marriage counseling!) Think about it: Sarah was ninety years old and Abraham was one hundred, and they did not have a master-slave relationship. That is probably the reason why God visited their home in the flesh and let Sarah know that by sleeping with her husband, she would enjoy the pleasure of conceiving a child in spite of their age.

Check out this family argument between Sarah and Abraham (formerly called Sarai and Abram). These verses help to give us insight into their relationship:

> Now Sarai, Abram's wife had borne him no children, and she had an Egyptian maid whose name was Hagar. So Sarai said to Abram, "Now behold, the LORD has prevented me from bearing children. Please go in to my maid; perhaps I will obtain children through her." And Abram listened to the voice of Sarai. After Abram had lived ten years in the land of Canaan, Abram's wife Sarai took Hagar the Egyptian, her maid, and gave her to her husband Abram as his wife. He went in to Hagar, and she conceived; and when she saw that she had conceived, her mistress was despised in her sight. And Sarai said to Abram, "May the wrong done me be upon you. I gave my maid into your arms, but when she saw that she had conceived, I was despised in her sight. May the LORD judge between you and me." But Abram said to Sarai, "Behold, your maid is in your power; do to her what is good in your sight." So Sarai treated her harshly, and she fled from her presence.
>
> Genesis 16:1–6

I think it is clear that Sarah was not a passive doormat that Abraham walked on. She was a powerful and beautiful woman who struggled at times to honor her husband's relationship with God when the Lord's promise to them seemed impossible. Yet ultimately, Sarah conceived by faith because she pressed through her circumstances and apprehended the promise (see Hebrews 11:11).

Abigail and King David

Let me make one final point on the subject of submission. We can learn a significant lesson from the life of Abigail, as told in 1 Samuel 25. Abigail was an intelligent, beautiful woman married to a rich fool named Nabal. Her husband was such a jerk that he refused to feed David's starving men. But Abigail usurped her husband's command and brought food to David and his men. God honored her actions and punished her husband with death, then made her the wife of King David. (Yikes! Thank You, Jesus, that we do not live under the old covenant anymore.)

We cannot allow ourselves to be intimidated into accepting disrespect toward God or one another in our homes and churches. To do so under the guise of "submission" shows a perverted understanding of the Word. While unity is often a higher objective than being right in a situation, we need to be conscious that submission to God's righteousness often means standing up in boldness. We must always honor God above man's sinfulness, as Abigail did.

Dealing with Abuse

When people counsel women (or men for that matter) to stay in dangerous situations in the name of "submission," they need to have their heads checked. A wife was never called to be a zookeeper, a lion tamer or a punching bag. She was born to be protected, adored, cherished and empowered. Submission must be mutually experienced and unilaterally applied, or what results is a slave-master relationship, not a marriage. Submission is not powerlessness and fear hammered out on the anvil of mindless religion. It is truth forged in the furnace of servanthood and passion.

If a man abuses a woman and then tells her he loves her, he is a liar and a certified coward—period. Love is more than a bunch of words strung together in a sentence. I am not suggesting here that a woman divorce her domineering husband (although that may be the only solution in some cases), but Tarzan should stay in the jungle by himself until he can prove that he can be kind to animals. Then *maybe* he will be ready to try to slowly rebuild trust with humans, and more pointedly, with Jane, his wife. If Tarzan uses threats and manipulation to try to bully his way back into the relationship, he can stay in the jungle and live among the other gorillas.

All marriages require sacrifice, but forcing your wife (or husband) to be a sacrifice is a substitute savior and a false religion. Many substitute saviors who drink this Kool-Aid die of a broken heart in the arms of their abusers. Children who grow up in this environment are being trained as terrorists, not disciples of Christ.

Enduring abuse is not an expression of covenant love; it is a slow march to the death camps of the devil. I am convinced that some people who stay in dangerous and highly abusive marriages have a martyr complex. These people honestly believe that Jesus requires them to stay in a cruel relationship. I think these people are reading the Bible through the eyes of self-hatred and a lack of self-respect.

I do understand that some people call any conflict "dangerous abuse" and use this as an excuse to walk away from what might otherwise be a workable situation. In no way am I trying to encourage divorce. As of this writing, I have been married 38 years, so I am a covenant man. But I am also the victim of two extremely abusive stepfathers. (Thankfully, one has changed his ways and is still married to my mother.) I could literally write a book entitled *A Practical Guide to Surviving a Violent Family*. I know very well the difference between conflict and abuse. There is no room in the Gospel for the latter.

The Gospel is always redemptive, so whenever we restrict or disempower people because of their sex, ethnic origin or social status, we have distorted the Gospel of the Kingdom.

The Rest of the Story

We have spent a lot of time talking about Peter's perspective on a wife's responsibility in marriage; now let's look at his exhortation to husbands. Peter wrote, "You husbands in the same way, live with your wives in an understanding way, as with someone weaker, since she is a woman; and show her honor as a fellow heir of the grace of life, so that your prayers will not be hindered" (1 Peter 3:7). Coming from a Jewish man, these are profound words. I understand women could get offended by Peter's suggestion that they are weaker, but Peter simply is saying, in the context of his letter about persecution and suffering, that men are typically physically stronger as it pertains to beatings and battles. Those were the circumstances Christians were facing when Peter penned these words. Conversely, I know very few men who are as strong as women are when it pertains to the matriarchal role and responsibilities, but that was not Peter's topic here.

Peter's exhortation for husbands to "honor" their wives as "fellow heirs" is a radical and profound countercultural statement, especially in the backdrop of first-century Judaism. Then the great apostle Peter drops another bomb on husbands in his closing declaration by saying, "so that your prayers will not be hindered."

The Greek word for *honor* in this passage means "to value, to pay a price, to think of as precious," and "to treat honorably." Let me give you the unauthorized Kris Vallotton translation of this verse: "Husbands, you may be physically tougher than your wives, but if you don't honor them as precious jewels and treat them as co-reigning equals, God is not going to answer your prayers!"

Nearly three millenniums ago, King Solomon captured the sheer essence of a wife when he wrote, "He who finds a wife finds a good thing and obtains favor from the LORD" (Proverbs 18:22). I tell men all the time, "Do you want to improve your relationship with God? Okay, then marry a King's daughter!"

There is something so inherently beautiful about the spirit of a woman that it attracts the favor of God Himself. God fashioned women to reign alongside men. We men need women to elegantly, gracefully, intuitively and compassionately join us in nurturing this ailing planet back to health. May creation itself rejoice as the daughters of God are restored to their predestined state of glory!

Epilogue

Powerful Women

My primary goal for writing this book was to be a Mordecai to the Esthers of the world and to empower women to fulfill their God-given destiny. As I got deeper into this project, I found myself struggling over the definition of the word *powerful*. My struggle was compounded by the fact that many people knew I was writing this book, and they kept asking me two questions: "Doesn't the Bible restrict women from leadership?" and "What does it look like for a woman to be powerful?"

I knew that I could answer the first question theologically to the satisfaction of any openhearted person. I have done that to the best of my ability in the preceding pages. But honestly, I was perplexed over the second question. It was not because I did not know powerful women. Quite the opposite is true. I know many powerful women, yet their strengths are so diverse that I found it impossible to define the word *powerful* with a single phrase or a certain personality type. The pressure to illustrate what a powerful woman is like grew with every chapter I completed. It came to the point where I was lying awake at night, trying to decide how to put my experience with this vastly diverse group of great female leaders into words.

I finally decided that the only way I can truly define what *powerful* looks like in a feminine leader is to share with you a little bit about five great female leaders whom I have the privilege of knowing very well. These five ladies, each of whom I will describe in a short paragraph, are incredibly different from each other in their leadership styles, personality and strengths. Their diversity will help me paint a picture of the various dimensions of the word *powerful*. If I had the time and space, I could write about a hundred more women I know well who lead impressively, yet differently than these five ladies. I want to make it clear that the strengths and personalities of these five women do not encompass the entirety of the word *powerful* as applied to female leaders, but they do demonstrate some of the diversity you will find in the strengths of womanhood.

Beni Johnson

First, I want to introduce you to Beni Johnson. Beni has been my friend and leader for 34 years. Beni is introverted, soft-spoken and gentle. She is a friend of God who walks with the angels. To Beni, *powerful* means to be unencumbered by the expectations of others, while not being weighed down by managing the daily activities of a ministry. She has to be free to fly, able to listen to the slightest whisper of the Bridegroom and able to respond to His beck and call. She needs the freedom to live spontaneously, to imagine, to dream and to draw outside the lines of predetermined expectations. Beni is an original—a beautiful person who inspires the misunderstood, loves the outcasts and personifies the beauty of a quiet spirit. She can soar with the eagles or walk with the broken. She is a free spirit . . . an almost mystical personality who personifies the mysteries of God.

Sheri Silk

Another strong leader I have had the privilege of walking with for more than three decades is Sheri Silk. Sheri and I have worked together for many of these years. Sheri is an outspoken leader who is fiercely loyal.

She is passionate, assertive and unrelenting in her pursuit of justice for the disenfranchised. She strengthens the weak and speaks up for those who have no voice. Highly intelligent, Sheri is an extremely capable leader who knows how to move mountains and get things done. She is a great people manager who has always been loved by her team as she inspires them to excellence. Sheri is a strong exhorter. When she takes the podium, the hearts of the people are stirred to action.

Kathy Vallotton

Next, I want to highlight Kathy, my wife. I have shared a couple of her stories in this book, but I feel it is important to use Kathy's life to illustrate yet another way in which powerful people carry out their God-given call. Kathy's life personifies stability, flexibility and resourcefulness. She can adjust to any circumstance, environment or culture and find a way to succeed. Kathy is an incredibly hard worker who refuses to give up on any person or task. She is innovative and creative, and she can figure out how to get things done long after everyone else has quit trying. It actually inspires Kathy when people say some task is impossible! Kathy also has an amazing ability to bring peace into tumultuous situations, which often results in people working together harmoniously even when they have never gotten along before. Kathy inspires people with her servant leadership style. She never complains, she has no enemies and she always sees the best in everyone. Kathy is so graceful that she can dine with royalty or split firewood with rugged men. Kathy has a God-given ability to see things as they should be. This gives her the capacity to organize complete chaos and administrate a multimillion-dollar organization.

Heidi Baker

One of the strongest people I have ever known is Heidi Baker. I have had the privilege of being close friends with Heidi and her husband, Rolland, for nearly a decade. Heidi is a unique person; she was born into wealth and carries herself like a princess. She is extremely intelligent and highly educated, having obtained her Ph.D. in systematic theology from the King's College, University of London. To say Heidi Baker is a visionary would be like saying Albert Einstein was intelligent—a gross understatement. Heidi's visionary quality is often hidden under her extreme humility. Yet the truth is that Heidi is possessed by vision that comes to her directly from the throne of God as she "soaks in His presence." Heidi, Rolland and their team oversee more than ten thousand churches in twenty nations. They are also building a hospital in the midst of the Mozambican jungle, as well as founding the finest university on the African continent—all of this while simultaneously feeding and clothing literally tens of thousands of children. I have been with Heidi when she sat in the dirt with the destitute and poor, and I have watched her minister to the rich, powerful and famous. Heidi is no women's libber and has no ax to grind with men, even though as a Christian she grew up in a religious system that often restricted women. Heidi is also a powerful speaker who motivates people through her intense compassion for the broken, the outcast and the poor. She is beautiful and walks gracefully as a very feminine woman who understands how to lead men and women through passion and vision, not manipulation.

Inese Šlesere

One of the most powerful and beautiful women I have ever had the privilege of knowing is Inese Šlesere. Inese is largely unknown to the Western world because she grew up in the former Russian country of Latvia. Latvia is one of the three Baltic states that escaped communism during the Singing Revolution in 1991. The communists placed no value on beauty, which was demonstrated by the fact that they literally painted all of their buildings gray. Latvia began holding beauty contests before its independence as a sign of revival, and in 1991, the year Latvia gained independence, Inese won the Miss Latvia contest. In 1999, she went on to win second runner-up at the Mrs. World Beauty Pageant. But Inese is much more than a beautiful face. Inese's father died when she was two years old, so she was raised by a single mother. Inese and her husband, Ainars, grew prosperous and powerful businesses as communism collapsed all around them. They constructed many beautiful hotels and established the finest shopping malls in the country. Yet Inese's passion to see the Kingdom established in her country led her to politics, where she has served several terms in parliament. Inese has led her country in reforming Latvian laws surrounding family values, moral principles and the care of the orphans. Inese has five children and a great marriage, yet she is not your typical housewife and mother. She is driven with intense passion to bring about cultural change throughout all of Europe. Inese's love for Jesus flows out of her so naturally that atheists and cultists are numbered among her best friends. She leads through the deepest kindness and most genuine compassion for people I have ever experienced in my life. Even politicians in the opposing political parties love her. Although she is highly educated and intelligent, it is actually her deep insight into the hearts of people and her unrelenting compassion for everyone she meets that make her a world-class leader.

Powerful and Free

Jesus set women free to be beautiful and powerful people who exemplify the feminine side of God. Women are so diverse in their strengths that it is simply impossible to explain with mere words the grace that flows from their lives. Yet my prayer is that if you are a woman, the lives of these extraordinary women whom I have mentioned would inspire you to be all that God calls you to be, and that you would refuse to be cloned or conformed into someone else's idea of a strong woman.

Strength comes in so many packages that comparing yourself to someone else will always lead you to feeling shortchanged. You can never be as good at being other people as they are at being themselves. When you imitate someone else, you just become a cheap copy of the original. Yet there is no one else created to be like *you*. As a woman, you are a one-of-a-kind, beautiful person who is part of the royal family of noble lovers of God!

Notes

Introduction

1. Rose Heyer and Peter Wagner, "Too Big to Ignore: How Counting People in Prisons Distorted Census 2000," Prisoners of the Census, April 2004, http://www.prisonersofthe census.org/toobig/gender.html. See also http://www.prisonpolicy.org.

Chapter 2: Hold On, Adam—Help Is on the Way

1. "Famous People: Mother Teresa," famouspeople.co.uk, 2004, http://www.famous people.co.uk/m/motherteresa.html.

2. James W Goll and Michal Ann Goll, *Compassion: A Call to Take Action* (Shippensburg, Penn.: Destiny Image, 2006), 122.

3. Ruth A. Tucker, "Ministries of Mercy: Mother Teresa," Christian History Biography, January 1, 2000, http://www.ctlibrary.com/ch/2000/issue65/4.20.html.

4. "Mother Teresa," Wikipedia, February 1, 2013, http://en.wikipedia.org/wiki/ Mother_Theresa_of_Calcutta.

5. Tucker, "Ministries of Mercy," http://www.ctlibrary.com/ch/2000/issue65/4.20.html.

Chapter 3: Who Was That Masked Serpent?

1. "Hebrew Dictionary (Lexicon-Concordance) Key Word Studies: H8596" Lexicon-Concordance online Bible, http://lexiconcordance.com/hebrew/8596.html.

2. *New World Encyclopedia* online, s.v. "Joan of Arc," August 29, 2008, http://www .newworldencyclopedia.org/p/index.php?title=Joan_of_Arc&oldid=794727.

3. "Joan of Arc," Wikipedia, March 3, 2013, en.wikipedia.org/wiki/Joan_of_Arc.

4. Ibid.

5. Ibid.

6. *New World*, s.v. "Joan of Arc," http://www.newworldencyclopedia.org/p/index .php?title=Joan_of_Arc&oldid=794727.

7. "Joan of Arc," Wikipedia, en.wikipedia.org/wiki/Joan_of_Arc.

Chapter 4: I Believe Every Word of the Bible

1. "Harriet Tubman," Wikipedia, March 7, 2013, en.wikipedia.org/wiki/Harriet_Tubman.
2. "Women in History: Harriet Tubman Biography," Lakewood Public Library online, March 7, 2013, http://www.lkwdpl.org/wihohio/tubm-har.htm/.
3. Clara L. Small, "Abolitionists, Free Blacks, and Runaway Slaves: Surviving Slavery on Maryland's Eastern Shore," University of Delaware home page, August 4, 1997, http://www.udel.edu/BlackHistory/abolitionists.html.
4. "Harriet Tubman," Wikipedia, en.wikipedia.org/wiki/Harriet_Tubman.
5. "Underground Railroad," Wikipedia, March 5, 2013, en.wikipedia.org/wiki/Underground_Railroad.
6. "Harriet Tubman," Wikipedia, en.wikipedia.org/wiki/Harriet_Tubman.
7. Ibid.
8. Ibid.
9. Ibid.
10. Ibid.
11. "Love, Faith, and Joy," Harriet Tubman Home online, 2009, http://www.harriethouse.org/love.htm.

Chapter 5: Jesus: Founder of the First Women's Liberation Movement

1. For more information on first-century Gentile women, see Christine Schenk, CSJ, "Jesus and Women: Women in the Gentile World," Future Church, http://www.futurechurch.org/wicl/jesuswomen2.htm.
2. Leonard Swidler, "Jesus Was a Feminist," God's Word to Women, 2005, http://www.godswordtowomen.org/feminist.htm.
3. For more information on first-century Jewish women, see Doug Weller, John Ortberg, Mark Foreman, and Scott Dudley, eds., "Life of Jesus—First Century Context of Palestine," JesusCentral.com, http://www.jesuscentral.com/ji/historical-jesus/jesus-firstcenturycontext.php. See also http://www.womenpriests.org/classic/tetlow1.asp; http://bible.org/article/daily-life-time-jesus; http://www.godswordtowomen.org/feminist.htm. Another good reference is Rick McKinniss's book *Equally Yoked* (Xulon Press, 2009).
4. Charles Marsh, *The Beloved Community: How Faith Shapes Social Justice from the Civil Rights to Today* (New York: Basic Books, 2006), 21.
5. "Civil rights icon Rosa Parks dies at 92," CNN.com, October 25, 2005, http://www.cnn.com/2005/US/10/24/parks.obit/.
6. Rosa Parks and James Haskins, *Rosa Parks: My Story* (New York: Dial Books, 1992), 116.
7. Shipp, E. R., "Rosa Parks, 92, Founding Symbol of Civil Rights Movement, Dies," the *New York Times* online, October 26, 2005, http://www.nytimes.com/2005/10/25/us/25parks.html, http://en.wikipedia.org/wiki/Rosa_Parks.
8. "Rosa Parks Biography: Pioneer of Civil Rights," Academy of Achievement, April 9, 2012, http://www.achievement.org/autodoc/page/par0bio-1.
9. Ibid.

Chapter 6: The Misunderstood Apostles

1. "The 15 Biggest Bestsellers EVER After the Bible," HUFFPOST Books online, May 25, 2011, http://www.huffingtonpost.com/2010/07/30/the-15-biggest-bestseller_n_664029.html#s115965&title=Quotations_from_Chairman.

2. David Padfield, *The Biblical City of Corinth* online booklet, 2005, 3, http://www
.padfield.com/acrobat/history/corinth.pdf.

3. Mark D. Roberts, "Ancient Ephesus and the New Testament," patheos online, 2011, http://
www.patheos.com/blogs/markdroberts/series/ancient-ephesus-and-the-new-testament/.

4. Sir William Smith, ed., *Dictionary of Greek and Roman Biography and Mythology*
(Rome: Taylor, Walton, and Maberly, 1849), 505–6.

5. Richard W. Hayes, "Should a Woman Have Her Head Uncovered in Church?," Bible History Online, November 28, 1996, http://www.bible-history.com/texts/women_head_covered
_rik_hayes.htm.

6. Out of 43 translations my assistant searched for this book, 11 of them use the words
husband and *wife* in translating 1 Corinthians 11:13. These include the Complete Jewish
Bible, the English Standard Version, God's Word, the Good News Translation, the Mounce
Reverse-Interlinear New Testament, the New Life Version, the New Revised Standard Version, the Voice, the Worldwide English (New Testament), the Knox Bible and The Message.

7. "Lexicon Results: Strong's G2228," Blue Letter Bible online, 1996–2013, http://www
.blueletterbible.org/lang/lexicon/lexicon.cfm?Strongs=G2228&t=KJV.

8. Loren Cunningham. *Why Not Women? A Biblical Study of Women in Missions,
Ministry, and Leadership* (Seattle: YWAM Publishing, 2000), 190–91.

9. "Board Members: Dave Meyer—Vice President," Joyce Meyer Ministries, 2011, http://
www.joycemeyer.org/AboutUs/DaveMeyerBio.aspx.

10. "What We Do," Joyce Meyer Ministries, 2011, http://www.joycemeyer.org/AboutUs/
WhatWeDo.aspx.

11. "About Joyce—President," Joyce Meyer Ministries, 2011, http://www.joycemeyer
.org/AboutUs/JoyceBio.aspx.

Chapter 7: Excavating Restrictive Foundations

1. Walter William Skeat, *An Etymological Dictionary of the English Language* (Oxford:
Clarendon Press, 1893), 170.

2. Linda L. Belleville, *Discovering Biblical Equality: Complementarity without Hierarchy*
2nd ed. (Downers Grove, Ill.: IVP Academic, 2004), 212–17.

3. Ibid., 209–10.

4. Ibid., 209.

5. Ibid., 219.

6. Richard Clark Kroeger and Catherine Clark Kroeger, *I Suffer Not a Woman: Rethinking 1 Timothy 2:11–15 in Light of Ancient Evidence* (Grand Rapids: Baker Academic, 1998),
Kindle electronic version Location 1035 of 2891.

7. Ibid., Location 1046 of 2891.

*Richard and Danielle Schmidt, "An Emancipation Proclamation: A Biblical Approach to
the Roles of Women in Leadership" (unpublished paper); "The Athanasian Creed," *Creeds of
Christendom, with a History and Critical Notes, Volume 1: The History of Creeds,* accessed
May 22, 2012, www.ccel.org/ccel/schaff/creeds1.iv.v.html; Matt Slick, "Arianism," Christian Apologetics and Research Ministry, accessed May 22, 2012, http://carm.org/arianism.

8. Origen, *Homilies on Romans* 10.17 (third century); John Chrysostom, *Homilies on
Romans* 31 (on Romans 16:1; late fourth century).

9. Daniel Mark Epstein, *Sister Aimee: The Life of Aimee Semple McPherson* (Orlando,
Fla.: Mariner Books, 1994), 15.

12. Cynthia Franklin and Rowena Fong, *The Church Leader's Counseling Resource Book: A Guide to Mental Health and Social Problems* (Oxford: Oxford University Press, 2011), 433.

13. Mark Eaton, "American Literary Supernaturalism," *American Literary History* 23, no. 4 (2011): 899–917.

Chapter 8: Women, Take Your Places

1. George M. Marsden, *Jonathan Edwards: A Life*. (New Haven, Conn.: Yale University Press, 2004), 498–505.

2. Steven Gertz and Chris Armstrong, "Jonathan Edwards: Did You Know?" CT Library online, January 1, 2003, http://www.ctlibrary.com/ch/2003/issue77/17.2.html.

3. "Burr, Aaron, 1756–1836," Biographical Directory of the United States Congress online, archived from the original on December 2, 2009, http://bioguide.congress.gov/scripts/biodisplay.pl?index=B001133.

4. Albert Edward Winship, *Jukes-Edwards: A Study in Education and Heredity* (Harrisburg, Penn.: R. L. Myers & Co., 1900), 74–86.

5. Ibid., 43.

6. "Biographical Directory of Federal Judges: Pierpont Edwards," Federal Judicial Center online, http://www.fjc.gov/servlet/nGetInfo?jid=693&cid=999&ctype=na&instate=n.

7. Winship, *Jukes-Edwards*, 55.

8. Ibid., 37.

9. H. D. Northrop, *Beautiful Gems of Thought and Sentiment* (Boston, Mass.: The Colins-Patten Co., 1890), 248.

Recommended Resources

Why Not Women? A Biblical Study of Women in Missions, Ministry, and Leadership by Loren Cunningham, David Joel Hamilton, and Janice Rogers (YWAM, 2000).

Powerful and Free: Confronting the Glass Ceiling for Women in the Church by Danny Silk (Red Arrow, 2012).

10 Lies the Church Tells Women: How the Bible Has Been Misused to Keep Women in Spiritual Bondage by J. Lee Grady (Charisma House, 2006).

Women in the Church: A Biblical Theology of Women in Ministry by Stanley J. Grenz and Denise Muir Kjesbo (IVP Academic, 1995).

The Hidden Power of a Woman by Bonnie and Mahesh Chavda (Destiny Image, 2006).

Man Down: Proof Beyond a Reasonable Doubt That Women are Better Cops, Drivers, Gamblers, Spies, World Leaders, Beer Tasters, Hedge Fund Managers, and Just About Everything Else by Dan Abrams (Abrams Image, 2011).

Scripture Index

Genesis

1 43, 44
1:1 41
1:2 55
1:21–28 41
1:26 57
1:27 124
1:28 42
16:1–6 231
18:12 231
2 43, 46
2:7–8 43
2:18 45
2:18–20 43
2:19–20 48
2:21–23 44
2:21–24 198
2:22–24 48
2:23 48–49
2:24 49
3:1–7 61
3:10 63
3:11 63
3:12 63
3:14–15 64
3:16 67
3:17–19 67–68
4:1 47
9:20–27 94
20 85

Exodus

15:20 183

Leviticus

18:20 47
18:23 47

Numbers

5:13 47
5:20 47

Joshua

2 113

Judges

4:4 152, 182
5:7 182

1 Samuel

25 232

2 Kings

22:14 183

Nehemiah

6:14 183

Esther

1 85
2 85

Psalms

51:7 66
68:11–14 65
91:11–12 95
103:20 149
124:8 46
139:23 47
146:5 46

Proverbs

1:1 218
2:1–2 118–19
2:11 118–19
2:16–19 118–19
6:20 217
7:6–27 119–20
13:22 86
14:6 83, 134
16:16 86
18:22 234
23:23 86
25:28 210
31 218–20
31:3 220

Ecclesiastes

2:13–15 86
2:21–23 86–87
3:19 87
4:9–12 87
7:16–18 87–88

Isaiah

1:18 66
2:2 82
2:4 82
8:3 183
14:11 58
14:13 55
14:15 55

Ezekiel

28:11–19 58–59
28:13 59–60
28:18 60

Malachi

1:2–3 82

Matthew

5:27–28 120
14:21 46
15:3–6 80–81
19:3–9 120–21
19:6 121–22
19:10 122
23:23 93
24:6–7 82
26:10–11 108
26:13 108

Mark

5:25–34 122
6:44 46
9:35 210

Luke

1:18 117
1:19–20 117

1:35 117
1:41–55 183
2:36–38 183
4:9–12 95
7:36–49 109
7:40–44 109
7:45 109
7:46 109
7:47 110
7:48 110
7:50 110
8:3 125
8:18 90
8:43–48 122
9:14 46
10:27 135
10:40 104
10:41–42 105
14:26 81
15 123
22:26 151

John

1:14 101
2:3 115
2:4 115
2:5 116
4:7 111
4:10 111
4:11–12 111
4:13–14 112
4:15 112
4:16–20 112
4:21–24 113
4:25 113
4:26 113
4:28–30 113–14
4:39–42 114
5:19–20 115
8:3–11 108
8:41 118
11:5 105
11:6 105
11:21 105
11:22 106
11:23–24 106
11:25–26 106
11:27 106

11:32 107
11:33–36 107
11:39 107
11:40 107

Acts

2:17 183
2:17–18 154
6 125
13:48 81
16:1–3 80
16:14–15 102
18:24–26 181
19:24–28 140
21:8–9 183
27:7–8 141

Romans

8:2 67
8:15–17 42
16:1 182
16:1–2 182
16:7 182

1 Corinthians

1:1–2 180
1:13 159
6:2 159
6:9 159
6:16 159
7 156, 225
7:1 142
7:1–7 142–43
7:2–5 223
7:7 50
7:12–16 142–43
7:13 144
7:16 144, 160
9:6 160
9:7 160
9:8 160
9:10 160
10:22 160
11 148
11:1–16 149–50
11:2–16 145–46
11:3 148, 150

11:11–12 148
11:22 160
12 50, 152
12:1–11 153, 157
12:28 185
13:13 93
14 154
14:1 154, 157
14:5 154
14:26–33 154–55
14:34–35 133, 141
14:34–36 155, 160
14:35 144
14:36 158, 160
14:37–38 155, 158–59
15:45 48

2 Corinthians

1:1 180
3:5–6 80
3:6 95
5:17 175
9:6 68
9:12–13 176

Galatians

3:26–28 136
3:28 148
5:1 89, 224
6:7 68

Ephesians

1:20–21 150–51
2 144
2:6 151
4:8–10 65
4:11–16 184
5:1 42
5:21–30 225
5:23 225
5:31–32 45
6:12 66

Philippians

1:1 182

Colossians

3:22 89
4:1 89
4:16 180

1 Timothy

1:1–3 180
2:4 81
2:8 177
2:11 176
2:11–12 116, 170
2:11–15 174
2:12 114, 178, 179
2:12–14 177
2:13 179

2:14 179
2:15 175
3:8 182
3:12 182

2 Timothy

2:15 79

Titus

1:1 181
1:4–5 181
1:10–13 141

Hebrews

1:14 149
8:13 182
11:11 232
13:17 152

1 Peter

1:1–2 229
2:18–25 228–29
3:1–6 228
3:4 210
3:7 191, 234
3:14 230
4:1 230
4:15 230
5:10 230

Kris Vallotton has been happily married to his wife, Kathy, since 1975. They have four children and eight grandchildren. Three of their children are in full-time vocational ministry. Kris is the co-founder and senior overseer of the Bethel School of Supernatural Ministry, which has grown to more than two thousand full-time students. He is also the founder and president of Moral Revolution, an organization dedicated to cultural transformation.

Kris is the senior associate leader of Bethel Church in Redding, California, and has served with Bill Johnson since 1978. He has written and co-authored numerous books, and his revelatory insight and humorous delivery make him a much-sought-after international conference speaker.

You can contact Kris or find out more about him and his other ministry materials at www.kvministries.com, or you can download the KV ministries app on your smartphone. You can also follow Kris and Kathy on their Facebook fan page at www.facebook.com/kvministries.

More from Kris Vallotton

To learn more about Kris Vallotton's books and ministries, visit kvministries.com.

With this book, Kris Vallotton turns the idea of spiritual warfare as we know it on its head. Through his personal story of demonic bondage and deliverance, Kris reveals the diabolical lies and strategies of the enemy—attacks and traps so subtle that we may find our souls and hearts imprisoned without even knowing it. But no more! You can win the invisible battle against sin and the enemy. Will you take hold of victory?

Spirit Wars

Few lives have had as significant an impact on the Vallotton family as that of Tracy Evans. From treating rebel guerillas while captive on an Asian island to sipping tea in a Mozambican hut while bullets whistled through the grass walls, Tracy has followed God's call into the most dangerous of places. In these pages you will find not only gripping true stories of Tracy's exploits around the globe, but the more amazing account of what God can do through one person's raw obedience and radical faith.

Outrageous Courage by Kris Vallotton and Jason Vallotton

✓Chosen